WHAT OTHERS ARE SAYING ABOUT

NICHE SELLING
HOW TO FIND YOUR CUSTOMER IN A CROWDED MARKET

"We're making an impact with our customers like never before. In uncertain economic times where customers proceed with understandable caution, we are much better equipped to take care of the customer and still achieve solid sales growth."

Nick Hiller
Group Personnel Manager
Sun Chemical Corporation

"Bill Brooks has pulled the rabbit out of the hat—by writing one of the most intelligent, insightful books on selling *in years*."

Jeff Davidson, MBA, CMC
Author of *Breathing Space:*
Living and Working at a Comfortable Pace
in a Sped-Up Society

"Bill Brooks crystallizes the need for, and simplifies the process of, achieving sales and marketing alignment with focus. *Niche Selling* deals with the essentials of making impact with customers. This is the key to success in the 90s."

Dan Harper
President
Mannington Wood Floors

"Strategies on how to address changes are a 'dime a dozen,' just ask anyone. For something as crucial as change, especially when it impacts your profession, a logical approach is a must for survival! In this fast-paced and changing world, the 'strategies for survival' in Bill Brooks' *Niche Selling* are logical and essential ways for salespeople to survive in their selling profession. It also provides insights on how to be the 'shining star' in a fast moving sales arena. *Niche Selling* is a must to read if you are at all touched by competition."

> Frank Goldback, CLU, ChFC
> Regional Sales Manager
> Nationwide Insurance Companies

"Must reading for all sales people if they are to succeed in the 1990s."

> Maurice Kent
> Vice President
> General Rehabilitation Services, Inc.

"[Bill Brooks] hit the essence of selling in a logical, concise, and understandable way. Too much effort and expense goes into 'smoke screen' selling when in reality the fundamentals are the missing ingredient. This book is mandatory reading for our entire sales force and all management personnel."

> John E. Skvarla III
> President and CEO
> Isotechnologies, Inc.

NICHE SELLING
HOW TO FIND YOUR CUSTOMER IN A CROWDED MARKET

William T. Brooks

Irwin/McGraw-Hill

A Division of The McGraw-Hill Companies

This publication is designed to provide accurate and
authoritative information in regard to the subject matter
covered. It is sold with the understanding that neither the
author nor the publisher is engaged in rendering legal, accounting,
or other professional service. If legal advice or other expert
assistance is required, the services of a competent
professional person should be sought.

*From a Declaration of Principles jointly adopted by a Committee
of the American Bar Association and a Committee of Publishers.*

Sponsoring editor: Cynthia A. Zigmund
Project editor: Gladys True
Production manager: Diane Palmer
Jacket Designer: Renee Klyczek Nordstrom
Compositor: Publication Services, Inc.
Typeface: 11/13 Palatino

Library of Congress Cataloging-in-Publication Data

Brooks, William T.
    Niche selling : how to find your customer in a crowded market /
by William T. Brooks.
        p.   cm.
    Includes bibliographical references and indexes.
    ISBN 1-55623-499-6
    1. Selling.   2. Consumers' preferences.   3. Consumer satisfaction.
I. Title.
HF5438.25.B745 1991
658.8—dc20   91–13213

Printed in the United States of America

8 9   BKM BKM   0 9 8 7 6 5 4 3

This book is most gratefully dedicated to my clients both past and present. Thank you for your insights. It is my hope that my work does you and your collective wisdom justice.

INTRODUCTION

What one-syllable word will redefine the very essence of the selling profession in the years ahead? What is the single most dominant concept that will direct and control sales success into the 90s?

That all-powerful word is *change*! The very same phenomenon that will determine the tone of politics, technology, and every other phase of the world structure well into the next century will also prove to be the major driving force behind the new face of professional selling. Permeating change will cause a new set of increasing and all-encompassing needs to appear in the marketplace. Sales professionals will need to anticipate and adapt to a series of events that will dictate their ability to meet the unique demands of the incredibly crowded marketplace of the 1990s and beyond.

Massive change will occur throughout our fast-paced world. Trends in the global economy will affect corporate and consumer spending patterns and behaviors in more direct and immediate ways than ever before. A key but still unknown variable is how well sales organizations and their sales staffs will respond to it. Change will require continual adjustment and course correction in the marketplace and in the ways in which sales professionals deal with its complexities.

This book will give you the insights and tools you need to keep your company, sales force, or personal selling career viable and vibrant throughout the 1990s and into the next century.

What are some changes that the crowded marketplace of the 1990s will bring? Here are just a few possibilities (each relates to a chapter in Part I of this book):

- *Focus:* Customer preferences for design, quality, flexibility, style, technical superiority, and even terms of purchase will become more important and will change on an unpredictable and more frequent basis. If the focus of your sales force is on your company's reputation or on the demonstration of your products, you may not notice the rapidly changing needs of your customers. In a crowded marketplace, the successful organizations and their sales forces will be those whose *focus* is on answering the customer's needs and preferences.

- *Leverage:* Economic trends will find their way to the marketplace more quickly and will be in full force almost immediately. You'll need to constantly monitor these rapidly emerging trends and search for ways in which your company's strengths can best serve them. This concept is called *leverage*. Leverage has always been an important tool; however, its specific application will change radically in the new world of highly niched selling.

- *Alignment:* The crowded marketplace will enable prospects and customers to respond to unsatisfactory customer service, poor treatment, or product dissatisfaction with vendor changes rather than tolerance. In light of this reality, your company's marketing strategy and your sales strategy will need to be in close *alignment*. If not, the inevitable conflicts caused by any misalignment of these two strategies will drive your customers to other companies.

Do you wish you had a crystal ball to predict exactly how these changes will affect your company? We cannot give you a crystal ball, but we can help a great deal. At The Brooks Group we've developed a set of principles, presented in this book, that will prepare your sales force to handle the forthcoming changes.

Your sales force can no longer afford to sell in a vacuum. Ever increasingly, the power of mass communications, macro- and microeconomic realities, consumer issues, value shifts, and even politics and global affairs will dictate day-to-day selling activities. As such, most traditional sales philosophies are outdated in today's crowded marketplace. The future belongs to the sales organizations that are *flexible* and *nontraditional* in their thinking.

Creative companies willing to adapt their concepts, thoughts, beliefs, and actions to the new marketplace realities will rule the economy of the coming decade. Companies who could not or would not adapt now litter the graveyard of business.

The companies of the 1990s that will end up in the graveyard are those that continue to use traditional selling techniques. Among the techniques that will turn companies into dinosaurs in the crowded marketplace are:

- Selling without consideration of the wants and needs of the customer.
- Canned, trite phrases; tricky closes; and coercive selling techniques.
- Scripted sales presentations geared toward a singular view emphasizing a company and its products rather than the customer's needs.
- Selling pure price instead of value.
- Adversarial selling.
- Complicated, confusing selling systems.
- Failure to investigate the market for qualified new prospects.
- Selling that is not backed by reliable service.
- Sales forces that do not understand the role of their company's marketing department.
- Marketing departments that neither address nor understand the needs of the sales force.

These approaches will not bring success to your company in todays crowded marketplace—perhaps they never have! Perhaps they only appeared effective because they were used in less crowded marketplaces—somewhat like the cliche about being "the only game in town." Getting away with using old-school selling techniques was once possible because some of your customers may have had little choice or knowledge but to buy from you.

Today, your secret or edge will not last long. Industrial intelligence reports are now readily available. Duplicating a successful product or service is so simple that product differentiation is a thing of the past. If you have found a winning combination, someone in the next town (or country!) will find out about it and will find a way to usurp your efforts. When this happens, your competitor will have the advantage of avoiding the mistakes you made and will, in addition, bring in a fresh perspective.

The closest we can come to offering you a view through a crystal ball is to say that regardless of whether you have been the only game in town, the newcomer will get a cool welcome if you have diligently and honorably served the long-term needs of your customers. Your job is to ensure that when the newcomers arrive—and rest assured they will—your customers will not be willing to give up the value and integrity they know they can count on with you. The most successful sales organizations and individual salespeople in the 1990s will be those who can most effectively sell two things: trust and value.

The decade of the 1990s will be the most demanding, fast-moving era in history for sales professionals. Yet at the same time it will present the most new opportunities. The secret to seizing these opportunities will be to understand this concept of change as it relates directly to the world of professional selling. This understanding is a concept that winning sales professionals and companies need to leverage to their advantage. Those who fail to recognize or deal effectively with this changing sales environment will quickly fall as easy prey to those who do.

There are three fundamental strategies to guarantee your survival, and I address each separately in the three parts to this book:

- **PART I: KNOWING YOUR ORGANIZATION AND YOUR MARKET**—In this introductory section I show you how to *focus* on your customer, *leverage* your talents and resources, and *align* your sales and marketing strategies for maximum IMPACT.

- **PART II: KNOWING YOUR CUSTOMERS**—By itself, the decision to align your sales and marketing will get you nowhere. To tap the power inherent in alignment, you need to base that alignment on a solid, proven plan. In this core section of the book, I present a clear and effective game plan. Here, you will learn the highly effective IMPACT Selling system that will guarantee you a prime niche in the crowded marketplace.

- **PART III: KNOWING YOURSELF**—A solid game plan alone is ineffective unless it is executed by highly *skilled*, *motivated* people who will make it work. I show the crucial difference between the old-school philosophy of hiring people who *can* sell—those with "sales personalities"—and hiring people who *will* sell—the kind of individuals whose value structures will enable them to become committed, IMPACT Selling professionals in a decade filled with unparalleled change, challenge, and competitiveness.

William T. Brooks

ACKNOWLEDGMENTS

Fortunately, most of my life has been spent as a member of some sort of team. The lessons that I have learned from those experiences have been invaluable. Perhaps the most precious of these is that nothing worthwhile is ever accomplished alone. That includes this book.

My deepest gratitude goes to the skilled and caring team at IRWIN Professional Publishing. To Jeff Krames for his confidence and belief; to Cindy Zigmund for her patient attention to detail; and to Kate Wickham for her creativity and understanding in grappling with the complex issues with which she must deal.

My heartfelt thanks also go to the highly competent support team of Bonnie Joyce, Debe Day, and Ronald Wagner. The technical expertise provided by Chuck Jones is also most appreciated.

The deepest appreciation of all, though, must go to my wife, Nancy, and to our greatest team effort, our two sons, Will and Jeb. Only those three people can really know the pain and loneliness of living with a 20th-century Quixote. Only I can know how much their love, support, and patient understanding have inspired my efforts.

CONTENTS

PART I

KNOWING YOUR ORGANIZATION AND YOUR MARKET

CHAPTER 1

FOCUS ON FOCUS

Great thoughts are from the heart.
Marquis deVauvenargues

The most common error in selling occurs when salespeople are so focused on what they or their company wants from a sales relationship that they lose sight of what their prospects want from it. This fatal orientation will lose more sales more quickly than ever before in the *buyer's markets* of the 1990s. Buyer's markets are crowded markets; crowded markets are filled with buyers who are confused and far too many sellers who use outdated, "me-too" marketing techniques.

Because of the crowding in today's markets, buyers are now prone to view similar products or services as similar when they merely give the appearance of similarity. The key to success in a crowded market is to determine what buyers value most, and then to point out those unique advantages of your product or service that address those values. When you focus on what the *customer* values most, you create perceived value that makes your product stand out from the crowd and that leads to a positive buying decision.

In the 1990s, the successful sales professional will be a master at *needs analysis* and *application selling*. Simply defined, needs analysis is understanding and selling to the buyer's needs rather than selling a product or service to meet a quota, win a contest, or "make a quick buck." Application selling is showing, in easy-to-understand terms, how a particular product or service can fulfill the buyer's most pressing needs.

Focusing on the buyer's needs results in better alignment of your product or service in the marketplace. Conversely, continued reliance on traditional selling techniques will result in poorly positioned products. For example, strong, aggressive, and insensitive closing tactics will lead to more closed doors than closed sales.

Focus is defined as a sharp, clearly defined center of interest or expenditure of time, energy, or dollars in order to maximize a return on any or all of the above elements.

Traditional sales techniques have never focused on the customer's needs. Instead, they have focused on the product or the company behind the product, or, worse yet, taught salespeople to focus on themselves. If the sharp, clearly defined center of interest or activity in your sales career has been on self, company, or product, then your career has been languishing.

Most companies focus on everything except the customer, a situation that leads to what I call *institutionalized insulation*. If you never strip away that insulation and shift your focus to place the customer's needs at the top of your list, you will always remain in the doomed, "me-too" marketing crowd that will become the selling dinosaurs of the 1990s.

Here is a story that clearly illustrates a salesperson with a misplaced focus.

I had already decided it was time for a new car, and I knew exactly what I wanted. My dream car was a top-of-the-line Volvo 940GLE. When I walked into the dealer's showroom, a young, enthusiastic salesman greeted me. I figured that I would make his day, giving him the easiest sale he had ever had.

"Look," I began, "I'm going to make this easy for you. I want a 940GLE. I want it in silver with the blue, crushed velour upholstery. I want the four-cylinder, turbo-charged engine and four-speed automatic transmission with overdrive. I want the best Volvo stereo system, an electric sunroof, and aluminum wheel covers."

What do you think his response was? Excitement? Disbelief at how well-informed I was? No. He paused for a moment, feigned deep thought, then said, "Did you know that the Volvo is the safest car in the world? Did you know it's got an all-steel body with steel beams in the doors? Did you know that the front end is designed to deflect around the passenger compartment in a collision, so that the occupants will not get hurt?"

Where was his focus? On product! He probably got an "A" in his sales-training class because he knew his product as well as anyone I have met, but he was intellectually and emotionally distanced from me as a customer. His response showed me a clear case of institutionalized insulation and, as a result, I did not buy the car from him.

If he had trained under a customer-focused, value-based sales system, he might have said, "We have one of those in stock right now. Do you mind if I ask you a few questions so I'll know better how to serve your needs?" Then he would have waited for my answer. I always answer "yes" to someone who wants to learn how to serve my needs. He might then have asked when I wanted to take delivery, or if I had a trade-in, and how I planned to pay. Instead, his training clearly forced his focus onto the product.

Getting to the top of a crowded market niche—and staying there—will not be easy. The secret to reaching and remaining at the top level is being attuned to change. Successful sales professionals will be in a constant state of adjustment. Because your market, your customers, and the world are constantly changing, you need to analyze, anticipate, and adapt to the changes that you face.

If your focus is on product, you most likely emphasize product demonstration. Your demonstrations may highlight how terrific your company's latest model is but will show a customer how to meet his needs only if you are lucky. In a crowded marketplace, you want to get your salespeople to stop thinking *"demo"* and start thinking *application.*

By definition, demonstration selling forces the focus onto the product. All that accomplishes is to make you look just like everybody else, so you fade into the crowd in your market. The difference between demonstration and application selling, although subtle, is critical to success in crowded markets. The shift toward application selling is an early step toward casting aside institutional insulation and adapting the new philosophy of customer focus.

DON'T OUTNUMBER YOUR CUSTOMERS

Think of where to direct your focus in this way; There are four areas on which you can focus—self, company, product, or customer. If you focus on the first three, your customer is outnumbered three to one. People who are overwhelmingly outnumbered feel confused and uncomfortable. People who are confused and uncomfortable rarely make buying decisions.

Most sales organizations have rallied their troops against their number one adversary: their customers! The reasoning has

FIGURE 1–1
The 80/20 Rule

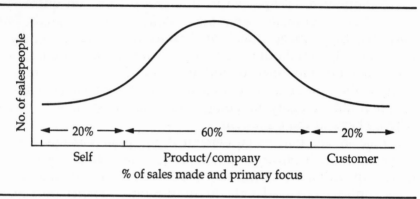

been that if the sales force is trained to maximize personal gains, if the traditional sales pitch demonstrates a hot, new product, and if the company makes bold claims about itself, then the customer will fall like prey to a hunter.

The Pareto principle, or the 80/20 Rule as it has come to be called, helps describe what goes on in selling today. Conventional research confirms that nearly 80 percent of salespeople today conduct presentations with a focus on self, product, or company. Our firm's studies also show that this group—those who are institutionally insulated from their customers—accounts for only 20 percent of the sales made in the marketplace.

Conversely, the remaining 20 percent of sales representatives focus on the needs and wants of their customers. This group accounts for fully 80 percent of all sales! Failure to focus on customers' wants or needs will place you in the bottom 80 percent of sales professionals or sales organizations, who generate only a small fraction of the sales they could be enjoying. The 80/20 Rule is illustrated in Figure 1–1.

CUSTOMER FOCUS OR DIE!

At the bottom of the non–customer-focused group, "the bottom 80 percent," we see salespeople who are survival-driven. These people worry that if they do not make a sale today, the electricity will be turned off tomorrow. The paradox is that no one wants to buy from someone who is desperate, particularly in the face of an abundance of other options. Customers themselves cannot survive by acting as a welfare agency to hard-pressed salespeople.

Self-oriented salespeople in this group focus on quota. To them, it does not matter what the customer wants or needs, but only that they "meet quota" on *Product X*. Quota focusers often achieve the minimum to get by—nothing more, nothing less. They have no emotional commitment to their jobs; they are just doing as they are told. In a crowded, competitive niche, the salespeople in this category are going to lose their customers to those who go beyond the minimum.

Also in this bottom 80 percent is the predominant Group: those who push *products*. Often these salespeople have been hyped up with a sales contest. We believe strongly that, at best, sales contests can lead only to short-range victories and may have seriously detrimental effects on long-range success. You can identify product-driven salespeople by their well-practiced and smoothly delivered sales pitch. They have been trained to believe that if they deliver their presentation with consistency, someone will eventually buy.

Others in the bottom 80 percent focus on *company*. You may hear them brag about their company, saying "we're the biggest in the industry," as if that alone will make customers buy. From Hertz and Avis, to IBM and Apple, to CBS and CNN, every industry is replete with companies who erroneously believed that sheer size and industry position would guarantee market share. If your standard presentation is always focused on your company's size or reputation, what will you sell if a competitor outgrows you, or if bad publicity should tarnish your company's reputation?

The only sales reps and sales organizations that will prosper throughout the 1990s are those in the top 20 percent, those that focus on their customers' wants and needs. And, even the top 20 percent has a hierarchy of its own. Within that group, we discovered that those in the top 5 percent accounted for 60 percent of sales. The remainder of the group—15 percent—accounted for 20 percent of sales. While that is as much as the entire bottom 80 percent, it is still only a fraction of the per-person results enjoyed by the top 5 percent. This remarkable finding prompted us to dig further in order to identify the cause of such disparity in sales effectiveness. Here is what we found:

> While all sales organizations and salespeople in the top 20 percent focused on their customers, the difference between the two

groups was that the top 5 percent focused on their customers' *needs*, while the remaining 15 percent focused on their customers' *wants*.

Both groups within the top 20 percent are successful sales professionals. Both have a focus that is outer-directed toward their customers and never inner-directed on themselves, their products, their company, or a quota. Both will survive in the crowded markets. Still, the very top performers are those who identify the deepest *needs* of their customers and find ways to fulfill those needs.

An outer-directed orientation produces top performers in any field, not just in sales. Here's an anecdote to help illustrate the observation. The Brooks Group has had the opportunity to work with leaders from two top-flight organizations: the Atlanta Hawks and the Detroit Pistons. The Hawks have had some great players and from season to season are able to achieve some outstanding successes, but they haven't been able to make a consistent title run in a long, long time.

The Pistons, on the other hand, also have very talented players. We've gained some valuable insights through our work with the Pistons' coaching staff. The coaches say their best players have a unique ability to rise above an inner-directed focus, delivering an effort that transcends their own short-term, immediate needs. Their focus is more on the team than on themselves, and that outer-directed focus can be clearly seen through the results it has delivered: championships!

It is as true on a basketball court as it is in a sales presentation: Top performers are outer-directed, focusing on the needs of others. The idea of shifting your focus to the customer is not a deep philosophical issue, though it is more of an emotional issue than an intellectual one. It is straightforward and produces easily measured results. Inner-directed salespeople are at the bottom; outer-directed ones are at the top. Within the bottom group, those who are merely average focus on their company or their product. The least successful focus on themselves. Within the top group, many highly successful salespeople focus on their customers' wants. The cream of the crop, however, consists of those exceptional sales professionals who focus on their customers' deepest needs. Figure 1–2 is an illustration of sales focus.

FIGURE 1–2
Sales Focus

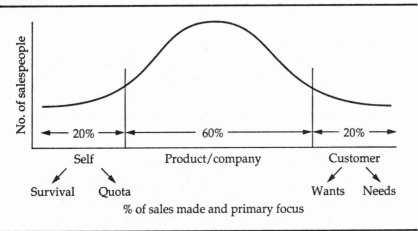

% of sales made and primary focus

HELPING OTHERS HELPS YOU

A by-product of helping others to achieve focus and direction is that your own focus and direction improve as well. A young medical equipment salesman named Randy was only a year out of college. His company had come out with a new product that was innovative, creative, and state-of-the-art. This new machine automated the analysis of spinal injuries and generated a detailed report that expedited the doctor's work tremendously. Though very expensive, it was clearly the best product on the market. Its capabilities were so exceptional that it could increase a physician's business and income by drawing patients from a wider area.

One day Randy called on a prominent neurosurgeon in Tuscaloosa, Alabama. The doctor had a large practice and a national reputation that brought him all the patients he could handle. He quickly told the salesman he had no interest in a machine that would draw more patients. Randy, though still new to sales, remained focused on his target. He continued to ask questions of the surgeon, probing for the doctor's most dominant needs. By persisting, he discovered that though the surgeon did not need to enhance his practice, he was looking for ways to reduce the time he spent handling what he already had. Randy discovered that one of the doctor's most time-consuming tasks was giving court depositions, though they added little to his income.

Although Randy was focused on his prospect's needs, he also knew his product well. He quickly told the surgeon about the ability of his product to display its data automatically in an objective format that was easy to understand and would be accepted in court depositions. The real kicker was that the machine produced the data in color, which was the most important need the doctor had in handling court depositions. As you guessed, the doctor placed an order with Randy.

Randy's story is a good example of something that few would have seen as a major selling feature: the production of data in color. Yet, by focusing on his prospect's needs, he hit the target dead-center and got much more than the commission from making a large sale. That surgeon no longer thought of Randy as a salesperson, but as a trusted business colleague who had helped him fulfill one of his most pressing needs. By helping someone else find direction, Randy enhanced his own sense of direction, too. The keys for Randy were knowing his product, being on top of a rapidly changing industry, and focusing on his prospect's dominant needs.

FOCUS ON YOUR CUSTOMERS AND NEVER LOOK AWAY

Almost anyone is receptive to new ideas when they have the time to listen. Often, though, there are periods in everyone's life when everything seems to be falling down around them. During those struggles, most people drop back to a survival mode. New ideas seem like something best put off for a day when the wolf is not baying at the door. This shifting of focus is a natural response to hard times in our lives.

In business, the same thing happens. Hard economic times often cause companies to retrench into a survival mode. During those retrenchments, there is a natural tendency for salespeople to shift their focus away from customer's needs to *income, survival,* or *quota.* The logic may be, "It won't matter whether our focus is on our customers' needs if we go out of business. For now, we've got to meet our quota for this quarter; *then* we'll worry about the customers!"

While that is a natural tendency, *never* let it take your focus off the only thing that will bring you success in today's crowded marketplaces: fulfilling your customers' needs.

If you are retrenching, everyone else probably is, too. They will most likely shift their focus to themselves and concentrate on survival. That is the best time to ask yourself, "How can I serve this prospect's deepest need?" Your customers are probably retrenching, too. More than ever, they need someone who will focus on their needs, which may be getting desperate.

A downturn in the economy, therefore, can be used to leave your competitors in the dust. Since even fewer salespeople will be focusing on your customers' needs, you will stand out more than ever before when you refuse to lower your focus. The reputation you build for yourself during tough times will long be remembered.

THE FASTEST WAY TO REVENUE

The more you need the money, the more narrowly you have to focus on customer needs. I learned that the hard way, struggling for several years before finally seeing the light and making a permanent change.

In 1983 my fledgling company was among several that were trying to market a sales-training program to the Chevrolet Division of General Motors. Back then, The Brooks Group consisted solely of a part-time secretary and myself, though I was closely counseled by my mentor and close associate, Ron Willingham.

General Motors had expressed the desire for a complete new sales program to guide each of its 27,000 Chevrolet sales representatives in the United States. In short, it was an enormous undertaking, and to me the contract represented the very foundation of The Brooks Group.

With Ron's guidance, I worked for nearly three years on selling General Motors that training program. During that time we built terrific frequent flier mileage accounts from our trips to Detroit, placed hundreds of long-distance phone calls, and wrote countless letters. Each step of the way, Ron and I tried to keep our focus clearly on what General Motors truly needed. We had to—that was the very concept we were selling!

Our company did well in the competition for the contract. We took the lead and soon stood at the top of the crowd. It appeared that we were actually going to win the contract and my dream was going to come true: teaching Ron's customer-focused, needs-based selling system to thousands of salespeople.

At that point, something happened: I found it extremely difficult to get my mind off those dollar signs. They were going to pay the contract on a "per-head" basis! Can you imagine how much money that totaled? It was more than I had ever dreamed. We were going to be very well paid. Predictably, we began to encounter snags with the contract. During the negotiations, I fortunately realized that my focus had shifted from their needs to my revenues, and I understood the danger such focus represented in nailing down the contract.

Recognizing how my focus had shifted, I refocused on the needs of General Motors; I made more visits and phone calls and got things back on track. Intermittently, my lack of experience and discipline allowed my focus to drift. I began, once again, to think about the new car I might soon be able to buy, the new house I could plan, and the better life I could provide for my family.

It was during this period that I began to understand why my focus kept shifting and I was able to learn the discipline to redirect my focus. I fixed my focus once again on the needs of General Motors and kept it there until we won the contract. Throughout that entire consulting assignment, the only time that the proposal went smoothly was when I focused on their needs instead of my own. Like most things in life of any value, the assignment went badly every time I focused on myself.

Paradoxically, the more you need the money, the more diligently you must focus on your customers' needs. Customer focus is not a fad; it is the only certain formula for success in the 1990s. Today's crowded marketplaces truly demand it. Your customers' needs will *never* include making you rich or raising the value of your company's stock. Ironically, we have found that nearly every salesperson we meet already knows at least the basic needs that their products or services can fulfill. Yet few of them truly understand that using that knowledge is the best way to sell their company's products or services.

Clearly, I had a much greater impact on General Motors when I focused on their needs. Much of what I learned in winning and servicing that contract has helped me to develop my IMPACT Selling plan, which is based on customer-needs focus.

NEEDED: A NEW DIRECTION IN SALES TRAINING

Traditional sales training does not focus on customer needs; instead, most sales training focuses on outdated approaches that work only for short-range goals. If you have felt frustrated by failure to attain long-range success, you may have experienced one, if not all, of the basic fallacies of current sales training. These are the most common misconceptions we find in today's training philosophies:

Regarding product training as sales training—This idea assumes that the only thing salespeople need for success is to learn the features of their company's products or services. Though product training is vital, it is not the whole picture. Any company that calls its sales force in merely to acquaint its people with new products is sending them out with only one weapon to fight a multifaceted war. As I have pointed out before, long-range successful selling cannot be viewed as adversarial. Your products are not weapons with which to wrest dollars out of your customers' pockets.

Using a motivational speaker to get salespeople hyped up—Motivational hype merely revs up the engine without shifting into drive. Motivation without a reliable plan only generates frustration and produces the long-range effect of sales burnout.

Using complicated sales training systems—Many current systems rely on clever buzzwords that have little meaning to the average person, complex ideas that turn salespeople into amateur psychologists or sly manipulators, and closing techniques designed to trap prospects into saying "yes." Even the salespeople who master them often discover that such arcane systems conflict with their personal values, since these systems bombard salespeople with myriads of techniques designed to equip them to regard the customer as an adversary, or perhaps even an idiot, and close in for "the kill." Customers who are naive enough to fall for yesterday's trick closing techniques will not be in business long enough to give you a long-range career even if you could keep fooling them. Buyers today are highly sophisticated and demand an entirely different focus from those of even a decade ago.

THE SALESPERSON'S GREATEST FOLLY

Most traditional sales training is based on inflating salespeople with self-serving slogans and high-sounding talk. Not surprisingly, then, focusing on the customer's values is often the last thing on the mind of a typical salesperson when he or she faces a prospect. The focus is instead most often on the salesperson talking his or her way into a sale. The following gem of wisdom from a highly successful professional football coach illustrates the salesperson's greatest folly.

In a game during the NFL's 1990-91 regular season, the Philadelphia Eagles humiliated the Washington Redskins on ABC's "Monday Night Football." Before a huge national audience, the Redskins, who had won the Super Bowl less than three years earlier, were thoroughly trounced and suffered the more calamitous defeat of having nine players knocked out of the game, many of them removed on stretchers. By the final quarter of the game, Washington ran out of quarterbacks and had to substitute a rookie running back to steer their offense.

The Redskins went home and found that the humiliation was not over. The Eagles continued to taunt Washington in the press. The insults boiled to a fever pitch when Washington and Philadelphia were scheduled to play in the first round of the championship playoffs seven weeks later. The Eagles had set a record that season for knocking opposing players out of games and they prided themselves on this ability. In pre-playoff-game hype, the Eagles advised Washington to bring "body-bags" to Philadelphia.

Despite all the hype, Washington coach Joe Gibbs continued to run his team in the cool, level-headed style that has become his signature. The Redskins said nothing in the press about Philadelphia, choosing instead to direct their energies toward the true task at hand: winning Saturday's game. The tactic paid off. Before a huge national audience, the Redskins avenged the earlier defeat and won the game that counted, knocking the Eagles out of the playoffs with a solid 20–6 victory.

Before the game, a *Washington Post* reporter had questioned the Redskins for being so quiet, suggesting they were intimidated by the Eagles. A Washington coach gave him an answer that is one of the best gems I have ever heard:

> *Most of the things that can go wrong in life happen when your mouth is open.*

Salespeople who have been brainwashed at sales meetings and then turned loose on prospects need to remember that NFL playoff story. Never fall victim to the salesperson's greatest folly: trying to talk your way into sales. Here is how it can work against you in selling:

"Hi! I'm Mary Smith with the XYZ Company. I can see from your left hand that you are a married woman, so let me tell you about a wonderful new perfume that is guaranteed to make your husband sit up and pop both eyes wide open when you walk into the room. May I come in and show you...?" bubbles the enthusiastic saleswoman.

"Good! I hope it will do all you say," says the stunned prospect. "My husband died last night, and I thought you were from the funeral home."

Trick door openers, canned sales pitches, and speed-talking approaches rely on the element of surprise and rely on the salesperson to do all the talking. Unfortunately, in today's crowded marketplaces it is most often the salesperson who gets surprised.

Perhaps that explains why one-third of all salespeople are looking for different jobs at any given time, and why it is not unusual for sales organizations to have an annual turnover rate of 125 to 175 percent of their sales force. Sales organizations that use trick ads to lure unemployed and disillusioned people to "unlimited futures" in selling by intimidation rob many capable people of their great potential for an honorable selling career and perpetuate the myth of the *quick buck* sales career.

If selling has become an unpleasant chore for you because you close so few of the sales you attempt, you may need to look no further than the way you approach prospects. Stop talking and start listening! Focusing on your prospects' needs will raise more than your closing rate; it will raise your self-esteem.

CUSTOMER FOCUS MAKES NEW DEMANDS

The new demands that your intense focus on customers' needs will place on you, on your entire sales force, and on other departments in your company are addressed in the next two chapters. As is emphasized in Chapter 2, these demands include having sales staffs leverage all resources available in support of identifying and fulfilling customer needs; anything short of an all-out effort will lead only to mediocrity. We will show you more about leverage in the next chapter.

Chapter 3 discusses the importance of alignment. Your entire company needs to focus on its customers; it will not be enough for you or your sales force to do it alone. If your marketing department does not align with you and does not focus on the same target, you will still fail or produce mediocre results, at best.

Part II, beginning with Chapter 4, contains a complete explanation of IMPACT Selling to help you implement and maintain an appropriate outer-directed orientation and to teach you specific customer-focus techniques. IMPACT Selling will eliminate problems caused when you fail to put customer needs first and think beyond your own needs. Once you have the IMPACT Selling process working for you, you will be free to focus entirely on the needs of each customer.

In Part III, I discuss how a focus on customers demands more from a salesperson than the stereotyped "sales personality." Since much of IMPACT Selling is based on a vision of long-range goals and a strong outer-directed focus, its successful use requires a person with a deep-seated value structure whose focus is on a higher goal than making a quick buck.

KEY TIPS

☑ In the 1990s, the successful sales professional will be a master at *needs analysis* and *application selling*. Needs analysis is understanding and selling to the buyer's needs rather than selling a product or service to meet a quota. You must shift your focus to place the customer's needs at the top of your list. Application selling is what you do with the information that you gather through needs analysis.

☑ There are four areas where you can focus—self, company, product, or customer. If you focus on the first three, your customer is out-numbered three to one. People who are over-whelmingly outnumbered feel confused and uncomfortable and rarely make buying decisions.

☑ The only sales organizations and sales reps who will prosper throughout the 1990s are the top 20 percent, who focus on their customers' wants and needs. But the very top producers—the top 5 percent, who will garner 60 percent of the market—are those who focus only on their customers' *needs.*

☑ Never let an economic downturn take your focus off the only thing that will bring you success in today's crowded market-places: fulfilling your customers' needs. Your customers are probably retrenching, too, and that is the best time to ask yourself, "How can I serve my prospects' deepest needs?" More than ever, your customers need someone who will focus on their needs, which may be getting desperate. A downturn in the economy, therefore, can be used to leave your competitors in the dust.

CHAPTER 2

LEVERAGE

Give me a lever and a place to stand and I can move the world.
Archimedes

To employ leverage one needs three things: a tool to use as a lever, a fulcrum to pry against, and an object to raise. As a concept, leverage is nothing new in business. The traditional concept of leverage, however, only encompasses maximizing your time, talent, and resources.

At The Brooks Group, we have refined the traditional idea of leverage by stressing that in order for leverage to work properly, it needs to be applied against the right fulcrum and must lift the right object. In the sales world, leverage means using your time, talent, resources, and advantages to deliver maximum value to your customers.

To be successful, your leverage must be adaptable to fit specific prospects and customers. You will use your strengths to help customers apply your products or services to create maximum value. We found a model example of sales leverage at work through one of our clients, Cellular One.

Cellular One's prominence in the market is due to its emphasis on quality, service, and value; it never focuses on price. The company does not compete with people who sell discount telephones, because that is not its business. It leverages its time, talent, and resources against the type of customer it wants. Cellular One uses the leverage of its guaranteed service to go after quality customers.

Cellular One offers a money-back guarantee and loaner phones when repairs are necessary. Its salespeople leverage this unique warranty and full refund pledge to create value for customers, focusing mainly on meeting the needs of cellular phone customers rather than on the physical product. If your company does not have this level of customer focus, you should encourage modifications of current service and warranty policies that you can use as sales leverage. Here are some more examples of leveraged strengths we have found in our consulting work:

- A tire dealer in Boston who offers free loaner cars to his customers. He does not have the lowest prices in town, but he enjoys runaway success because he focuses on a crucial need for his customers. The loaner policy adds value to the dollar price his customers pay.

- A commercial truck dealership in Pennsylvania that keeps extra trucks in standby reserve in case a customer's truck breaks down. The spare trucks are delivered and loaned out until repairs are complete. Thus, from this dealer, customers do not buy a truck; instead, they buy *the use* of a truck, which is what their true need is.

- A floor covering store in Virginia that offers its Do-It-Yourself customers free tools and training on how to lay floor coverings. Although the products do not sell for the lowest prices, the business is highly successful because the employees never sell price. Instead, they sell value by helping their customers save on installation, thereby getting a lower total price for the completed job.

Before you can implement leverage as a sales tool, you must create each of the three elements of leverage. You must first create the lever and the fulcrum, and then place your fulcrum in your selected niche market. The third element—the object you will raise—is customer value. The fulcrum itself—what you apply opposing pressure against—is your competition. What, then, is the lever itself? It is you and your sales force.

YOU ARE THE LEVER IN LEVERAGE

The *actual* amount of time, resources, and energy we have is finite, yet the way we use what we have can dramatically change the *effective* amount of each. At a recent high school reunion, I saw a terrific illustration of the ways different people get different effective results from a commodity they all have in relatively equal amounts. While there, I observed four ways in which my classmates had used their time, resources, and energies over the last quarter century. With our time, talent, and resources, each of us is free to

Invest: For which we get a return.

Spend: For which we may get little or nothing in return.

Waste: For which we get nothing in return.

Abuse: For which we suffer a loss.

I saw these four ways of using time, resources, and energy in the lives of people I had grown up with. Those who had invested their lives were easy to spot; it was visible in their body language even from across the room. When I met them and we talked, it became even more clear that they had invested their lives wisely, in return earning the dividends of success and happiness in abundance. The 80/20 Rule was highly evident at my class reunion in my observations of those who had invested their lives.

Most of my classmates were clearly part of the crowd. They were average—those in the middle of the bell curve. It is hard to distinguish between those who had spent what they had and those who had wasted it, because either group may have received nothing in return. This large middle group is analogous to companies that get by from day to day, yet never prosper.

Classmates at the other end of the bell curve—those who had abused their lives—were as easy to spot as those at the top. Alcohol and drugs had often been their best friends, turning them into the human equivalent of bankrupt companies.

Most likely your company has people in all four categories as well. The spenders have limited selling skills and are hard at work making cold calls. The wasters are the time-wasters, those who are experts at clock-watching techniques. The abusers are those who complain and sulk about failures, blaming outside circumstances for their troubles and often turning to alcohol or drugs for comfort.

Naturally, to achieve long-range success we must be in the top category. We must be investors. In the 1990s, any business that spends, wastes, or abuses its time, resources, or energies will be overrun by better-disciplined competitors. Leveraged salespeople are those who do the right things at the right time in the right place with the right people for the right reasons.

Here are some tips that will help you spot the classic activities in which salespeople either spend or waste their time:

- Meeting with prospects who have no need, ability, or authority to buy nor have any sense of urgency.
- Spending excessive time getting organized instead of systematically employing a proven plan.
- Working with prospects whose demographic characteristics are inconsistent with those of the most common customers within your niche.
- Horizontal prospecting ("the shotgun approach") instead of vertically integrating your product or service into existing clients, customers, or markets.

Sounds like standard sales practices, doesn't it? Very few salespeople employ value-based leverage, but I will show you how to integrate leverage into your sales.

HOW TO BECOME A LEVER

We will demonstrate sales leverage by making the process analogous to the manufacture and use of a steel lever. There are three basic stages in making a steel lever: The first step is mining the raw materials; next, refining the ore into steel; and finally, forging the steel into the finished tool. Your knowledge will form the raw materials; you will refine the raw materials with your selling skills; and your confidence will forge the final product—leverage in your market niche. Let's look at each step in detail.

Knowledge—Mining the Raw Materials

This is the dirty work of sales leverage, but nothing else will happen if you do not possess the raw materials. Before you and your sales staff can become instruments of leverage, your knowledge must include a well-versed understanding of:

- Products and services offered by your company and your competitors.
- Pricing information and financial facts and figures for your products and those in your prospect's industry.

- Familiarity with the demographics and geographics of your territory.
- The procedures and policies of your company and your prospect's company: the "ins and outs."
- Marketplace know-how such as trends, shifts, history, emerging players, and economic forces.
- Networking experience that includes formal and informal relationships within market niches and trade associations.
- A long-range macro view of the marketplace and a longitudinal view of future needs.
- Common mistakes made in the past by other companies within your niche such as giving poor service, growing too rapidly, or taking customers for granted.
- A realistic assessment of how much time you can devote to new accounts without degrading the quality of your service to existing accounts.
- Current profitable accounts, so you can identify new prospects in your territory by comparing them to the ones you now serve successfully.
- What has traditionally been the single best source of your most productive accounts in the past.
- The needs your customers and prospects have that you can help fill better than anyone else.

In Part II and especially in Chapter 5, I give you in-depth help on unearthing the raw materials, introducing you to methods that are akin to detective work and investigative reporting. For now, I want to remain on the subject of how you use the information in sales leverage. Once you have mined the raw ore of leverage, you will be ready to begin the refining process.

Professional Skills—Refining the Steel

Your skills, both natural and learned, will enable you to apply your knowledge so that you produce a finished tool that will maximize your investment of time, talent, and resources. Throughout this book, I cover many specific examples of how to enhance your professional skills. For now, I will simply break these skills down into three basic categories:

- Marketplace and Product skills.
- Selling skills.
- Personal skills.

Each of these key skills relates to one of the three parts of this book:

Marketplace and Product Skills (Part I): Focusing on customer needs rather than on product; leveraging your time, talent, and resources to provide maximum benefit to your customers; and aligning your sales strategy with your company's marketing strategy.

Selling Skills (Part II): Knowledge of your competition and your product's unique advantages and weaknesses; perception of your company and your product within the marketplace; focus on the needs of prospects in your market niche and mastery of the IMPACT Selling plan: Investigating, Meeting, Probing, Applying, Convincing, and Tying-It-Up.

Personal Skills (Part III): Personal values and motivation, goal setting, time management, territory management, listening skills, and planning skills.

Before you can become a sales lever, these skills must be refined to a high professional level. Your salespeople must be able to draw on each of these skills instantly and apply them to greatest advantage. Salespeople who lack these skills will suffer lost sales, an eroding position within their marketplace, and a market niche that will be hard to defend against those who have the skills.

Confidence—Forging the Lever

Confidence comes as a natural result of knowledge and skills. When a salesperson possesses accurate market knowledge and consistently applies the right skills, he or she will discover that confidence abounds. One secret to successful selling is to move confidently and quickly with a clear focus. The salespeople who have the most knowledge, coupled with the correct skills, will emerge in the 1990s as the dominant players in their market niche.

Once you become a sales lever, your efforts will become highly effective. And effective you must be, for there will be no time to go back after near-misses. Your effectiveness must make you a laser-guided missile of the sales world. When you become a lever forged from all your knowledge, skills, and confidence, you will succeed as Luke Skywalker did in *Star Wars* when he put the missile right down the middle of the exhaust port on the Death Star. Luke and his ragtag Rebel forces succeeded because of leverage. With enough leverage you can do anything.

BUILDING THE FULCRUM

Levers must act *against* something. When pressure is applied to one end of a lever, the opposing downward force is concentrated on the fulcrum. Applying your knowledge, skills, and confidence against an identified objective—your fulcrum—will maximize your output (sales and income) and minimize your costs (time, talent, resources, and energy).

Just as a military commander gathers intelligence to decide where to apply maximum pressure, your objectives will be identified by the intelligence you gather on your market niche. This intelligence gathering will show you where to put the fulcrum. Once you have carefully and accurately placed your fulcrum in your chosen market niche, your competition will take the downward pressure, or your leverage.

The intelligence-gathering efforts that will help you build the fulcrum should include analyzing your marketplace to learn

- What are my market segments? How do the segments differ? Do their needs differ? Are some segments destined for obsolescence because of changes in the market?
- Which segments within my niche are prosperous? Are any of them recession-proof? Recession-sensitive? Which are doing poorly? Why? You should always be in tune with financial and business publications.
- Which segments of my niche are most price-sensitive and competitive? Which are most profitable?
- What trade journals in my market niche are the best, the most comprehensive, and the most objective? Subscribe to every relevant publication.

- What can I learn from our own suppliers that can help me serve the needs of my niche? Your suppliers may have uses for their products that you never thought of.
- Are any of my competitors exhibiting any behavior that seems strange or unusual? If so, what are the true reasons behind it?
- What must I do to become a recognized expert within my niche? Are there any certification mechanisms for which I can qualify? Associations I need to join? Groups in which I might need to assume a leadership role?

Having intelligence information on your market can be likened to knowing the rules of the game. When you know the basics, you are ready to gather scouting reports on other teams in the league. Here's an example of how important it is for you to know your competitors as well as your prospects.

When I was a college football coach, my teams were not blessed with the most talented players on our schedule, but we leveraged the talent we had by spending many hours learning about our competition. We studied thoroughly all the other teams on our schedule through film analysis, scouting reports, computer reports, and statistical analysis. We used everything we could to figure out what they were *really* doing. We had to determine how much of what we heard about them was gossip, how much was intentionally put out as propaganda, and how much was accurate. We needed the truth.

Whenever we had accurate intelligence on our competitors, we could leverage our own strengths and weaknesses against theirs and apply the most concentrated, effective pressure we could muster. In sales, you must do the same or be relegated forever to .500 seasons. Some of the information you need from intelligence reports on your competitors is

- Their basic sales philosophy. Are they needs-based? High pressure? Focused on short-range or long-range goals?
- Sales force training, technical expertise, and turnover. Do they always seem to have ads in the classifieds for sales positions?
- What, precisely, is the niche they have identified for themselves? How, if at all, does it differ from yours?

- Their public relations image. What is their history of damage control scenarios in the light of bad publicity?
- Their delivery systems, availability of their product, and their product "glitches." How quickly can they fill a buyer's order?
- Pricing history, in good times and in bad. Are they knee-jerk price cutters?
- Quality control systems and their history of success. How do consumer magazines rate their products?
- Research and development capabilities and limitations. Do they offer public tours of their facilities so you might see how theirs compare to yours?
- Customer service philosophy and mechanisms. Do they have money-back guarantees?
- Internal mechanisms, politics, and strategies. Are their salespeople happy or dissatisfied? How about their delivery staff, customer service team, and other support personnel?

Simply being in contact with any market niche will enable you to pick up much of the intelligence we recommend. Yet, you must be careful of its accuracy. Do not rely on word of mouth; instead, aggressively seek information yourself. What travels through "the grapevine" is often "sour grapes." You will also find much of it to be second-hand knowledge or highly inaccurate. Never take the risk of leveraging the best you have against information that is, in reality, what one person *thought* they heard another say about something they *thought* they picked up last week. You should trust only direct and reliable sources. There are plenty available:

- Subscribe to competitors' technical or trade journals.
- Pick up competitors' promotional materials.
- Get copies of the guarantees and service policies of your competitors.
- Remain continually vigilant for newspaper or magazine articles on competitors or their products.
- Buy a share of their stock to get their company reports.
- Check out government data or secure it from Better Business Bureau reports.

- Dig into general industry data such as stock analyst reports found in libraries.

Once you gather your complete scouting report, you must make an *honest* assessment of your competitors' strengths and weaknesses as compared to your own. Their strengths will indicate areas in which you also need to excel; their weaknesses are like holes in a defensive line through which you can reach your goal. However, I want to urge caution on the use of your competitors' weaknesses.

USE YOUR LEVERAGE CAREFULLY

Be sure your scouting information is accurate, and never use any negatives you learn as a club to beat up on your competitors. Rarely will your customers *need* negative information about your competitors and, if they did, they would not rely on you for it. Your sales leverage will be most greatly enhanced when you apply it toward positive goals. Your advantage must come only from using the lever of your strengths to apply maximum pressure against your competitors' weaknesses so that your leverage applies maximum efficiency toward raising the value to your customers.

RAISING CUSTOMER VALUE

Once you have forged a lever and built a fulcrum out of scouting reports on your competitors, it's time to put your leverage abilities to use. What we want to do with our leverage is to use it to raise customer value.

It is difficult to raise something you cannot see, and customer value is not visible. But it can be measured. To help you build value for your customers, we have created a formula to use as a measuring device. Throughout Part II of this book, you will learn specific techniques where you apply this formula. Our value equation combines three basic elements into a single formula:

Value (*V*): Value becomes measurable when you prove to your prospect that your product or service is worth more to him or her than its cost in money, time, effort, risk, or commitment. Each customer has a personal definition of value. One may be interested purely in "the bottom line," while another may weigh in psychological factors such as the increased prestige the purchase will bring.

Perceived benefit (*PB*): Perceived Benefit is an advantage or benefit that a particular feature of your product or service provides toward best fulfilling the needs of your prospect. You have to remember that each customer will perceive benefits differently. What may be a critical need for one may be of no interest to the next.

Perceived price (*PP*): Perceived Price is the true cost of your product or service to your prospect. It is much more than a dollar figure because, as with *PB*, it is relative to each prospect. Usually the true cost of a purchase represents more than dollars. It often includes some risk, possibly a threat to the prospect's reputation if he or she makes a poor decision, and could include down-time on equipment while yours is installed. There will frequently be training costs and initial declines in productivity. Also, the payback ratio on any purchase will vary for every customer.

When these three factors are combined properly, they produce my formula for measuring value:

$$V = \frac{PB}{PP}$$

When expressed as directly as in this formula, it becomes clear that *V* increases as *PB* increases, or as *PP* decreases. Sales are closed when the ratio is greater than one-to-one. The higher the value is, the easier the sale and the more satisfied the customer will be. When salespeople prove to prospects that their products or services provide *PB* worth more than the *PP* they are ready to tie up the closing of the sale.

Most "old-school" selling programs focus only on decreasing price, concentrating on only half the equation by *making deals* like traders on the floor of a commodity exchange. Yet, as you can well imagine, we are not the first to see that increasing benefits also increases value. Our improvement is in the application of the formula and in our use of *PB* that relies on a needs-based focus on your prospects. Often salespeople approach prospects with assumptions about their product's benefits that may have no weight with some prospects. Customer focus will ensure that you always increase *PB*. Part II of this book illustrates specific techniques for increasing *PB*.

After you have completed the three steps to create a lever (knowledge, professional skills, and confidence) and have built the fulcrum in your market niche, the properly applied leverage will:

- Position you favorably with other major players in your market niche.
- Distinguish you in the marketplace as someone your prospects can trust.
- Maximize your sales opportunities by identifying the right people to see and when to see them.
- Prove the advantages of your product, service, or company to your prospects.
- Raise the value of your products to the key prospects in your market.

If in today's crowded markets you do not serve your customers with the power of maximum leverage, you can rest assured someone else will. It is central to your success that you use these key elements to leverage your time, talent, and resources:

- Learn all you can about your market niche, its needs, its competitive factors, and its current delivery systems.
- Realize that there is a finite limit to the *actual* amount of time, talent, resources, and energy you have, but that leverage will increase their *effective* amount.
- Deliver effective solutions that fulfill specific needs of prospects in your market niche.

Part I concludes with a topic we call *alignment*. Alignment is actually a specialized form of leverage that coordinates your sales leverage with the leverage of your company's marketing efforts. The result is a concept that we call *positioning by alignment*. After Chapter 3, you will have mastered the fundamental philosophy required to prosper in crowded markets, and you will be ready to move on to apply it to your own personal sales effort as well as in your sales training activities.

KEY TIPS

☑ To implement leverage as a sales tool, you must create each of the three elements of leverage. You must first create the lever and the fulcrum, and then place your fulcrum in your niche market. The third element—the object you will raise— is customer value. The fulcrum—what you apply opposing pressure against—is your competition. The lever itself is you and your sales force.

☑ To be in the top category and to enjoy long-range success, we must be investors of our time, talent, resources, and energies. Leveraged salespeople can be investors by doing the right things at the right time in the right place with the right people for the right reasons.

☑ You must become a highly effective sales lever because the crowded markets will leave you no time to go back after near-misses. You must become a laser-guided missile of the sales world.

☑ Gather scouting reports of accurate intelligence on your competitors. So that you can leverage your own strengths and weaknesses against theirs, apply the most concentrated, effective pressure you can muster. In sales, if you don't leverage against your competition, you'll be relegated forever to .500 seasons.

☑ Be sure your scouting information is accurate, and never use any negatives you learn as a club to beat up your competitors. Your sales leverage will be most greatly enhanced when you apply it toward positive goals.

☑ Use the value equation to focus your leverage on increasing perceived benefit to your prospects while decreasing their perceived price. If you do not serve your customers with the power of maximum leverage in today's crowded markets, you can be certain that someone else will.

CHAPTER 3

ALIGNMENT

A canoe is paddled on both sides.
Yoruba (Southern Nigeria) Proverb

Carefully coordinated linkage between your company's sales strategy and its marketing strategy is crucial for long-range success in a crowded market. This chapter reveals the importance of having your entire company focus on its customers. In company after company, I see it is not enough for sales to fly solo. If your sales strategy is not closely linked with the strategy of your marketing department, your company will fail or produce mediocre results at best.

First, let's clarify the difference between sales and marketing—many salespeople do not understand the distinction:

> *Marketing strategy is what gets you to the customer's door in the best possible light. Sales strategy is what you do when you are inside.*

Many marketing departments regard salespeople as something akin to peddlers. Today's highly competitive, crowded markets will no longer be forgiving toward those companies who are so divided internally. You need to present a unified message, both outside and inside the customer's door.

A successful sales strategy is one that focuses on the customer and leverages your time, talents, resources, and advantages. That focus will show you how to position yourself as a selling professional in a way that is consistent with your marketing department. Few sales forces use a successful sales strategy. Even fewer are aligned with their company's marketing department. Some don't even have any idea of the responsibilities of a marketing department.

Learning International of Stamford, Connecticut, recently completed a study in which it polled corporate marketing executives and sales managers to compare how they would answer the same questions. One question asked the respondents to list what they thought salespeople needed most. Among marketing executives, "selling skills" ranked at the top of their list, while that choice on the sales managers' poll ranked nearly last. Instead of "selling skills," the sales managers placed "marketing strategy" at the top of their list. Clearly, companies with such gross discrepancies in their answers to a survey are not employing the power of alignment.

THE POWER OF ALIGNMENT

Though they are very closely related, selling is merely one component in a company's total marketing system. Marketing and sales must be closely aligned to meet the new demands of today's markets. Creative salespeople have discovered that they can dramatically improve their alignment by learning from at least two types of marketing specialists: marketing research and advertising.

Marketing research concerns itself primarily with finding out what people want, whereas advertising seeks to interpret how products and services will give people what they want. Both functions are highly sophisticated in today's complex business world, yet the principles behind them are simple.

Marketing strategists use polls, interviews, and a host of other tools to determine the needs of the people they hope to reach with their products or services. The advertising specialists then develop ad campaigns to convince potential customers that their products or services will meet those needs. It is a highly effective combination. Yet, marketing sometimes misses its targets and can be fine-tuned or even revamped completely by using input from salespeople.

Because market researchers must rely on generalities, and because advertising people must address masses of people with their campaigns, salespeople often have an advantage over marketing specialists. Salespeople talk directly with individual prospects daily, probing for their deepest needs and desires.

Salespeople must not merely uncover their prospects' deepest needs; they must also find out how each of them perceives those needs. The perceived need is usually a more powerful motivation for buying than the actual need. Here is an illustration of the difference between perceived needs and actual needs, and how aligning sales and marketing with that difference can have a dramatic impact on a company's success.

According to management expert Peter Drucker, half a century ago International Business Machines was struggling to survive in the highly competitive office machines market. Its primary customers seemed to believe that they had all the business machines they needed and showed little interest in buying more from a relatively unknown firm.

Fortunately for the company, its top salespeople took a value-based approach to selling and began to ask their potential customers what they perceived their needs to be. "We need better ways of processing information," summed up the substance of their needs. No one said they wanted to buy machines, yet they had plenty of work to do that could be done by office machines.

International Business Machines translated this newly revealed perceived need into an actual need for more business machines. With that knowledge, the entire company revamped its selling approach, aligning itself with the information gathered by its sales department. The name of the company was changed to IBM. Marketing began to advertise its products as "data processing systems and information management systems" instead of office machines, whereas the sales department began providing professional assistance to increase office productivity and to set up the systems to do it.

Thus, by addressing its customers' perceived needs instead of relentlessly pushing its products, IBM soon began to dominate the same market where it had nearly failed earlier. Imagine where it would be today if its sales force had not interacted with marketing to change the alignment of the whole company! The aligned coordination between the two departments became a powerful lever that transformed a struggling company.

Many companies have salespeople running all over the country while the right hand (sales) does not know what the left hand (marketing) is doing. Marketing usually operates in one area, sales in another, and never the twain shall meet. The two never talk to each other. They are not *in sync*, not *aligned*. When that occurs in a crowded marketplace, your sales will flounder. The sales staff has to carry the marketing banner. There has to be consistency. When the two are aligned, the resulting consistency always produces improved sales. As the survey by *Learning International* revealed, alignment is a real challenge for sales managers to address.

Any sales or marketing strategy can be either focused or diffused. The key to alignment is for both sales and marketing to work from the same focused strategy. Success cannot be expected if alignment coordinates two departments with ineffective, diffused strategies. Here are the distinctions between focused and diffused strategies:

Focused Strategy	**Diffused Strategy**
• Clearly defined	• Unclear
• Well-known	• Unknown
• Accepted	• Not accepted

The strategy we've developed, entitled IMPACT Selling, covered completely beginning with Chapter 4, is an example of a *clearly defined* strategy. Of course, any strategy has to be customer-focused to succeed, but it must also be plainly identifiable and complete with training mechanisms for your staff.

Identifying a successful, clearly-defined sales strategy will naturally be of no use if it is not known, accepted, or used by your sales force. Once you train your entire sales force, then your strategy will have the second element of being *well-known*.

An important third element is that your sales staff also *accept* the plan you use. It is our hope that the demonstrated successes we have seen with IMPACT Selling will give you an easy job of convincing your salespeople of its value. Once your staff accepts IMPACT Selling, you will have all three elements of a focused sales strategy.

THE STRATEGY ALIGNMENT MATRIX

The possible strategies a company's marketing and sales departments may employ can be depicted in four ways. First, both the marketing and sales strategies can be focused. Clearly, this is the most effective combination. It is also possible for either one to be focused while the other one is diffused. And least effective, both strategies can be diffused.

FIGURE 3–1
Strategy Matrix

Marketing strategy

		Diffused	Focused
Sales strategy	Diffused	Failure **1**	Conflict and low sales **2**
	Focused	Marginal success **3**	Long-range success **4**

Figure 3–1 illustrates the four possible combinations of marketing and sales strategies:

On the left side of the Strategy Matrix chart you see the two possible sales strategies. Then, across the top of the chart, I have placed the two possible marketing strategies. The intersections of each heading in the matrix correspond to the predicted outcome of using one of the four possible combinations. I will now examine each of these four possibilities, providing anecdotes to illustrate each situation.

Diffused Marketing and Diffused Sales Strategy
Result: Failure

Box number one shows that if *neither* your company's marketing strategy nor its sales strategy is clearly defined, well-known, and accepted both inside and outside of your organization, your company is *doomed* to failure. Your company will disappear in the crowded marketplace of the 1990s. Failure due to misalignment is not something new, but has been a fact of business life for centuries. I have merely given it a name and a place in the matrix.

Finding companies to study where marketing and sales are both diffused is difficult because they do not last long. I won't bother including examples of that *lose-lose* combination. If you want to read about some on your own, check your local courthouse for the latest Chapter 11 bankruptcy filings.

Focused Marketing Strategy and Diffused Sales Strategy
Result: Conflict and Low Sales

In greater abundance are companies whose marketing strategies are focused while their sales strategies are diffused. The most notable characteristics of this common situation are internal corporate conflict and low sales. These companies represent a large proportion of that bottom 80 percent I discussed in Chapter 1. They may plod along for years, but their misalignment will ensure that they never prosper.

In these companies, marketing has done a terrific job of identifying prospects and may well have developed strategies that bring customers through the door in droves. The problem, which the companies usually cannot understand, is why sales are not being closed. Internal corporate conflict develops, and relations between sales and marketing rapidly deteriorate to finger-pointing and accusations.

The well-focused marketing department in one of these companies usually believes it is saddled with the worst sales department in the world. While it may appear that way from the marketing side of the fence because the right customers are being reached, the real problem lies with upper management. It has not ensured that both strategies are aligned. Here is a story that provides a good example of how misalignment of even a single salesperson can hurt sales performance.

We consulted with a car dealership that was having trouble with a new salesman named Jim. His poor performance was a surprise to the sales manager because Jim had been the sales leader at a nearby Toyota dealer. For years, he had set regional records and had had a tremendous impact on the success of the dealer. In fact, Jim had used his exceptional performance to leverage his career, advancing to our client, a Porsche dealership. Once at his new job, though, his performance suddenly dropped, and a deep conflict developed between Jim and his sales manager.

Jim had a finely honed sales strategy of his own which gave him great confidence. However, his poor closing rate led his manager to question Jim's talents. The sales manager did not believe that Porsche's marketing strategy was at fault.

Clearly, Porsche's marketing strategy is well-focused. The company is masterful at targeting prospects who might buy high-end, high-performance luxury cars. It was equally evident that Jim was a top-notch professional.

The immediate problem at this dealer was that the sales manager had not aligned his new hire with Porsche's marketing strategy. The missing element was that the Porsche sales strategy was not yet known or accepted by Jim. Jim had continued using a sales strategy that had served him well for years, but it met the needs of buyers who were more economy-minded. His former prospects had a completely different idea of value in an automobile than did Jim's new Porsche prospects. Once we pointed out the misalignment, the sales manager worked with Jim to change his selling strategy to fit in with Porsche's marketing strategy. Shortly thereafter, Jim's sales performance jumped dramatically.

Here is a truism that I have emphasized to countless sales managers:

> *Both the company and the salesperson need to understand the power of positioning by alignment, and the salesperson needs to understand the power of* personal *positioning by alignment.*

Though the Porsche sales manager had a good sales strategy, it was not well-known to Jim. You can see in our Strategy Matrix that this problem put them in the box where conflict reigns. Had this former Toyota salesman immediately focused on the needs of his new customers, he would have automatically realigned himself *personally* with the well-focused Porsche marketing strategy.

Diffused Marketing Strategy and Focused Sales Strategy
Result: Marginal Success

Let's examine box number three on the grid and describe another type of company that floods the ranks of the bottom 80 percent group, and as such merely gets by.

When marketing and sales are out of alignment in this direction, we find marginal success and marginal profits at best, but little or no growth. A company in this category may stay in business for years and be a well-known brand name, because it will usually maintain moderate success. Still, its lack of alignment will never allow it to enter the top 20 percent.

The obvious question is, "Why do these companies survive better than when the misalignment is in the other direction?" That question has a simple answer: Good salespeople can sell anything! I have done it; you have done it. When you turn a good sales staff loose with a good product and good product training they will make sales. Salespeople who are well-trained can make things happen.

Companies that rely on the natural instincts and capabilities of their salespeople will experience limited success but will continually fall short of their long-range goals. Eventually, customers tire of pushy sales pitches. Even worse, one of those customer-focused, "top 20 percenters" arrives on the scene.

We saw a great example of this in our own offices with a saleswoman who called here. She worked for a collection services agency and came in to see if we needed what she was offering. We let her proceed because we were eager to see what would happen.

Initially, she asked a couple of polite questions, but only because somebody had trained her to do so. Then she began to pitch her product in the classic sense. She was a stereotypical, high-energy salesperson and probably could have sold a fan in a windstorm. She seemed to be on a roll.

About halfway through her well-rehearsed pitch, she stopped, looked me straight in the eye, and said, "If everything looks good to you, Mr. Brooks, is there any reason why we couldn't do business today?" I knew immediately that she had been through extensive—though outdated—sales training. But I knew just as well that her company did not have a focused marketing strategy. Clearly they had made no marketing efforts to find prospects who needed their services.

While the saleswoman may have sold us if we'd had a need, her company's approach, diffused marketing and focused sales, always leads to a low closing rate. She was not *personally* aligned with anything but her archaic sales training.

This story shows why I see alignment as an extension of leverage. The diffused marketing strategy of the saleswoman's company had put her in a position where she was not making the most effective use of her time, talent, or resources. She was simply going about a daily routine, hoping for something to happen. I liken a salesperson in this category to a spider in its web. The small flies and bugs that land there will be quickly entrapped and wrapped up. The spider will suck the living juices out of its catch to survive (i.e., cash that commission check) before it gets away.

The spider settles for whatever comes along (i.e., waits for someone to answer the ad). If the flies are not buzzing, the spider does not eat (i.e., there is a downturn in the economy). Worse, the really big catches that could feed the spider for life will go right through the web so that it will just have to weave another web and wait. Of course, this could be interpreted as a real genetic strength of the spider. And it is. However, human beings are genetically engineered to far exceed the performance of a spider!

I see the problem of a diffused marketing strategy and focused sales strategy capsulized in an aphorism that has been around for years:

> *You may need to take whatever comes along, but you have to go after whatever you want.*

Your path toward getting whatever you want begins when both your marketing strategy and your sales strategy are aligned. Only then will you experience success through long-range growth and high profits. Let's now look at the alignment order that will put you in that top 20 percent of salespeople, tapping you into 80 percent of sales.

Focused Marketing Strategy and Focused Sales Strategy
Result: Long-Range Success

This is the master key to long-range success in the crowded marketplaces of the 1990s and beyond. Your marketing strategy and sales strategy need to be developed in tandem from the ground up, with both focused squarely on the needs of your prospective customers.

Your sales strategy has to be linked with marketing to leverage the advantages and opportunities that develop as a result of the advertising of your products or services. Linkage will be difficult unless the two strategies are developed concurrently.

The power of alignment can be illustrated by comparing two prominent companies in the lady's hosiery business. Industry leader *L'eggs*, with a focused marketing strategy and a focused sales strategy, has a solid lock on the top spot, despite having higher prices than competitors. This piqued our curiosity, so we studied its success. Here is what we found.

At L'eggs, both marketing and sales are well-focused, targeting the high-end of the market. *No nonsense* is number two in the industry, though it clearly beats L'eggs on price. No nonsense has a focused marketing strategy that targets the same high-end customers as L'eggs, yet its salespeople always push price because they do not believe they can compete with L'eggs.

The expectations of the No nonsense sales reps seem to continually come true, although not for the reasons they imagine. The true problem is that No nonsense salespeople mainly push their price advantage over L'eggs, which is in direct conflict with the marketing thrust of No nonsense. If the buyers were looking solely for discount hosiery, they could get even better deals from generic products. No nonsense should instead focus its salespeople where its marketing is—on delivering a high-quality product to those customers who demand it. If the company adopted that strategy, then store buyers would readily see that No nonsense offers a better value.

The struggles of No nonsense in the hosiery industry are a classic example of the internal conflicts we always find when marketing is focused and the sales department is not aligned with that marketing. Here's a truism you can bank on: *Price alone is rarely a key factor in buying decisions.* Instead, the key factor in any buying decision is the perceived value to be gained by the buyer. Perceived value is the reason why companies with the highest priced products and services in many industries often garner most of the market.

We continually see lower-priced competitors scratching their collective heads in amazement at how they are continually beaten, though they offer the same product at a lower price. People rarely buy products; they buy value, and most are willing to pay a fair price for the value they receive.

MARKETING AND SELLING CELLULAR PHONE *SERVICE*, NOT CELLULAR PHONES

The cellular phone industry has recently become a crowded marketplace. It has already reached the easy sales prospects; the people who had to have cellular phones made their purchases early and will continue to use them. Also, the market is flooded with an every increasing number of companies producing cellular phones.

The industry's challenge now is to tap the next level of buyers—the hard-sell customers—yet the sales staffs of most companies in the cellular phone industry are out merely peddling phones. Most cellular phone customers have little need to own a *cellular phone;* what they need is *cellular phone service.* Most cellular phone companies have a properly focused marketing strategy that correctly emphasizes cellular phone service. Still, their traditionally oriented sales forces are out peddling phones because that is how salespeople are compensated. When a phone gets installed in a car, a salesperson gets paid. These companies suffer greatly from internal conflicts because marketing pushes services, and sales pushes phones; the sales strategy is *out of sync* with the marketing strategy.

Cellular One, one of our clients, is a notable and highly successful exception to the norm. It has carefully coordinated both sales and marketing strategies. When making sales calls, the company's salespeople focus on the needs of their prospects while emphasizing the "quality, service, and value" of Cellular One.

Cellular One offers long-term, money-back guarantees, outstanding service with credit for bad connections, and *loaner phones!* That is an advantage that no other company offers, and the sales staff has used that advantage as *leverage* to improve the value of the Cellular One product to customers. If you buy a Cellular One phone, you will probably pay a higher *price* than if you used a competitor. Yet, if the cheaper phone breaks down and you end up driving for days with a nonworking phone in your car, what do you have in terms of *value?* Instead of selling *cellular phones,* Cellular One sells its customers continuous, reliable, and satisfaction-guaranteed *cellular phone service.*

When both your marketing strategy and your sales strategy focus on customer needs *and* on customer-perceived value, your unified efforts will enjoy a high degree of long-term success.

PERSONAL POSITIONING BY ALIGNMENT

Complete alignment of a company's marketing and sales strategies culminates in well-positioned, one-on-one *personal* sales presentations. Even if your company has the most highly focused marketing strategy ever devised and you use a highly focused sales strategy, individual salespeople can diminish the effectiveness of the whole organization if they do not personally align themselves with the corporate thrust as they face prospects. The company can help to get the salesperson inside the door. Once inside, however, the individual needs to assume control and maintain a strict focus on customer needs; this is *the power of personal positioning*. In Part II, especially in Chapter 5, I cover specific actions for individuals to use for personal alignment.

Too often traditional sales training focuses on tricks and techniques to use once the salesperson has a foot in the door. One of my mentors, the salesman on whom I leaned most in my early years of selling, told me to stick my head in the door instead. His reasoning was that if they slammed it on me, I had less to lose. Salespeople trained with inner-directed selling plans will have little to lose if their heads are slammed in doors when they are using traditional sales tricks.

PUTTING IT ALL TOGETHER: FOCUS, LEVERAGE, AND ALIGNMENT

The key to survival in the 1990s is to ensure that your entire sales force uses their heads for more than a doorstop. To succeed, they need to know everything they can about their prospects and their products. They must then use that knowledge to employ the three fundamentals presented in Part I.

Indeed, focus, leverage, and alignment remain the dominant themes I present in the rest of the book. Furthermore, I believe that ultimately someone in your market will learn the IMPACT Selling orientation or something similar, apply it, and chew up the competition. I want that someone to be you.

To ensure that you are that someone, I have developed another chart that will help you always keep focus, leverage, and alignment in mind. I have combined all three into an integrated formula for success, as is illustrated in Figure 3–2.

Here are all three ideas in summary:

- Focus every activity on the needs of your prospects and on ways to increase value to them. There are four areas on which you can focus—self, product, company, or customer. If you focus on the first three, your prospects are out-numbered three to one.

FIGURE 3–2
Focus, Leverage, and Alignment Formula

Where is my focus?	Am I leveraged?	Where am I aligned? Marketing strategy		
			Diffused	Focused
• Self?	• Time?			
• Product?	• Talent?	Sales strategy Diffused	Failure	Conflict and low sales 2
• Company?	• Resources?			1
• Prospect?	• Advantages?	Focused	Marginal success 3	Long-range success 4

- Leverage your own time, talent, and resources. Leverage the advantages of your product and service offerings to raise value to your customers. Leverage your strengths against the weaknesses of your competitors.
- Align yourself with your company's marketing strategy by using a proven, outer-directed sales strategy. Always present a unified image to your customers. This is positioning by alignment.

Once you understand the power of this integrated focus, leverage, and alignment formula, you are ready to learn how to turn the theory into practical action steps. We will now move on to Part II to explain the IMPACT Selling plan that will separate you from all the "me-too" marketing approaches that your prospects encounter daily.

KEY TIPS

☑ Marketing strategy is what gets you to the customer's door in the best possible light. Sales strategy is what you do when you're inside.

☑ Any sales or marketing strategy can either be focused or diffused. The key to alignment is for both sales and marketing to work from the same focused strategy. Successful alignment coordinates the two departments with effective, focused strategies. A focused strategy is clearly defined, well-known, and accepted both inside *and* outside your organization.

☑ Both the company and the salesperson need to understand the power of positioning by alignment, and the salesperson needs to understand the power of *personal* positioning by alignment.

☑ You may need to take whatever comes along, but you have to go after whatever you want. When both your marketing strategy and your sales strategy focus on customer needs *and* on customer-perceived value, your unified efforts will enjoy a high degree of long-term success.

☑ Complete alignment of your marketing and sales strategies culminates in well-positioned, one-on-one, *personal* sales presentation. You can diminish the effectiveness of the whole organization if you do not personally align yourself with the corporate thrust. The company can help get you inside the door, but once inside you must assume control and maintain a strict focus on customer needs.

PART II

KNOWING YOUR CUSTOMERS

CHAPTER 4

IMPACT SELLING

Knowledge is more than equivalent to force.
Samuel Johnson

The best way to boost your customer impact is to cultivate an empathy with the customer by understanding his or her needs, interests, and desires, and by knowing how to get for the customer what he or she wants. I based that idea on the wisdom I learned from an inspirational salesman who taught me the greatest secret of success in selling.

THE GREATEST SECRET IN SELLING:
Show people what they want most, and they will move heaven and earth to get it!

That secret comes from an anonymous source and was first revealed in print by Frank Bettger, who learned it from what he termed "an old-timer." Mr. Bettger used its power to make more than a million dollars in selling during the early years of this century. One of Mr. Bettger's stories that illustrates just how powerful this secret is.*

As a life insurance salesman, Frank Bettger called on a successful businessman named Scott and asked him for five minutes of his time; promising to leave after that unless the client asked him to stay longer. Mr. Scott agreed but assured him it would be a waste of time for both of them, since he was 63 years old and had long before quit buying insurance. Mr. Scott further explained that all his children were grown, his wife was well-protected

---

*From the book, *How I Raised Myself from Failure to Success in Selling*, by Frank Bettger (1977, 1949) Used by permission of the publisher, Prentice-Hall, Inc., New Jersey.

with paid-up life insurance, his business was well-covered, and his estate plan and will had all been carefully prepared.

That would have been enough to send most insurance salespeople packing, but not Frank Bettger. Mr. Bettger applied the secret he knew about selling. He had done his homework and knew that Mr. Scott was a highly benevolent man who had often given generously to worthwhile causes. "Mr. Scott, a man who has been as successful as you surely must have some interests outside your family and your business," Mr. Bettger suggested. "Perhaps a hospital, religious work, missionary, or charitable work," he continued. He then listed a few he knew Mr. Scott had supported. "Did you ever consider that when you die, your support will be withdrawn? Wouldn't this loss seriously handicap or even mean the discontinuance of some splendid work?"

At that, the salesman glanced at his watch, noted that his time was up, and thanked his host for his time. But Mr. Scott invited him to stay and talk some more. Frank Bettger used the additional time and the confidence he had gained very carefully. Instead of seizing the moment to spill out everything he knew about insurance, he continued to ask questions.

Those questions revealed that the work nearest and dearest to Mr. Scott's heart was the work of three missionary teams in Nicaragua that he supported. Mr. Bettger also learned that one of those teams included Mr. Scott's son and daughter-in-law, and that he was soon planning to visit them.

"Mr. Scott," he finally asked, "when you go down to Nicaragua, wouldn't you be happy to tell your son and his young family that you had just guaranteed that if anything ever happens to you, a check will come to them *every month* so that their work may continue? Wouldn't you also like to write to the other two missionaries, giving them the same message?"

There was a long silence. Mr. Bettger waited. Then Mr. Scott thanked Frank Bettger for helping him discover a serious oversight in his planning. No pressure had been applied, and no tricky closes had been used. The old pro had simply shown his prospect what he wanted most, and the prospect had made a decision to buy. Mr. Bettger had not tried to sell insurance; he had shown Mr. Scott that what he really wanted was for the missionary work to continue after he could no longer support it.

After tying down the sale, Frank Bettger walked out of that man's office with a check in hand for $9,000, back when $9,000 was a whopping insurance premium. That is impact selling—and it works!

Thousands of salespeople use that secret daily to close sales in nearly every business you can name: insurance, capital equipment, automobiles, industrial supplies, real estate, and so on. Yet, for every salesperson who uses it, there are ten who do not and yet wonder why they close so few sales. Let's review that secret one more time: *Show people what they want most, and they will move heaven and earth to get it!*

That simple secret will revolutionize your selling career if you memorize it and use it on every sales call. Your prospects will move heaven and earth to buy from you, but only *after* you show them what they want most. To understand what your prospects want most, you must first connect with their highest values.

I will now explore how you can make the greatest secret in selling work for you on an individual, customer-by-customer, prospect-by-prospect basis within your market niche.

HOW TO MAKE THE VALUES CONNECTION

Before you can show people what they want most, you must discover what their wants and needs are. You will never talk your way into an in-depth understanding of a prospect. To find out what people want most, you must listen.

We all share certain basic needs, interests, and desires—to live, to be loved, to be happy, to have security and adventure. Yet the different ways in which we define those elusive conditions, and our ideas of how to obtain them, are enormous and uniquely personal. These different perceptions and the actions we take to satisfy our desires are what shape our individual value systems.

How do you connect with a prospect's deepest needs, most compelling interests, and greatest desires? It's just like staying in good physical condition—relatively simple, but not always easy! Discovering what people want most involves asking the *right* questions, listening *carefully*, and being totally aware of everything that expresses your prospect's *values*.

You will later learn how to hone your listening skills, because they are vital to every high IMPACT salesperson, and they add tremendous power to your persuasion. For now, though, we will continue to explore value-based selling.

USING CUSTOMER NEEDS TO PROFIT
FROM VALUE-BASED SELLING

Once you discover what your prospect wants most out of life, you are in an excellent position to employ value-based selling. You can then tailor your whole presentation to appeal to your prospect's greatest desire by concerning yourself with what is most important on his or her own personal priority list of desires. We consistently find that most salespeople do not custom-tailor their presentations because they believe it takes too much time. We hear several common excuses.

First, they feel it takes too much of their own time.

"Man, I don't have time to waste talking to every prospect I see about all those things," a salesperson once said to me. "I have to call on at least 20 people every day to meet my quota. You've got to get in, tell your story, and get out," she added. "The more people you see, the more money you make...it's a numbers game, everybody knows that. Besides, if people are really interested, they'll buy without all that.'

"How many sales a day do you average?" I asked her.

"I always try to make at least two sales a day," she said.

"Would you like to make half as many calls and sell twice as much?" I challenged her.

"You bet I would!" she quickly acknowledged.

Her closing ratio had been running at only 10 percent of the sales she attempted. I told her that many salespeople we have trained in customer-focused, value-based selling were closing 40 percent and more of their sales. If she were only able to match that, she would still close four sales a day while only calling on 10 clients.

Second, most salespeople feel their customers do not have time for value-based selling approaches.

"People are busy. You've got to get right to the point, say what you want to say, and get out," is a typical response to a question we often ask about how much time salespeople spend with their average prospect. That typical answer is correct, too; people are always too busy to waste time doing anything they do not really want or need to do.

The secret to breaking through that barrier is expressed in the first of three *value-based selling principles* we have developed.

VALUE-BASED SELLING PRINCIPLE #1:
People always find time to take care of something they need, value, or truly want.

People always manage to make time to do what really matters to them. For example, most people can find a thousand ways to avoid spending time in a dentist's chair—unless they happen to have a throbbing toothache. Struck with an immobilizing pain, a person will easily find the time it takes to go to a dentist.

The nerves you hit through value-based selling will not be as sensitive to your prospects as the ones a dentist hits, but your impact can be surprisingly similar and powerful. If you fully explore your prospect's needs, you may discover his or her biggest business toothache. The time spent getting in touch with and speaking to your prospect's need will go a long way toward capturing his or her attention and will pay big dividends for you.

Once you discover what your prospect perceives his or her most pressing need to be, you can build your whole presentation around that need. This is application selling at its best. Tailored presentations save time because they keep you from wasting time educating customers on products that may never serve their perceived needs. Application selling puts you in touch with your prospects' strongest motivations for buying. It forms the difference between trying to create a need and helping the prospect find a much desired solution to a problem he or she has.

This truism is embodied in a second key selling principle.

VALUE-BASED SELLING PRINCIPLE #2:
It is always easier to sell to a prospect's perceived need than to create a need in the prospect's mind!

Failure to understand and use that simple principle causes most salespeople to work much harder than necessary, to miss many sales they could close, and to fail when they could succeed at selling. Value-based salespeople always concern themselves first with how the prospect perceives his or her needs.

Wish-Fulfillment Selling

Some of the most effective value-based selling in America today is done by the people who produce commercials for network television. Have you ever noticed that AT&T never asks you to make a long-distance call? Instead, they invite you to "Reach out and touch someone." The hamburger chains never peddle sandwiches; they say, "You deserve a break today," and "Have it your way." The Kodak company never advertises film; they urge you to "Trust your memories to Kodak."

Traditionally, the style of sales appeals such as those is called "selling the sizzle instead of the steak," but it goes deeper than that. We call it *wish-fulfillment selling*, and it has some solid psychological reasoning behind it. Studies have shown that if you tell people something they want to believe and keep repeating it, they will begin to remember it and act upon it. The American private enterprise economy has improved the tastes and quality-of-life level of the average citizen. Wish-fulfillment selling has played a major role in that growth and vitality.

In comparison with other cultures, Americans have few unfulfilled needs. While we share the same need for food with people of all nations, we do not *need* instant foods in nearly every imaginable variety. American food sales now focus on convenience, simplicity, ease of preparation, and a host of other intangible values people are willing to buy. Fortunes have been made by discovering what people want most and showing them how to get it.

The food industry has one terrific example of the concept of meeting perceived needs. How many people would buy a jar of monosodium glutamate? Can you imagine an ad that peddled MSG? "We've got the highest quality MSG on the market and we've been in business for more than 75 years!" Yet, when the same substance is labeled *Accent* and its ad tells consumers it "wakes up food flavor," it suddenly meets people's needs.

Your challenge in value-based selling is not merely to show off the features of what you are selling, but to make your prospect believe that what you are selling will fulfill his or her wishes. That challenge can be expressed in a very important principle.

VALUE-BASED SELLING PRINCIPLE #3:
All values are equal until someone points out the difference!

This is particularly true when selling inside a carefully carved niche because competition narrows and becomes highly intense. The need to differentiate values becomes essential as your niche concentration narrows and wish-fulfillment selling becomes even more critical.

The key to wish-fulfillment selling is to connect very solidly with the deepest aspirations and hopes of every prospect you call upon, and to know your products and services well enough to see how to fulfill those desires. Though value-based selling takes a lot of creativity, imagination, and an innovative spirit, it is a dynamite sales approach. Moreover, the increasingly crowded marketplaces of the 1990s will require it. To sum up the three key points of value-based selling:

- Connect with and sell what your prospect values the most.
- Uncover your prospect's needs, as he or she perceives them, and show him or her how to meet those needs through what you are selling.
- Connect with deepest hopes and aspirations of every prospect you call upon, and know your products and services well enough to identify how they can fulfill those desires.

Although these three points are simple to understand, integrating them into your entire force is not easy. I will now begin to present a simple but powerful formula that will enable you and your sales force to use value-based selling with every prospect within your niche. You cannot build a successful sales force through the application of traditional motivational techniques alone. It takes much more than that today. Motivation without a plan leads only to frustration.

YOU MUST HAVE A PLAN

Without a plan, salespeople set goals, push hard to reach them, and yet never seem to get anywhere. They begin to doubt the value of what they are selling, to question their abilities, and to think of other careers. Or, even if somewhat successful, they may hit a slump and feel stuck.

If you have ever had any of those feelings, you have one of these two problems:

- You do not have a simple, effective selling system that works well for you.
- If you have a plan, you are not following it precisely.

When I was coaching college football, I discovered that the only way my teams would win consistently was for me to (1) establish a simple, well-conceived *game plan* that took maximum advantage of the unique skills of my players; (2) drill it so firmly into my players' heads that they could follow it *instinctively*; and (3) insist that they follow it in every detail.

The more clearly I defined and believed in my game plan, the more my players believed in it. The more they believed in my plan, the closer they followed it. The better we stuck to the game plan, the more games we won. It was that simple!

Using a game plan in successful selling is equally simple. IMPACT Selling is a unique, simple sales game plan that is easy to learn and extraordinarily effective.

Keeping pace with the ever changing value systems of today's crowded marketplace calls for a highly adaptable approach to selling. You need a sales plan whose key points align perfectly with the values and needs of today's crowded markets. A successful value-based plan must be

- Dynamic enough to meet the challenges of selling in the ever changing environment of the 1990s and beyond.
- Adaptable to any product, service, or selling situation.
- Founded on basic principles of human relations so you will know the *why* behind every *how*.
- Integrity-based so you will never have to violate your own value structure.
- Filled with many practical ideas you can begin to use immediately.
- Easy to learn and simple to implement so that anyone can do it.

THE GREATEST MYTH OF SELLING

The greatest myth of selling is that some people are simply "born salespeople." This misconception has kept countless talented people—who didn't have the "right" personality—from pursuing a sales career, and has filled the profession with many people whose highest qualification is being a "natural" for sales. There is an old story about a man who was an obstetrician for many years. "I've delivered thousands of babies over the years," he once said, "but I've never delivered a salesperson."

Selling is a science, based on documented principles that can be learned by anyone of average intelligence. As a science, it has an underlying view of human nature, a concomitant set of principles that are learned by study and experimentation, and effective applications to daily life.

Like any science, selling is constantly changing as it challenges old assumptions, embraces new discoveries, and adapts to new situations. Through the IMPACT Selling process, you will find a blend of the best of the tested and proven techniques as well as challenging new concepts that are working well for thousands of salespeople with whom we have worked and trained to be successful in today's new selling environment.

OUR GAME PLAN

There are six phases to the IMPACT Selling system, and each is introduced and presented sequentially in the next six chapters of this book. Completing Part II will show you exactly how to implement value-based selling from prospecting through closing the sale. The six powerful phases of our game plan are:

1. Investigate. Discover who may need your products or services, identifying them as prospects; gaining appointments.

   - To give you a large range of qualified prospects for what you are selling.
   - To give you all the information you need about those prospects in order for you to be most convincing.
   - To enable you to prepare your strongest and most persuasive presentation.

2. Meet. Engage prospects personally; turn resisters into listeners.

   - To set up the best selling situation.
   - To make your prospects feel important and relaxed.
   - To start them talking about themselves or their key interests.
   - To gain rapport.

3. Probe. Discover what prospects want, need, and value most and under what conditions they will buy it.

- To discover what your prospects want most.
- To uncover real and perceived needs.
- To get prospects involved in the selling process.
- To get prospects to tell you their deepest needs.

4. Apply. Build value for your prospects by showing them how your products and services will meet their needs.

- To show prospective buyers that you understand their needs and desires.
- To present the product or service in a light that will fulfill those needs and desires.
- To let them experience how the product or service will meet their needs and desires.
- To make sure they understand all the benefits they will receive from ownership.

5. Convince. Prove to prospects that they can fulfill their needs and wishes by buying your products or services.

- To prove every claim you have made.
- To answer any questions prospective buyers may have.
- To justify the price through emphasizing value.
- To reemphasize the importance of customers' desires and relieve any fears of buying.

6. Tie it up. Close the sale and reinforce the buyer's decision.

- To negotiate a win-win agreement.
- To welcome, identify, and answer all objections.
- To reinforce customers' positive feelings about buying.
- To close the sale.
- To get referrals and introductions after earning the right to do so.

That is the whole IMPACT Selling System. Later on in this chapter, I will show you how this process can be clearly and easily followed through the assimilation and application of a simple, yet easy-to-follow graphic representation of the actual sales process.

This process has been laid out in a way that has proven to be a success formula for literally thousands of sales professionals. What you sell and to whom you sell it is most critical. However, the process has been designed so that it is clearly superior to all other approaches when used in a competitive, tightly niched marketplace.

Though you may use many of these individual steps already, our system provides a convenient plan for coordinating them in the most effective way. Every step sets up the next one, steadily moving the prospect toward a buying decision without making him or her feel pressured in any way. The three principles of focus, leverage, and alignment blend naturally into a values-based selling system that ensures long-term success within your niche.

IMPACT Selling Is Not a Canned Pitch

Canned sales presentations are insulting to today's educated and alert consumers, many of whom are professional buyers. Also, such presentations guarantee failure within a specialized niche.

More significantly, a stock-in-trade approach disregards the greatest advantage of having a talented salesperson call on prospects—the advantage of one unique human being connecting with another. Because IMPACT Selling taps the power of personal connections, it is a strategy that can be used by any salesperson to sell anything to any prospect.

Yet, some will argue, "Who needs it? I just play it by ear." Unfortunately, most of those who say they "play it by ear" usually play it by *mouth* and talk themselves out of many sales they could close if they followed a simple, adaptable plan. Once you learn IMPACT Selling and practice it a few times, you will use it intuitively. You will then be free to concentrate on what really matters in closing the sale—the customer.

Adapt; Don't Throw Out the Plan!

If it seems I am contradicting myself, I understand how you feel. On the one hand, I have said you must recognize that every customer is different. On the other hand, I am now saying that you should follow a system. We have discovered that during this early stage of learning about IMPACT Selling, many people feel confused. Nonetheless, the two concepts are compatible. Over the years, I have found that this football analogy helps clarify how.

Every opponent my college team played against was unique. Each opposing team had a different style, the talents of the players varied from team to team, and some of our key players occasionally had bad days while other players seemed unusually adroit.

The temptation was always there to throw out our basic game plan in order to take advantage of the weaknesses of a specific opponent or to compensate for weekly differences. Yet, as we learned the hard way, we were always most effective when we stuck to those things we did best and concentrated on doing them even better. Although we prepared differently for each of our opponents by adapting our plan slightly to compensate for weaknesses and to take advantage of our opportunities, we never departed from the basic plan.

You must do the same in selling. Incorporate the IMPACT Selling system as your basic game plan, then adapt it to take advantage of opportunities and to compensate for problems. For example, if you know a prospect very well and consider him or her a friend, you will not need to spend much time in the Meeting phase where you establish rapport with the prospect. Instead, you can move quickly into an interview, which we call the Probe phase. You will not have abandoned the basic plan merely because the first two phases are unusually brief. *Always* follow the IMPACT sequence.

CUSTOMER IMPACT: THE WINNER'S EDGE

Winners and losers may remain close throughout a race—even finishing neck and neck. When it's over and they take their winnings home, however, the losers are often far behind. Here is a typical example that illustrates the difference in the distance between winners and losers on and off the track.

A few years ago, a racehorse named Achmed became one of the first horses in history to win more than one million dollars in a single racing season. During that same season, there was another horse that came in second in nearly every race Achmed won.

Interestingly, Achmed won 15 times as much money as the horse that consistently came in second. Later, the champion was sold for ten times more money than the second runner. Does that mean that Achmed was 15 times faster than his nearest competitor?

That question intrigued a sportswriter, so he studied the times logged by the two horses. Achmed's finishing times averaged only 3 percent faster than the second best horse, yet that brought his owner 15 times more prize money and ten times as much long-range value.

For most salespeople, income is directly proportional to the number of sales made. Some may be able to change jobs often enough to remain ahead of a draw or jump from one salaried selling job to another and keep some income flowing. Eventually, however, merely being a journeyman player catches up with them. Simply playing the game will only serve short-range goals.

In the Super Bowl, each losing player walks away with a large check just for playing. Making a sales presentation, of course, is not the Super Bowl; no prospect will ever pay you just for being there and making a good sales pitch. Regardless of the methods you employ, this truism will always remain:

> If you don't close sales, you won't make a living as a salesperson.

Our game plan is clearly not about "making a living"—that is the loser's mentality. Losers feel privileged merely to be in a big game, but winners always play to win it.

As a college football coach for 14 years, I learned that I could predict the outcome of a championship game by listening to what the coaches and players said before game day. The 1986 Super Bowl offers a good example of how I made my predictions.

In 1986, Super Bowl XX featured the New England Patriots and the Chicago Bears. The Patriots brought a great team to the championship game. They had many talented players and excellent coaching, and they had overcome great adversity by beating some very strong teams on their road to the biggest NFL game of the year.

Despite their steady path down the championship trail, the Patriots seemed surprised that they had made the play-offs, shocked that they had won their conference, and amazed that they had earned the right to play in the Super Bowl. "We're just glad to be here and to have an opportunity to play in this game," several of their players told the press in the week before the big game.

The difference in the two teams had been clear throughout the season. The Bears had decided before the season began that it was to be their year to win it all. They believed they could win every game they played that year, and they did win all but one. "No team in football can beat us!" boasted their cocky quarterback, Jim McMahon, before the big game.

The Bears confidently took the field and turned their dream into reality. They backed up all their claims with a dazzling performance, winning decisively. When it was all over, they were clearly the champions.

If you find someone who will pay you to make traditional "sales pitches" and if you enjoy the work, you will never need IMPACT Selling. Those of you who are not paid a runner-up fee need to remember this adage: *Don't just show up for the game; play to win!*

WHAT MAKES A WINNER? THE 80/20 RULE EXPANDED

I discussed the well-known 80/20 Rule earlier: 80 percent of all sales are produced by only 20 percent of the salespeople. This truism applies to most areas of human endeavor and has spurred many people to success in a wide range of enterprises. Yet, as powerful as its message is, we discovered a startling enhancement to that rule when it was found that:

> More than 60 percent of all sales are made by the top 5 percent of all salespeople.

We wondered why that was true and began asking salespeople we worked with, "Why is it that more than 60 percent of all the sales are made by the top 5 percent of all salespeople?" We got a wide spectrum of answers. Some typical ones were

"They've got products that are in great demand."

"They've got good territories."

"They just work harder."

"Some are born lucky."

We have found studies that refute every one of those claims. Most salespeople in the top 5 percent would do well selling almost anything almost anywhere, and they often work fewer hours than most of the salespeople in the bottom 20 percent. The studies found that the true answer to why the top 5 percent of all salespeople have become the real champions in selling is simply this: *They have and use the winner's edge of customer-focused, value-based selling.* In other words, they possess and use the power to convince people to buy.

If all things are equal within your niche, the sales force with the most IMPACT will enjoy the most success. Let's now find out more about what customer impact is, discover how it can give you the winner's edge, and learn how to get it.

WHY CUSTOMER IMPACT WORKS

A great way to understand customer impact is to put yourself in the customer's shoes. Here is one scenario that is easy to envision.

Your doorbell rings. You answer it and discover that there is a salesperson who wants to come in and show you a miraculous, new can opener that can be yours for a phenomenally low price. You are courteous, but you quickly get rid of that salesperson. If he or she gets pushy, you might even speak abruptly and slam the door.

Yet, later that evening an insurance salesperson keeps an appointment with you, and you spend more than an hour soaking up every word of the presentation. When it is over, you commit yourself to spend thousands of times what you would have spent on the can opener.

What is the difference? Why is it that we will listen intently to everything one person says, whereas we will not give another the time of day? The obvious answer is that you were more interested in insurance than you were in a can opener. Yet, that is only a surface answer that raises an even more important question: How does any salesperson awaken a prospect's interest and convince people that it is to their advantage to invest time in listening to a sales presentation?

There are countless techniques that would enable you to hold someone's attention long enough to rattle off a traditional sales pitch. Remember, though, techniques are for short-range goals. To succeed for a long-range career, you must ground your attention-getting methods on principles. We have developed four principles that make the answer to the "What is the difference?" question absolutely clear.

CUSTOMER IMPACT PRINCIPLE #1:
We pay attention to people we believe have something important to tell us.

The beginning of utilizing customer impact in your career will come with your capacity to *convince* people that what you have to say is important to them. Your customers live in a world where they are continually bombarded by people who *claim* to have something important to say to them. Your challenge is to *convince* them.

Again, put yourself in a customer's shoes.

All day long, people are trying to gain your attention. The boss wants you to hear or read instructions; family members want you to do things for them; friends and neighbors have ideas they want to share; television, newspapers, and radio blitz you with appeals to buy things. You live in a never ending barrage of hype. Communications experts have found that the typical American receives about 1,800 messages a day that press for some form of action. That totals 9,000 messages in one normal work week, and you are only one of those messages.

Americans have learned to tune out most of this stream of unwanted messages. We have learned to filter out all but those messages we think are important to us. In order to be successful, salespeople must have the capacity to break through those thousands of other messages and convince a prospect that what they have to say really matters to him or her. How can that be done? Though the process of breaking through listening barriers involves many steps, we have found another impact principle that provides a basis for the process.

CUSTOMER IMPACT PRINCIPLE #2:
People buy for their own reasons—not for yours or mine.

Champion salespeople know that prospects typically could not care less if they have a chance to win a trip to Hawaii, or a new car, or even a yacht. We all have an inner radio that is pretuned to pick up only one station—WII-FM. That stands for What's In It For Me? Every prospect you call on has his or her own needs, interests, and desires, and the only place where they hear ads about how to fulfill them is on WII-FM.

During training experiences with thousands of salespeople, we have observed that the greatest single selling error occurs when salespeople consistently fail to broadcast their messages over their prospects' personal station, WII-FM. Salespeople who use traditional selling techniques broadcast in a buyer *blindspot*, focusing on why *they* want to sell, instead of *who would want to buy what they're selling*.

This blindspot in salespeople's attitudes often results in a preoccupation with handling objections. Traditional sales training has preached that we should continually read, study, and practice techniques to "overcome objections," rather than find out how to connect with what the customer needs and how we can supply it. The top 5 percent of the selling profession always remembers WII-FM and continually broadcasts the fact that they know how to help people get what they need or want.

A single-minded focus on this one concept, that of viewing yourself as a needs-fulfiller for every prospect, will easily place you in the top 5 percent. That one insight alone makes this entire book worth its cost and the time you will invest in reading it. Throughout the IMPACT chapters in Part II, you will notice that I continually reemphasize that vital principle: *Nothing else can give you more customer impact than knowing how to direct every appeal to the prospect's self-interests.*

That leads us to the next vital insight into what gives a salesperson impact.

CUSTOMER IMPACT PRINCIPLE #3:
People do not want to be sold; they want to buy.

Have you ever noticed that when someone proudly displays a purchase with which they are pleased the most common expression is "I bought it from..."? It is only when we are unhappy with a purchase we have made that we say, "That XYZ Company *sold* this trash to me!" In a crowded market niche, a few customers who make statements like that will quickly ruin your reputation.

People resent feeling coerced, manipulated, or tricked into doing or buying anything. We will listen to, and even appreciate, information about a product, service, or company that interests us. We will ask questions about things we don't understand. We will even welcome some gentle persuasion to help us make up our minds. Yet, the moment we feel someone is trying to manipulate, intimidate, or dominate us, our defenses take over and we prepare to put up a good fight. Tricky selling maneuvers are an invasion of personal space and propriety, and people will defend their personal space almost to the death.

True sales champions know that when a salesperson and a customer get locked into a war of the wills, the salesperson always loses. The emphasis must remain on helping prospects make the decision to buy, never on selling. When you are meeting someone's needs or offering what they value most, you never trigger negative emotions; instead, you become a welcome aide.

CUSTOMER IMPACT PRINCIPLE #4:
Buying is basically an emotional response.

The two most fundamental reasons any of us buy anything are the desire for gain and the fear of loss. We buy because we hope to gain something from the purchase or because we want to avoid a loss we are currently experiencing or that we expect may occur. Buying is primarily an emotional response.

Our purchases may be guided by common sense and reason. We may temper our purchases with logic. We may be delayed by conflicting interests. Yet, what causes us to sign on the dotted line is emotion. That principle suggests several important aspects of customer impact that we should consider.

First, it suggests that people buy benefits for themselves, not features, products, services, or even corporate reputations. People seek benefits that will fulfill their desire for gain or protect them from the loss they fear.

Second, the principle suggests that a strong empathy with the customer is absolutely vital for success in selling. Since buying decisions always involve emotions, you must be intuitively insightful into what the prospect is feeling.

Third, it means that you must be the sort of salesperson people enjoy doing business with. During an emotional experience, no one needs a salesperson pouring more into the flood they already feel.

Your customer impact will rise sharply when you put your heart into your work. Learn how to connect with your customers' feelings and how to help them find and fulfill their desires or overcome their fears. Benjamin Franklin stated it best when he said:

> In persuasion, talk of emotion, not reason.

Customer impact is the ability to gain and hold the attention of the right people and to influence them to buy. It is your capacity to get people to filter your message out of the 9,000 other messages they will hear during their workweek and eventually follow your lead in a buying decision. If you do that, you will make more money, have more control over your life, and gain greater recognition in selling than in nearly any profession available to you. Having high customer impact is the dominant factor that separates the winners from the losers in the selling profession.

PRINCIPLES-BASED SELLING

Value-based selling is not a technique; instead, it is a philosophy based on sound principles. Techniques serve short-range goals and must be altered continually to keep up with the environment in which they are used. Sound, philosophically-based principles, on the other hand, are timeless and will always apply.

Countless selling techniques have been invented and amended, written about and taught, memorized and forgotten, loved and hated. Countless more selling techniques that we have not yet heard of will follow. Techniques in selling are like weapons in war: Develop a hot, new one and it will produce great results until the other side develops either a defense for it or builds an improved version, based on what they learned from yours. That works fine with weapons, because wars are short-term and adversarial by definition. Your selling career, however, should be long-term and never viewed as a confrontation. Almost every selling technique ever created approaches selling as if it were a war, pitting salespeople against buyers.

The prime reason techniques-based selling no longer works is described in the aphorism, "There is nothing new under the sun." The marketplace of the late twentieth century is crowded with salespeople and has been in operation a very long time. As a result, nearly every effective technique has been so overused that the defenses went up long ago. In today's marketplace you will meet hardened buyers, concerned with getting top value for themselves or their companies, who have heard it all before. Most of us are highly unlikely to come up with a new killer sales technique, and, even if we did, it wouldn't be long before massive overuse would make it trite.

The only sales plans that will enjoy long-range success are the ones based on sound principles instead of coercive techniques. People will always buy what they want or need, but clever, tricky sales techniques may get them to buy things they do not need—once. Word of such tricks will travel quickly in a tightly segmented, small market niche, and your customer sources can evaporate like a puddle in July.

However, a sales plan that is based on the unchanging principle that people will always fulfill their needs with what they value most will succeed regardless of the techniques used to implement it. The principles behind the IMPACT Selling process keep you focused on the fulfillment of the customer's needs, so you will enjoy long-range success and find prosperity in the crowded marketplaces of the 1990s and beyond.

Our principles-based plan was developed over a period of more than 20 years. It has been tested and proven in virtually every segment of the selling world, producing impressive results. Whenever companies use IMPACT Selling there is a rise in sales and market share, whether the products are multimillion dollar leasing contracts or high-volume, low-priced novelty items.

FOCUS ON RELATIONSHIPS

Successful value-based, principle-based selling depends upon building and maintaining trust-filled relationships with prospective customers. Naturally, it includes being liked, yet it goes well beyond that. Having a great personality and getting along well with others is not the key to effective customer impact. I have met salespeople who were thoroughly likable but could not sell ice water in a desert. The prospect making the buying decision must trust that you are sincerely interested in fulfilling his or her needs and that he or she is getting a good value.

The ancient Greeks gave us a word that expresses the heart of a trusting relationship: *symbiosis*. It means "living together in a mutually beneficial relationship—a relationship that provides enough benefits for all the partners to view it as valuable." Symbiosis can ensure that you enjoy a *win-win situation* in your professional relationships. For the impact selling profession, that means always making sure that you fulfill your customers' needs by giving them enough value to more than justify what they invest. You cannot achieve symbiosis through personality. The person behind the personality is what gives IMPACT Selling its power.

AN EFFECTIVE PLAN NEEDS EFFECTIVE PEOPLE

You have surely met salespeople who seem to work shorter hours and enjoy their work more than most, yet make more sales and money that others of equal ability and training. What is the difference? Simply put, some salespeople are more effective than others. The next obvious question is, "What does it mean to be effective?"

I have three definitions of *effective* that help pinpoint the answer:

- Strikingly impressive.
- Ready for service or action.
- Capable of producing a desired outcome.

Combining those three definitions gives us a description of an IMPACT Selling professional:

THE IMPACT SALESPERSON
A strikingly impressive person, ready for service or action, and capable of producing maximum sales with minimum time and effort.

Each of those three phrases relates to the kind of person you are inside and goes much deeper than simply having a good personality or being a great joke teller. Remember that in symbiosis all partners must view the relationship as valuable.

Here is a detailed explanation of the three components of personal values that equate to being a highly effective salesperson.

Strikingly Impressive:
Who You Are

Impact grows out of the way you feel about yourself, about others, and about what you are doing. To understand your level of customer impact, you should ask the question, "What is there about me that would make people who are being constantly deluged by my competitors want to buy from me?" Strikingly impressive salespeople will have more impact on their prospects and influence more of them to buy. Part III of this book presents an in-depth study of this concept.

Ready for Service or Action:
What You Know

Your most valuable selling tool is not your mouth—as most salespeople have been trained to believe—but your mind. A high level of customer impact grows out of what you know about people, about your market niche, about the selling profession, and about what you are selling. You must master a value-based game plan that will give you the competitive edge to meet the demands of today's tough-minded buyers. The next two chapters in Part II will prepare you for service and action.

Capable of Producing Maximum Sales with Minimum Time and Effort:
What You Do

Nothing works unless you do, but there is more to it than that. Some of the hardest working salespeople in the world are also some of the least successful. IMPACT Selling involves doing the right things at the right time and in the right way within your niche in order to obtain the desired response. That can only happen when you put yourself in the prospective customer's shoes and understand his or her needs. The best way to do that is to use the four Customer Impact principles that I presented earlier in this chapter. For review, those are

- People only pay attention to those they believe have something important to say to them.
- People buy for their reasons, not for yours or mine.
- People don't want to be sold—they want to buy.
- Buying is basically an emotional response.

The last four chapters of Part II will show you how to put these four principles to work.

Every sales professional who embodies all three of the personal qualities I covered and uses our four customer impact principles will be at the top of his or her profession at the end of the 1990s and will be poised to stay there throughout a long and prosperous career. In other words, today's IMPACT Selling professionals will be tomorrow's sales leaders.

TAKE IT ONE STEP AT A TIME

You do not need to implement every one of these selling behaviors instantly. Integrating the whole plan one step at a time has enabled thousands of salespeople to double, or even triple, their sales. As you carefully assimilate each step, you can move on to the next one.

You will begin almost immediately to notice a rise in your sales success. Within a few weeks, you will have internalized the system so well that you will be able to accomplish each step instinctively. When that happens, your customer impact and sales will soar dramatically.

A system only makes sense when you can see the whole plan and understand how each part fits into the broader picture. That's what I do in Chapters 4 through 10, as I give you our entire game plan by thoroughly covering all six phases of IMPACT Selling.

But before I do that, we need to take an in-depth look at how this system works and how it can help you to gain positive control of your niche.

As a science, IMPACT Selling has a series of rules and a set of principles that formulate its practice. When implemented correctly, this science becomes an art that can be used creatively and can be personally crafted around the skills of the practitioner.

This is the result of observing thousands of salespeople, interviewing literally hundreds, training tens of thousands of others, and having the privilege of learning from some of the very best sales writers, theorists, and trainers in the world today.

The premise of IMPACT Selling centers around several key concepts:

1. Niche knowledge, prospecting, and a set of concentrated actions are the keys to successful selling in the tough demanding markets of today.
2. Contemporary selling mandates that professional salespeople sell three critical things: trust, value, and needs.
3. People can do things they see. Therefore, there is a graphic design of the sales process.
4. Any successful selling process must be simple, based on a set of sound principles and a set of easy-to-apply rules.
5. Application, rather than traditional demonstration selling, is the watchword in competitive markets.

This process is examined in Figure 4–1.

What forms this wall of apathy and/or resistance? Better yet, who is apathetic or resistant? Only the prospect? Of course not. It could also be apathy or resistance on the part of the salesperson.

A salesperson could be apathetic as a result of anything from a personal production plateau or personal problem to a lack of

FIGURE 4–1
IMPACT Selling Process

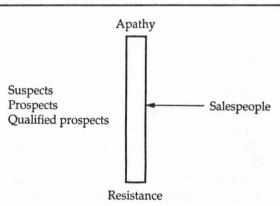

selling skills or product knowledge. That same salesperson could be resistant to attacking a new niche or segment or to dealing with an unknown circumstance. The list is endless.

How about the prospect? Apathy or resistance could be caused by any one or a combination of the following:

- *Lack of knowledge* about you, your company, or your product.
- *Skepticism* about you, your company, or your product.
- The need to *compare.*
- *Fear* that he or she will be taken advantage of.
- Having received an *incomplete story* from another salesperson.
- *Inadequate product performance* through hearsay or experience.
- *Prejudice* against you, your product, or your company.

The key is to attack the wall at precisely the right spot (fulcrum) with the right tool (lever), as shown in Figure 4–2. That tool will have a point or edge on it. The point will serve two specific functions: The first is to penetrate the wall, and the second is to serve as the honing device to locate the specific fulcrum. The specific spot earmarked for penetration will be identified by the location of a segmented niche within your specific market. In this

FIGURE 4–2
Targeting the Right Spot

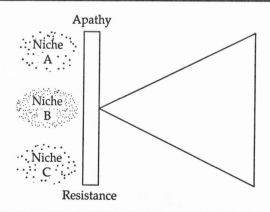

FIGURE 4–3
Wall Which Has Been Blunted

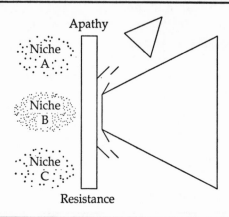

example, segment B is the targeted segment within our niche—the one that holds the greatest promise of penetration and profitability.

Should the point or cutting edge of the tool be removed, the wall will be blunted (Figure 4–3) rather than penetrated (Figure 4–4). A bullet has a point, as does an arrow. Even the nose of a rocket has a point in order to slip through the atmosphere with the minimum amount of resistance.

FIGURE 4–4
Wall Which Has Been Penetrated

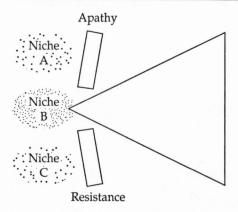

FIGURE 4–5
Time Invested in Each Step of IMPACT Selling

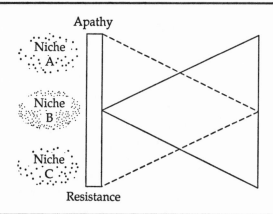

The amount of time that a salesperson will invest in each step of IMPACT Selling will be represented by the dotted line in Figure 4–5. As you will note, there is much more time invested early in the sales process than there is later.

The sales process itself will be represented by the six segments outlined in Figure 4–6. It is important to reiterate that the amount of time invested in each step will lessen as we move through the process. The amount of time invested in each step is represented by the circumference of each step. For example,

FIGURE 4–6
Six Segments of Sales Process

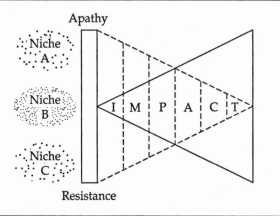

I = Investigate
M = Meet
P = Probe
A = Apply
C = Convince
T = Tie-it-up

FIGURE 4–7
Pushing Through the Wall

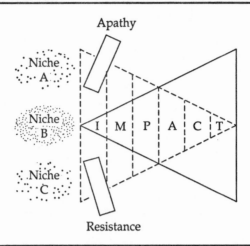

there will clearly be much more time consumed in Investigate than in the Tie-It-Up phase.

As each step is followed in sequence, a powerful scenario will unfold. As we complete the first step, we start to push the tip of the tool through the wall at precisely the right spot to attack our selected market segment. This is shown in Figure 4–7.

As we complete each step, we continually move through the wall (Figure 4–8). By the time we complete the process, the wall will eventually disappear and we will have engaged, absorbed, and captured the appropriately targeted segment of our market (Figure 4–9).

There are three very simple, easy-to-remember, and simple-to-apply rules for mastering IMPACT Selling:

1. Never skip a step.
2. Don't go on to the next step until you exhaust the prior step.
3. Make sure you and your prospect are in the same step.

There you have it. A clear picture of a sale. Much like a diagrammed football play, it is easy to see, to understand, and to do. In football, every play is designed to be a touchdown. In football games played in the real world instead of on a blackboard, though, that just doesn't occur. IMPACT Selling is designed with

FIGURE 4–8
Steadily Overcoming Barriers

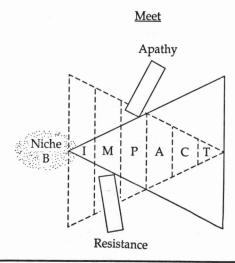

Meet

the same goal in mind—a sale every time! But sales are also a real-world experience...so a touchdown doesn't occur every time there, either.

FIGURE 4–9
Wall Has Disappeared

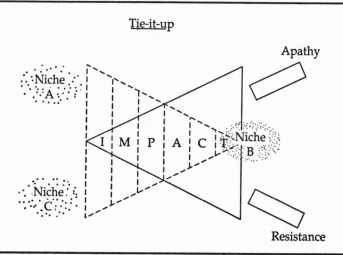

In tough, competitive, and demanding market niches sales-people face a stalwart defense: a defense of resistant buyers, aggressive competition, and price sensitivity. The result? Not scoring a touchdown or making a sale on every play! But what happens if salespeople get just a little better every time they practice and run their very best play? IMPACT Selling can become your "very best" play, too! But only if you learn it, assimilate it, apply it, and practice it. Let's take a look at how to do precisely that.

KEY TIPS

☑ "The Greatest Secret in Selling" from Frank Bettger, author of *How I Raised Myself from Failure to Success in Selling*: Show people what they want most, and they will move heaven and earth to get it!

☑ Discovering what people want most involves asking the *right* questions, listening *carefully*, and being totally aware of everything that expresses what your prospect really *values*.

☑ People always have time to take care of something they need or truly want. Since Americans have so few unfulfilled needs, it is always easier to sell to their perceived needs.

☑ More than 60 percent of all sales are made by the top 5 percent of all salespeople, because they have and use the winner's edge of customer-focused, value-based selling.

☑ People buy for their own reasons. Remember that every prospect listens to you over their own inner radio, WII-FM, What's In It For Me?

☑ Remember that people rarely want to be sold; they want to buy because buying anything—large or small—is basically an emotional response: *Talk of emotion, not reason.*

CHAPTER 5

INVESTIGATE

INVESTIGATE

A carefully devised strategy for the identification of qualified prospects. The game plan where all success in sales begins. The physical activity of prospecting where tangible results are achieved: Prospects are found, appointments are made, and effective, well-presented sales presentations are planned.

A wise man will make more opportunities than he finds.
Francis Bacon

The *Investigate* phase of IMPACT Selling is the foundation on which all your sales activities are anchored. Its primary function is to identify highly qualified prospects within your niche and to gather sufficient background information to build an IMPACT sales presentation. The most successful IMPACT salespeople will be those who pull out all the stops in the Investigate phase, compiling an in-depth study of their chosen market niche. Here is a truism that highlights the importance of a sweeping investigation:

> *In a crowded marketplace, all other things being equal, the one with the most information wins.*

As the competition heats up ever further, we can refine this already sound statement by adding that the winner is the one who possesses the most information and can apply it effectively. In other words, you must use the information gained as a result of your investigation to identify those prospects for whom you can create the most value. You will then apply this knowledge to create the highest perceived value for your customers. During this phase, you must remain constantly aware of your focus, use all your leverage, and make sure everything you do is aligned with your marketing department.

It is absolutely essential that this initial phase be carefully coordinated with your company's marketing strategy to ensure that you are both in alignment. For an illustration of why this is important, imagine two ships that depart from the same port. If one is on a course that differs from the other by only a single degree, there will be little distance between them initially. After 60 miles of travel they would be one mile apart, still close enough for visual contact and a course adjustment. After 180 miles of travel, three miles of ocean would lie between them. At three miles, the curvature of the earth prevents visual sighting and thus course corrections. By the time both have crossed an ocean, they may well land in different countries. The Investigate stage is the time for you to ensure that your sales strategy is closely aligned with your company's marketing strategy. You must make small course adjustments now, before you are too far apart to even see each other.

Failure to make continual course adjustments will quickly put your sales strategy and your company's marketing strategy out of alignment. For instance, imagine that your marketing department has just identified a highly qualified market for a new product and has targeted ads for that market without passing on the information to you. Without alignment, your sales staff may well continue to see a long-established list of prospects that does not include a single contact identified by the marketing department. Certainly some of your long-term customers may need the new product, but an Investigate phase that is carefully coordinated with marketing will produce a higher closing rate than would be possible by simply seeing current customers.

Failure to align your investigation with your company's marketing strategy will eventually result in the appearance of a problem in the closing ratios of your sales force.

THE KEY TO A SUCCESSFUL CLOSE
IS KNOWING HOW TO *OPEN*

In the Investigate phase, you and your staff will gather information that will enable you to change your sales opening so that the close is no longer a thrilling victory in a battle with a prospect, but simply the next step in a natural flow of events that is mutually beneficial to your company and your customers.

Here is a story that is typical of problems we have encountered repeatedly. It reveals how a closing problem may be caused by not knowing how to open. It began with a call to me from a frustrated sales manager.

The sales manager went directly to the point: "Bill, I need you to come in here and teach these knuckleheads how to close a sale!"

"Are you sure closing is the problem?" I asked.

"Of course it is. Their closing ratio is terrible. And I know my salespeople are not lazy," he explained. "They talk to a lot of people every day, they make a lot of presentations, and I see to it they know their products. They just don't get enough people to sign on the dotted line!"

"But do they consistently see the right people, and are they really ready when they go on a sales call?" I probed.

"What do you mean?"

Then I carefully explained the Investigate phase of IMPACT Selling, which asserts that the most vital part of a sale is seldom the close, but what takes place before the interview begins—in other words, the *opening*.

After a careful study of this sales manager's situation and talks with several of his salespeople, we concluded that their problem was not with closing skills. Our study revealed that most of the sales interviews they conducted were not potential sales to begin with.

Sure, they would "go out and find the people," and certainly they would "lay a mean 'pitch' on anybody who would listen to them long enough." They were extremely busy, and they were remarkably effective at getting in to see people. Furthermore, they were expert at every closing technique in the book. Most of them had been trained under the old-school method that said, "If you tell your story to enough people, some of them will buy." The problem for them was that in today's crowded marketplace there were just not enough hours in the day for them to succeed.

That sales manager had a difficult time accepting our suggestion that he and his entire sales staff attend a seminar on prospecting. At first he believed that we did not understand his problem. We did, but he did not know it yet. He had called us seeking a seminar on closing, but because we kept our emphasis on what he really needed, he finally accepted our analysis. Six months after his sales staff had taken one of our sales seminars, he reported that their closing ratio had immediately risen sharply and had been climbing steadily ever since.

This sales manager was not initially interested in teaching his sales force more about prospecting, because he was limited by outdated, superficial views of it. His salespeople became more successful after we taught them our highly sophisticated version of that old term "prospecting," which we call *Power-Packed Prospecting.*

POWER-PACKED PROSPECTING: MANDATORY FOR THE 1990s

The real issue in a crowded market niche is not how often you tell your story. It is how and to whom you tell your story. It is the difference between looking everywhere for opportunities and creating your own opportunities.

Good prospecting is hard work. Consequently, most salespeople find it easier to run around and shoot off their mouths than they do to approach presale investigating as a science and to work at it consistently. It is much easier to learn a product demonstration by rote and to memorize a canned sales pitch, then hit the streets with demo products and piles of sales literature. It also feels good. There is a sense that something is being done. Your sales force is out there beating the bushes. Beat enough bushes long enough and eventually you will flush something out. Right? Not anymore. There are not enough hours in the day to keep up with competitors who do a better job of prospecting and preparing than you do. The more in-depth your investigating is, the better your chances of closing sales will be.

Prospecting as Investigation

"But investigation sounds like work for a detective, not for a salesperson!" We have heard that objection countless times, yet it is not a bad comparison. A good detective always follows several guidelines that are equally applicable to *Power-Packed Prospecting*. Think of your sales force as detectives when you read this list:

- A good detective always looks beyond the obvious, but never overlooks the obvious.
- A good detective asks a lot of questions.
- A good detective follows a set plan.
- A good detective makes detailed notes and keeps accurate, up-to-date records.
- A good detective uses every means available to check out every possibility.
- A good detective manages time carefully so he or she is always at the right place doing the right thing at the right time.
- A good detective follows up every lead.

In the Investigate phase of IMPACT Selling, an effective salesperson does everything a good detective does yet must do even more because of one significant difference between the goals of a sales professional and those of a detective. A detective is looking for one guilty *suspect*, while the salesperson is looking for as many qualified *prospects* as possible.

In selling, a suspect is a person:

- You have opened limited communications with.
- Who may have a need you can satisfy, although he or she may not yet know it.
- Who may or may not have the resources to buy.
- Who may or may not listen to you.

To properly use leverage, you must dig deeper than finding suspects. You need qualified prospects. A qualified prospect is a person who:

- You can establish or have already established rapport with.
- Has a need you can satisfy and is aware of that need.
- Has the resources, ability, and authority to satisfy that need.
- Has a sense of urgency.
- Has agreed to listen to you.

Most salespeople traditionally spend their most productive selling time—their *prime time*—attempting to sell products to suspects instead of making presentations to qualified prospects. Unfortunately, your closing average with suspects will always be much lower than it would be had you invested the same amount of time with properly researched, highly qualified prospects.

In Search of Qualified Prospects

Because we continually see closing rates climb after sales staffs have shifted their thinking toward intelligent openings instead of hard-nosed closings, we have developed the first principle of *Power-Packed Prospecting*:

POWER-PACKED PROSPECTING PRINCIPLE #1:
The better job of finding qualified prospects you do, the higher your closing average will be!

A sales force can significantly boost its selling impact simply be making it a habit to spend its prime selling time with the most qualified prospects they can find. To do that, they will need to readjust their schedules (with proper guidance) by using *peripheral time* to search for suspects to try to move to the category of qualified prospects.

For example, if your prime selling time is from 9:00 A.M. until 4:00 P.M., you could set aside two hours before and two hours after that period each day to try to make prospects out of suspects. If the lunch period is not a good selling time for your clientele, why not invest that 60 to 90 minutes in taking suspects to lunch or doing other follow-up work?

Find the time in any way you can, because you will not long succeed beyond this phase if your investigation fails to turn up truly qualified prospects:

Your future success in selling depends on the quality and breadth of your prospect file.

The key words in that aphorism are *quality* and *breadth*. Otherwise, you will find yourself with wasted, idle hours during your prime selling time. Or, you may waste your prime time trolling for suspects who may or may not nibble on your sales presentation. Since I know you will not tolerate wasted time, I will now show you how to ensure that you find as many quality prospects as you can properly handle.

Six Tools to Locate Qualified Prospects

During literally thousands of training sessions and consultations with hundreds of business leaders, we have found unanimous agreement on one basic point: Lack of qualified prospects is the greatest single cause of failure among salespeople.

Prospecting is the toughest part of selling. It means much more than the traditional approach of finding warm bodies you might corral into listening to a standard "pitch." Instead, it means identifying qualified prospects, establishing enough rapport with them to gain a good hearing, and setting the stage (time and place) for you to make your best presentations.

We have seen how prospecting is similar to detective work, but there is another profession even more closely analogous to prospecting: investigative reporting.

A sharp investigative reporter always uses the six well-known tools of the journalism trade to track down a story. Those tools are the questions: Who? Where? What? Why? When? How? The reporter's standard toolkit is just as useful to the alert salesperson who is committed to the job of *Power-Packed Prospecting*.

This philosophy is not theory; it is a proven idea on which The Brooks Group bases another of its prospecting principles:

POWER-PACKED PROSPECTING PRINCIPLE #2:
The salesperson who asks enough of the right questions of the right persons in the right places will always have plenty of qualified prospects.

I will now present these six tools of prospecting in a general context to illustrate how they can work for you. These general ideas will work in many fields of selling. The task of a professional sales manager is to apply them to a selling situation and ensure that salespeople are well-trained in their use.

Power-Packed Prospecting Tool #1: Who?
An investigative reporter in a city of a million people will get nowhere if he or she assumes that every resident in the city is a likely candidate for a story. Instead, the reporter must

narrow down the field to those whose stories are truly news-worthy and then choose a few to focus on in depth.

In *Power-Packed Prospecting*, some excellent *who* questions for a salesperson to ask in order to convert suspects within his or her market into highly qualified prospects are

- Who has the most obvious need or desire for the company's products or services that we sell? For whom is that need or desire most compelling?
- Who are our ideal prospects? (Do not limit your thinking in this area to your current customer list. Think afresh of *ideal* prospects and describe them in detail.)
- Whom do we know that might fit that ideal description?
- Whom do we know now that might lead us to new people who fit that description?
- Who has the money to buy the products our company sells? Who has the money right now? Who has an urgent need for our products?
- Who has bought similar products or services before?
- Who has bought from our company before and might be ready to buy again?
- Who has influence on the prospects we identify?

If you approach your *who* questions creatively, you can develop a huge suspect list from those questions alone. An important source for your list will most likely be found in your company's marketing department. In planning the advertising campaign, they have probably already answered most of the questions on that list. This is clearly a major reason why you want to closely align yourself with the marketing department.

After your initial list is complete, a key to continued success is to keep asking yourself and your sales force the same questions, constantly looking for names you might have missed or for new names not available initially. This list must become a part of your permanent files. Keep it and do not give up on it too early. Here is a good reason why.

We found a recent study by the Thomas Publishing Company that revealed that most salespeople give up too early. According to their study, 80 percent of sales to businesses are made on the fifth sales call, yet only 10 percent of salespeople call more than three times!

Be careful in the way you handle your repeat contacts so that you appear as a persistent professional and never a pest. Many salespeople have reported stretching their contacts over more than two years, although one year is a good limit. Maximum effectiveness was found while the list was no more than six months old. So, we now know that a good source for *who* questions may be in your dusty business card file—and just think, this will be the first time you contact prospects while using a customer-focused, value-based approach!

Power-Packed Prospecting Tool #2: Where?

By asking enough *where* questions, you can turn up prospects beyond your current client list and probably way beyond your initial expectations. You will be amazed at how many lists of people you and your sales staff can find, many of whom will be logical prospects.

Here are some sample *where* questions that produce great prospecting results:

- Where do our ideal prospects live? Work? Play? Worship? Socialize? Relax?
- Where can we find useful mailing lists of people who fit the ideal prospects description we developed? (A properly conducted search will provide lists of people by professions, neighborhoods, types and frequency of purchases, credit ratings, dominant interests, property deeds, and so on.)
- Where can we find directories from which to assemble our own lists? (Include the business section of public libraries, clubs, social groups, and officers and directors of service organizations.)
- Where might we contact prospects? (Although the hottest new trend is toward exhibits and huge trade shows, do not overlook the traditional places in your daily life like country clubs and health and recreation centers.)

This is one area in which the crowded marketplace of the 1990s may work in your favor. Our fast-paced, crowded society has gone bonkers over lists. Computers have made it possible for those lists to be arranged by every conceivable category. Yet, those computer-generated lists are readily available to everyone.

They may also serve only to increase the number of suspects you have, thereby wasting your time. It is essential to choose carefully focused lists so that they produce highly qualified prospects. The more careful you are in selecting your lists, the more productive they will be for you.

Power-Packed Prospecting Tool #3: Why?

Why questions can help set priorities as you seek to transform suspects into highly qualified prospects. They can also help you decide which approach is best to reach a particular person or group of people.

The following *why* questions are helpful:

- Why would this person be likely to buy our product?
- Why would this person resist buying from us now?
- Why might this time be especially good (or poor) to approach this person?
- Why would this person be most likely to accept an appointment with a salesperson? (If the answer to this one is that they may only respond to a referral, can you get that referral?)

Be careful of your attitude when you are asking this type of question. If you approach the *why* questions negatively, they may make you feel too intimidated to call on anybody. To see how, reread the first question with a negative, cynical tone: "Why would this person be likely to buy our products?" When put the wrong way, some *why* questions can easily produce intimidating answers for inexperienced salespeople or even those who are cynical and experienced, thereby serving as an excuse for procrastination. If, on the other hand, you always approach the questions with a positive attitude, they will help show which suspect should get top priority, often pointing you straight to qualified prospects.

Power-Packed Prospecting Tool #4: What?

The family of *what* questions in your investigation can boost your prospecting impact by improving your focus on the most powerful content for prospecting. Each *what* question should focus on what it is that the prospect needs from you or your product.

Here are a few you might find helpful:

- What will this prospect find most beneficial about my product or service? What will he or she find least beneficial?
- What questions or statements are most likely to get your prospect talking about his or her needs? What questions is he or she likely to ask me?
- What more do I need to know about the person to ensure success in setting up an appointment?
- What is the formal and informal structure of this organization?
- What information should I try to gain from my initial contact with the prospect?
- What is the single biggest problem I can help them solve?
- What are they themselves up against in the marketplace today? Nearly every market is crowded, and your prospects most likely face many of the same survival challenges you face.

You should only invest time asking yourself the *what* questions about people you have identified as prospects. The higher the quality of your answers to the *what* questions, the greater your batting average will be in getting prospects to accept appointments.

Again, remember the Value equation from the Leverage chapter and use this time to find ways to build maximum value for your prospects. Your *what* questions should reveal what you can do to increase perceived benefits while reducing the perceived price.

A successful professional should be able to identify no less than 25 needs their prospects have. Of course, you will focus only on the three or four most dominant needs, finding ways in which you and your products will provide valuable benefits for those needs. If you cannot name 25 needs, you may be walking past golden opportunities. Failure to have a long list of answers to your *what* questions is similar to fighting with one hand tied behind your back.

Power-Packed Prospecting Tool #5: When?
Timing has a great influence on how successful you will be at prospecting. Too often, salespeople try to set up appointments

for their own convenience rather than at an optimum time for the prospect. Others have so few prospects that they jump at an appointment any time they can get one. You must strike a balance.

A positive and productive approach to balance is to blend your interests with those of the prospect and always shoot for the best time schedule for both of you. The answers to some *when* questions will help you schedule other activities appropriately. Answers to other questions will help directly in scheduling time for prospecting.

Questions like these can help you see the best balance for both you and your prospects:

- When is the optimum time for me to do my prospecting and not cut into my prime selling time?
- When is it most productive from the customer's viewpoint for me to try to contact suspects? When is it least productive?
- When is this prospect most likely to give me an attentive hearing? When am I at my best? When is a good alternate time that maximizes the answers to these two questions for both of us?
- When should I contact this prospect again if my first efforts are not successful?

One well-known example of a time waster, for instance, is calling on a busy executive first thing Monday morning. Successful sales professionals know that this is seldom a productive time for an executive, so they schedule other clients for that time. The most successful salespeople practice good time management habits. One good time management technique is to set up quality appointments. There is more to a quality appointment than merely meeting with a qualified prospect. The first three prospecting questions (*Who? Where? Why?*) show how to find quality prospects. The next question (*What?*) is designed to target your presentation to those quality people. The fifth question (*When?*) can maximize the quality of the time invested with the prospect by ensuring that both of you are ready to focus on the prospect's needs.

Power-Packed Prospecting Tool #6: How?
Your *how* questions are perhaps the most crucial of all the tools for prospecting because many of their answers will evolve from answers to the five other types of questions. You cannot ask many meaningful *how* questions unless you have explored the other five first. Notice how these are related.

Here are some *how* questions you will find very helpful:

* How can I be sure that I am doing a good enough job of follow-up in prospecting? (*Who?* Remember those old files.)

* How can I use my prospecting time more productively, including the few moments available to me right now? (*Where?* A long list of *where* questions will always give you some research to do during slack times.)

* How can I sharpen my prospecting skills? (*Why?* Always search for creative ways to put your products and services to use.)

* How can I best approach suspects and prospects? (*What?* Think of what they will most want to hear.)

* How can I make more time for prospecting without cutting into my prime selling time? (*When?* The leverage of time management is an essential sales tool.)

The key to making the *how* questions, as well as many of the others, work for you is to continually ask yourself these questions and revise your answers. The last *how* question is most productive for you when answered specifically for individual clients. The *how* of approaching suspects and prospects will vary greatly from one to another.

A Final Prospecting Principle

"He that questioneth much shall learn much," said Francis Bacon. Nowhere in IMPACT Selling is that statement more true than in the Investigative phase. We have shared with you some of the questions we continually ask ourselves. These questions have helped us and many of our clients to completely eliminate the problem of not having qualified prospects to call on at any given moment.

As reinforcement, I would like to add an important caveat to one of my earlier statements:

In a crowded marketplace, all other things being equal, the one with the most information, who applies it most effectively, wins.

We can sum up what have learned about the task of prospecting so far with the final prospecting principle:

POWER-PACKED PROSPECTING PRINCIPLE #3:
The most productive sentence in the salesperson's vocabulary always ends with a question mark!

Good prospecting is a matter of developing a solid game plan that works well for you and following that game plan to the letter. I will now present some pointers we have developed that will help you formulate your game plan.

PROSPECTING POINTERS

The following ideas for Power-Packed Prospecting have been tested and proven effective by leading salespeople in all fields. These are our *gems*, diligently collected through many years of experience in sales training and consulting.

Look over these pointers with an eye for how you can apply them. Although you may be an established sales professional, you should find many of them useful personally. Also valuable is to use them as training tools for your sales staff. Train them early to embrace these proven prospecting pointers:

1. **Treat prospecting as the lifeblood of your sales career.**
   Not the clichéd definition, but Power-Packed Prospecting:
   - Focus on quality. It is the only way you can spend most of your prime time with qualified prospects. It is also the only way you can have enough hours in a week to be successful.
   - Focus on quantity. Your success depends on having enough solid sales leads.
   - Focus on consistency. A steady supply of qualified prospects can enable you to avoid slumps and plateaus,

eliminate call reluctance and procrastination, and keep you from pressuring your current clients.

- Do it now. Increasing your prospecting effectiveness is the fastest single way to boost your sales and income.

2. **Treat prospecting as your most valuable time management tool.** *Remember that you are always looking for ways to better leverage your time:*

- Use it to avoid wasting prime time on people who are not qualified to say "yes."
- Use it to ensure that you will always have enough qualified prospects to keep you productively busy.
- Avoid wasting time through sloppy or haphazard prospecting.

3. **Take an organized approach.** *Never keep leads on scraps of paper or self-adhesive note pads. You can buy a computerized system or create one of your own. Whatever you choose, choose something that ensures you will never:*

- Lose or forget about valuable leads.
- Be late on promised follow-up calls and visits.
- Waste time looking for lost information.
- Improperly value your prospect inventory.
- Fail to do mailings and other footwork because of a disorganized prospect list.
- Become a compulsive procrastinator when it comes to developing your prospect inventory.

4. **Remain alert for suspects who have the potential to become qualified prospects:** *In today's fast-paced society, people's needs may change rapidly and radically, giving you prospects where you had never thought to look.*

- Develop a prospecting mind-set that automatically asks, "Is this person a prospect?"
- Assume all suspects are prospects until proved otherwise.
- Keep looking for new places to find prospects.
- Cultivate mutually beneficial relationships with everyone who can give you leads or open doors for you.

- Take full advantage of every effort made by your company to generate leads. Maintain close alignment with your company's marketing department.
- Make it your policy to always secure referrals from satisfied customers.

5. **Stay in constant touch with active prospects through phone calls, periodic mailings, and personal contacts.** *Keep in mind the "Top of the Consciousness Principle," which states that:*

- The only certain way to ensure that your customers think of you first is through frequent, repetitious contact.
- Others are always competing for your prospect's attention and dollars.
- You never know when your prospect's motivation to buy will suddenly, dramatically increase.
- You need to be sure that the prospect thinks of you or your product first when he or she evaluates how to fulfill his or her business needs.

6. **Rework your suspect inventory regularly to try to upgrade suspects to the status of qualified prospects.** *A good filing system will help tremendously:*

- Learn to use the telephone in a professional, pleasant, and business-like manner. Then use it regularly.
- Constantly search for people who can give you a referral for every suspect on your list. Or, better still, will they make a contact for you?
- Look everywhere for the slightest clue indicating that the suspect's buying status might be changing.

7. **Continually upgrade your prospecting system and strategies.**

- For a steady flow of fresh ideas, you should read books, journals, magazines, and business news; listen to cassettes; attend seminars; and talk to other successful salespeople.
- If you are not using a personal computer, you should be. Your competitors are. Computers are remarkable

aids for prospecting and managing prospect information files. Make sure you get a system that will work
easily and well for you and will grow with your needs.

- Above all, maintain a positive attitude about prospecting. Make a game out of it.

Go back now and reread Power-Packed Prospecting Pointer
#1: "Treat prospecting as the lifeblood of your sales career." It
definitely is, and here is a terrific story of the tremendous payoff
that may await good sales detectives everywhere. Perhaps you
will soon be one of them.

At one of our seminars we learned of a truck salesman from
Indianapolis (I will call him Rich) whose investigative reporting
paid off very well. Rich's regular investigating uncovered an arti-
cle in the newspaper about a local towing and recovery company
that had just been awarded an exclusive contract to handle all
towing for downtown Indianapolis. But Rich had a sales dilemma
on his hands: He sold Isuzu trucks, whereas tow truck companies
traditionally have a particularly *macho* culture where big American trucks prevail: the bigger the better!

Instead of seeing this as an impossible market, Rich continued to use his investigative skills and turned up a potential
glitch in the contract for the towing company. Operating in the
tight confines of crowded downtown streets, the company was
required by contract to hook up and get out in less than ten
minutes, or it could face penalties for adding to traffic conges-
tion. When Rich learned that, he knew he could get the sale. His
extensive investigative files included information he had
stashed away earlier about an equipment manufacturer that
had a special tow truck device that reduced hook-up time to
less than five minutes. Furthermore, his trucks were of a small,
medium-duty, "cab-over" design that made them short and
highly maneuverable.

Rich put the two together and showed the towing company
how to meet a very pressing need. Combining the resources of
his investigative files, he was able to structure a sales opening
for that tow truck dealer that practically ensured a sales closing
before Rich walked in the door. This is a perfect illustration of a
truism I gave you earlier in this chapter:

The key to a successful close is knowing how to open.

TO SUM IT ALL UP...

In the first chapter of Part II, we discovered that the greatest secret of IMPACT Selling is:

> Show people what they want most, and they will move heaven and earth to get it!

Before you can show people what they want, you must get in touch with their needs and desires and discover how you can fulfill those needs and desires through what you are selling. That is what prospecting is all about and what makes it the most vital step in the selling process.

Unfortunately, few sales professionals understand that that principle revolves completely around the customer, instead, they look for "suspects" to whom they can "sell." As a result of our experience and research, we have taken the traditional old prospecting ideas far beyond their normal roles. That is why we call it investigating.

Investigating is highly sophisticated. It is not simply finding anybody who might easily be roped into listening to you as you spout off the virtues of what you are selling. Investigating means finding a sufficient quantity of qualified prospects who have a need and desire for what you are selling and who have the authority and financial resources to satisfy that desire. It not only involves finding qualified prospects but includes finding out everything you can to help close the sale.

Once you have made a thorough investigation to obtain all the information you can about a qualified prospect, you are ready to move one step nearer to the close through that all-important second step: Meeting your prospect.

ACTION STEPS

List at least three ways in which you can apply the "Investigate" techniques outlined in this chapter to advance your old prospecting techniques to a higher level than ever before:

1. _____

_____

_____

2. _____

_____

_____

3. _____

_____

_____

KEY TIPS

☑ The better job of finding qualified prospects you do, the higher your closing average will be! Your future success in selling depends on the quality and breadth of your prospect file.

☑ The most productive sentence in the salesperson's vocabulary always ends with a question mark! The salesperson who asks enough of the right questions of the right persons in the right places will always have plenty of qualified prospects.

☑ Always use the reporter's toolkit of journalism questions: Who? Where? What? Why? When? How? All other things being equal, the one who has the most information and applies it most effectively wins.

☑ Treat prospecting as the lifeblood of your sales career because it is! Not the clichéd definition, but Power-Packed Prospecting.

☑ Treat prospecting as your most valuable time management tool. Remember that you are always looking for ways to better leverage your time.

☑ Take an organized approach. Never keep leads on scraps of paper or self-adhesive note pads. Buy a computerized system, but whatever you use, continually upgrade your prospecting system and techniques.

☑ Always keep alert for suspects who have the potential to become qualified prospects. Now is the time to contact those *dated* names you had intended to get back to someday.

☑ Stay in constant touch with active prospects through phone calls, periodic mailings, and personal contacts. Keep in mind the "Top of the Consciousness Principle."

CHAPTER 6

MEET

MEET

Engaging prospects personally. Turning resisters into active participants. Breaking down mental barriers and involving prospects in the sales process. Reducing tension, establishing trust, and building rapport to lower mental and emotional barriers. Starting a successful sales presentation.

> When you look into a mirror, you do not see your reflection; your reflection sees you.
> *Daedalus*

This chapter presents ways to break through mental barriers and get your prospects involved as active participants in what you want to happen. Also consider this chapter as further refining your time management skills. In the Investigate phase, you learned to improve your time management by narrowing your prospect list down to highly qualified clients. Now your time management will improve even further as you learn to maximize the value of the time you spend with those clients you decide to see personally. Getting your prospects involved in what you want to happen will leverage your time.

In learning about the Meet phase of IMPACT Selling, you will discover how to

- Get your prospects to lower their mental/emotional defenses so you can become personally acquainted.
- Reduce tension and establish a strong trust bond between you and your prospect.
- Build a warm and cordial rapport with each other.
- Make a natural transition to a successful sales dialogue.

After your Investigate phase has produced a list of highly qualified prospects and identified when it is best to schedule appointments, it will be time to meet the prospects. In IMPACT Selling, however, meet means more than the casual introduction and handshaking we normally associate with meeting people, and far more than the antiquated concept of "selling yourself" to the prospect.

The old school of sales training called this "the warm-up." Conceptually, it was considered as "setting the prospect up for the kill." The plan was to tell a few jokes and then, while he or she was in a good mood, move in for the close, get your money, and leave before Buyer's Remorse settled in. If a sales force tries that antiquated approach with today's sophisticated consumers, it will be in for a rude awakening. The old-school "warm-up" technique will not serve a customer-focused sale force.

Let us now look at a story I often tell to illustrate how deep-seated the bias is today against old-fashioned "warm-ups." This observation helped me see the need for my IMPACT Selling plan. Here's the story as I have often told it at seminars.

My father-in-law is a beef farmer in Virginia, and I've learned a great deal about selling from watching the way he responds to the many salespeople who drop by from time to time while I'm visiting with him on the farm. A true southern gentleman, he will go out of his way to be hospitable and will even chuckle at their jokes. But the moment they make their first sales overture, he gets that glassy-eyed look on his face and withdraws into his own little world. Usually, the salespeople who try the old-school warm-up routine on him fail to get to first base. Yet, I have also noticed that salespeople who show a genuine interest in getting acquainted with him and meet him in his world of farming find him willing to listen to almost anything they have to say.

If my southern gentleman father-in-law turns to ice when the old-school methods are used, you can certainly expect the same reception from harried, time-pressed executives.

The warm-up technique does nothing to get clients involved with what you want to happen. For salespeople who follow the traditional sales methods, selling sometimes feels like combat. All too often it degenerates into a we/they situation, a war of the wills in which everybody loses. Selling never has to be that way for you again.

Granted, it is not always easy to break through the sales resistance, competitive demands, and frenetic pace of life to get people to listen to you. Still, the fact that thousands of successful salespeople all over America do it every day is proof enough that it is possible. Their success proves that those sales winners do more than just get a foot in the door—they get people involved in what they want to happen.

That is the whole purpose of the Meeting phase of the IMPACT Selling system—to change prospects from defenders against your selling efforts into active participants in the selling process. I will now show you how to get your clients actively involved in what you want to happen, which will help you and your staff leverage your time.

BUILD RAPPORT BY GETTING PEOPLE ACTIVELY INVOLVED

Have you ever tried to talk your way out of a traffic ticket while the officer just kept on writing? He may half listen and occasionally nod his head, but he just keeps on writing the ticket. Of course, you may not be able to talk him out of the fine anyway, but you will make no progress at all until you can get him to stop what he is doing and pay attention to what you are trying to tell him.

Selling works the same way. You cannot begin selling until people start listening to you, and they will not listen to you until they really want to hear what you have to say. In short, you have to get their attention and pique their interest.

The best way to gain a prospect's attention is to get him or her actively involved in what you want to happen. The quickest way to get people involved with you is to first get involved with them. While it sometimes requires creativity, you can usually turn even a distraction into a common meeting ground. Here is a terrific example from my personal anecdotes.

Early in my direct selling experience, I watched an old pro do something that amazed me. He was making a presentation to a family with a three-year-old boy who was a holy terror. The father was only half listening and half watching TV. The toddler was dismantling the salesman's briefcase. His mother was busy trying to keep the child under control. I expected the old salesman to give up at any moment and beat a hasty retreat.

But I was in for a surprise! Almost before I knew what was happening, the guy was sitting on the floor, asking the little fellow to help him find a book in the sales kit. Soon he was reading a story from the book, while the little boy sat in rapt attention and sheer delight.

The father was astonished that his little terror sat still to hear a story and soon became deeply involved in what was going on. The mother then relaxed and started asking questions. Within a matter of minutes, we left that house with a check and a signed order.

That salesman knew that the most important thing in that couple's life was the little guy, so he found a way to get the whole family involved. He did that by getting involved with the one object of their affection.

The moral of that story is simple: If something is important enough to your prospects to distract them, it also has the potential for getting them involved with you. A key in getting your client to focus attention on you is to know what already has his or her attention.

A second technique for getting your clients involved with what you want to happen is to gain eye contact and to use your intuitive insight to plug into the emotions of your prospect. Try to connect with everything that person is feeling. Some questions you might ask are

- How does he or she feel about my being here?
- What other things are going on in his or her life now?
- What about life in general?
- What about the business at hand, and how can I provide him or her with a benefit he or she needs?

The answers to personal questions such as these can often be found inside the prospect, through the window of his or her eyes. Put yourself in that person's shoes and see how you look from his or her side of the table. When you do that, two remarkable things happen. First, you begin to feel a genuine empathy with what the person is feeling. Next, the empathy you feel is transmitted to the other person through your eye contact with him or her. The prospect will sense your sincerity.

You will get people involved with what you want to happen when you show them you have a real understanding of their feelings. The intuitive insight you gain through eye contact is a powerful instrument in understanding others.

Another technique for getting your prospects involved with what you want to happen is to ask them questions, encouraging them to start talking about themselves or about something in which they have a strong interest. Most people will talk with you about themselves or their deepest interests even if they will not talk with you about anything else. Nothing gets a prospect involved in the selling process more quickly or effectively than inviting them to talk about themselves or the things they value most deeply.

We found that these three keys can help make this idea work:

- Ask questions that draw your prospects out. "That's a beautiful painting! Tell me about the artist!"
- Truly listen to their answers. Looking people straight in the eye and paying attention to everything they say is a highly effective way to show your interest in them as human beings. It also provides a great opportunity for you to pick up intuitive insights into your prospects that will help you meet their needs.
- Show a genuine interest in what they tell you by offering feedback. "I'm sure you're very concerned that your industry is changing so dramatically."

Here I have given you three techniques for getting people involved in what you want to happen. These are intended merely as examples. Use your imagination and come up with other methods that will apply directly to your situation. You never know when you will meet an important new customer, as this story proves.

A truck salesman in Springfield, Missouri, named Mike specialized in heavy-duty trucks. Though his prime method of meeting prospects was to go out and meet them on their sites, he had an office in the dealership. From his office he could see the display floor. One day a man came in, dressed so shabbily one would not have expected him even to have had a job. As he wandered around, the regular floor salespeople ignored him.

Mike scooted back from his desk and walked right up to the man to meet him. Things did not go well initially since the man realized he was being ignored because of his looks. Mike persisted with our Meet principles and built a good rapport that helped lower the prospect's emotional defenses and eliminated the tension. Mike's respectful attitude paid off.

This dirty, tattered-looking man owned his own sanitation and waste disposal company. He looked so bad because he had been helping his men work overtime to cover his rapidly burgeoning business. He did not have enough trucks to cover his new contracts and to meet future needs. Within a few minutes that man bought a $40,000 truck, making a $20,000 *cash* down payment. And Mike had a new long-term customer who would soon buy many more trucks.

What is truly important is that you do whatever it takes to build rapport. Rapport is essential to get clients actively involved in the selling process. No real selling can take place until that happens. Therefore, rapport is essential to successful IMPACT Selling. Rapport also sets the stage for soothing that almost inevitable tension your prospects feel when facing a sales presentation.

HOW TO REDUCE TENSION AND ESTABLISH TRUST

Most of your prospects see a sales call as an interruption of things they regard as more significant or productive. A salesperson is often viewed as an intruder, as a money-grabber, as a beggar, and sometimes even as an inconsiderate, unethical villain. At best, many polite prospects tend to feel that they are being nice to a fellow human or doing you a favor. Unless you can change that basic attitude and atmosphere, you are doomed before you get started.

Before successful selling can begin, tension must be greatly reduced. Completely eliminating tension is impossible and not necessarily desirable. A certain amount of tension is healthy and normal in an effective sales relationship. However, your prospects do need to feel that you are a trustworthy person, that you have something important to say to them, and that they might benefit enough to justify the time they invest in listening to you. That is a tall order, yet we will add another dimension to make it even taller:

You have only a matter of minutes—possibly only seconds—to establish your credibility and convince a prospect that time spent with you will be productive.

Let us now look at two very effective strategies used regularly by successful IMPACT Selling professionals to reduce tension and establish trust: *winning the inner game and creating trust.*

To Reduce Tension You Must Win the Inner Game

Prospects can read you like a book. They can instantly sense your confidence level, your attitude toward selling and what you are selling, your feelings toward them, and how comfortable you are being with them. It shows in your eyes, in your gestures and movements, and even in your tone of voice.

You simply cannot consistently fake your way through the inner game of selling and be a winner in the outer game.

"But I can't change the way I think and feel!" is one protest we hear repeatedly. Hold on, we have good news for you! You can change even your most basic attitudes and thoughts.

It starts when you begin replacing your negative, self-limiting thoughts with positive thoughts and insights. You will experience a real change in the way prospects respond to you when you begin feeding your mind with positive thoughts. Remember, if you are a sales manager your attitude affects far more than your own career. Here are some thoughts that will be especially valuable for you personally as well as for your entire sales force.

- Selling is an honorable profession that is worthy of my best efforts.
- I am a capable and confident salesperson.
- My purpose for being here is to enable this person to discover what he or she wants most and how to get it.
- I am a value generator for this person and for all of my clients. I concentrate on value and constantly seek to deliver it.
- The company I represent is a solid firm that seeks to deliver greater value than it receives in payment for its products and services.

- •What I am selling has a greater value to people than the money they will pay for it. I will see to it that they get what they pay for, and more.

- • I will not rely upon using high pressure to make this sale, but will concentrate on having a significant *impact* upon this customer.

- • When I finish this interview, I will leave behind a happy customer who will feel good about my company and me.

When you begin to see yourself in the positive light presented in that list of statements, you will be happily amazed at how much more warmly your prospects will receive you. More importantly, once you come to embody every one of those statements, you can spread them to your salespeople. Increased self-esteem will reduce tension among your clients and build their trust in you. That powerful development will leverage the selling time of an entire sales force as your customers become interested in what you want to happen.

You Have to Create Trust

The natural condition that exists at the beginning of any selling situation is tension, even when your prospects are close friends or relatives. We could build a seminar around all the factors that cause such tension, but you have probably experienced enough of it to know how real it is.

High levels of tension may exist between your prospects and you until you take action to reduce it. So, we will focus now on what you can do about it. Here are three techniques we have developed that many sales professionals find very helpful.

First, eliminate any unnecessary tension inducers before you make the sales call. That includes things like being neat in appearance and dressing in a way that will make your prospects feel you are one of them.

"This is a free country," a novice salesperson once told an old pro. "I can dress as I please, wear my hair as I please, and drive any kind of car I choose—and no one can stop me!"

"You're right!" responded the seasoned veteran. "And that prospect can exercise his freedom to say 'no'—and nobody can stop him!"

All you need to do is be aware of your reaction to the way strangers look and you will agree how important it is to make a good first impression.

Second, look for tangible ways to help your prospects relax. A quiet manner, a mild sense of humor, and a warm smile can go a long way toward breaking down barriers between you and your prospects.

A short, humorous, personal story that identifies you as a real human being can often do wonders to help people relax, especially if you listen while they tell you a story in return.

Notice that we said humorous, personal stories, not *jokes*. Be extremely careful about telling jokes. Most people do not tell many jokes, and they feel uncomfortable around salespeople who do. Besides, it takes special skill to tell jokes that really score a hit with everyone. Moreover, because of today's hypersensitivity to "politically correct" language, it takes a genius to tell one that will not be offensive to someone. If your customers wanted to buy from comedians, they would go to a night club and find a really good one. You are a sales professional, not a stand-up comedian.

For the same reasons, use one-liners very cautiously. If you start out by telling a big joke or just set up a series of one-liners and nobody laughs, where do you go from there? Unless you have a ready sense of humor that most people can easily identify with, concentrate on selling. Otherwise, you may look ridiculously awkward trying to make the transition from failed jokes to your product.

Consider the whole idea of salespeople as comedians in light of how it may impact your credibility. By starting with jokes, the subtle message to your customers is that you know what they will find funny. If they do not, then what will they think when you change the subject and tell them you think you know what they want in their business?

Third, be a good guest. When you are in someone's office, home, or workplace, you are on their turf. You are bound by etiquette and common courtesy to observe the "house rules."

For example, you might feel comfortable putting your feet on a coffee table, but if you do that with some prospects, they will immediately identify you as insensitive and start looking for ways to get rid of you and your bad manners.

Smoking cigarettes is a serious turnoff for many people these days; in many workplaces, smoking is forbidden. A cigar is rarely acceptable. If you smoke, never light up unless your host does and then only after asking for permission.

Your bad manners can turn off even an otherwise determined buyer. This illustration will show you how your demeanor can affect your sales.

Recently, I was called upon by a seasoned salesman, a veteran of more than twenty years of selling. He wanted to show me his line of exclusive—and very expensive—custom-designed suits. His products were beautiful, impressive examples of excellent craftsmanship and he knew the business and his line of products very well. Yet, while I was admiring the workmanship and his knowledge, he dragged his briefcase carelessly across my desk—scratching it slightly—and then used my phone to contact another prospect, expecting me to wait patiently for him to finish. I didn't really mind his being on the phone, though, because when he wasn't tying up my line, he dominated the conversation with boring, trite stories and a steady stream of stale jokes.

As impressive as his suits were, I couldn't stand to keep him in my office long enough to place an order. I thanked him for coming and then asked him to go. The idea that your manners can make or break your sales career is not some theory we've dreamed up; it's a completely valid and unforgiving concept. By all accounts, this highly experienced sales professional should have known better than to be such an offensive guest. However, in sales it is a real truth that theory is a far cry from practice.

That is enough of the negatives. This topic began with a list of positive things you can say to yourself. I will finish now with another.

One of the best ways to gain trust is to receive graciously any hospitality your hosts offer. To many people, offering a drink or snack is a way of saying "Let's be friends." Turning down an offer of kindness from a client can be interpreted as saying, "No! I'd rather be a stranger." This is yet another way in which you can let the customer leverage your own skills. Allow them to like you.

Remember, tension is a natural state that exists in the selling situation. It will never be reduced without your efforts. You must take positive steps to create a level of trust that will reduce the natural state of tension before IMPACT Selling can begin.

HOW TO START SUCCESSFUL SALES TALK

The final stage of the Meeting phase of the IMPACT Selling plan is to introduce the subject that you want to occupy the center stage of the session with your prospect, that is the selling of your product.

Shifting gears to sales talk can be very awkward, both for you and your prospect. Many of the salespeople who attend our seminars confess that this is the most uncomfortable part of the whole interview for them. I have already given you many techniques to help you focus the early stages of the Meeting phase so that the transition becomes a natural next step.

Setting the Stage for Action, Not for Reaction

The shift from friendly conversation to active sales talk is one you must make naturally. When you make it you want a positive response—not a reaction. One helpful image that illustrates how to do this is that of seeing yourself as building a bridge across a chasm. The best way to move a prospect from friendly chitchat to a business sales talk is to give him or her a firm foundation to walk across.

Obviously, the most crucial factor in building a bridge is knowing where you are coming from and what your destination is. Two factors that cause many salespeople to fail at building that bridge are that they start from the wrong place or do not clearly see where they are going.

Starting with a tricky foot-in-door tactic and trying to set up the prospect for the close is one way to start in the wrong place. I have already shown that a better approach is to start from a position of trust and strong rapport. Establishing the latter of the two will firmly anchor one end of the bridge.

Seeing the customer as an adversary to be conquered is one way to have the wrong destination. This can be tough to overcome, however, in a demanding, highly niched market in which your competitors are constantly dealing on price alone. Some prospects *believe* they prefer an adversarial relationship because they think it will give them a negotiating advantage. Your approach, however, should always be that your purpose is to convey value. If you always focus on the needs of your customers, you will clearly see where the other end of the bridge should be anchored, regardless of the prospect's initial reaction.

One anchor of the bridge is to create a strong trust bond. The other end is to convey value to your prospects through whatever you sell. You must see these two principles as the mental foundations of the IMPACT Selling plan in order for me to show you how to build a bridge between those two points. The rest of the IMPACT Selling plan will show you how to finish that bridge.

To get started in that direction, here are some pointers on how the real winners in the IMPACT sales plan begin building their bridges between the foundations of trust and value.

Get to the Point of Your Visit Quickly

Four things are uppermost in the prospect's mind from the moment you knock at the door:

- Who are you?
- Whom do you represent?
- What do you want?
- What's in it for me?

The quicker you can answer those questions, the sooner the prospect can relax and allow you to make the transition to the sales talk. When you answer those initial questions you display your customer-focused orientation for the first time. Subtly, by focusing on their needs, you will begin to show your prospects where you've laid the foundations of your bridge.

Avoid Being Abrupt

Amateurs or poorly trained salespeople often say things such as "Well, I know you folks don't have all day to talk and neither do I, so let's get down to business." Or, they may have been trained with the outdated techique of asking a startling question that is out of touch with everything that has been said up to that point. Such poor initial tactics show a lack of respect for the people you meet and will strengthen the barriers between you.

The most successful selling professionals take a more gentle approach. They ask nonthreatening questions or make statements that gently open the door. They also use good manners that indicate respect for the person with whom they are talking.

Something like, "Do you mind if I ask a few questions so I can find out how to assist you better?" will show that you want to help the person and gets him or her talking right away, as you wait for an answer.

Make It Natural

Search for a common interest with your prospects, a point of personal pride or joy for them, or a way to express concern over a problem they might be experiencing, and use that as a launching pad for your shift into sales talk. Things have a way of becoming intensely interesting to us when they become personal. Once you have found a tangible way to identify with the prospect, let the transition to sales talk flow naturally from the rapport you have set in motion.

When you become personal with your clients in a nonthreatening way, you become very interesting to them. But sincerity is essential. Never fake an interest you do not have. False flattery, inane chatter, and insincere comments create tension rather than reduce it. If, on the other hand, your interest is sincere and you use a little creativity to find ways to express it, your prospects will return the favor of your attention.

This brings us to a basic tenet of selling in the 1990s:

Success in selling in a crowded marketplace requires a genuine interest in and understanding of people.

If your interest is genuine, you will find you naturally identify with your prospects. That, in turn, enables them to identify with you. Once your clients feel that you see life pretty much as they do and that you mean them no harm, you have mixed up a solid load of concrete to build a lasting bridge.

Test Your Bridge Before You Invite the Prospect to Walk Across

Many prospects who have seemed relaxed and comfortable suddenly lapse into morose seriousness or a deathly silence at the first effort to move toward sales talk. Sometimes they will turn into aggressive attackers. If one of those two things happens, you have just witnessed a nearly involuntary reaction by your prospect to what they see as the approach of old-school selling methods. The message for your intuition, then, is that you have not built a strong enough trust bond.

Building a trust bond leads to action and avoids reactions. Prospects often resist sales talk because they have been subjected to so much high pressure from manipulative salespeople that they are afraid to ask a question, volunteer any information, or show any sign of interest. Therefore, you must continually test the trust you have established. A highly effective way to do this is to introduce sales talk in stages while you remain intuitively aware of the prospect's reactions.

A simple step in that direction is to ask for a small piece of information, and then to monitor carefully how freely the prospect shares the information you seek. If you sense reluctance, the prospect is still holding back out of fear of how you will use that information. The prospect's reluctance will be a clue to you to back off and build more trust rather than push forward, adding to the tension. If, on the other hand, you get a warm and immediate response, you know it is safe to proceed.

TO SUM IT ALL UP...

Here's a good quotation I often cite in seminars: "All effective sales talk is dialogue. It is not monologue!" To have dialogue with people is to "get in touch" with them in a meaningful way. That personal touch will set in motion a two-sided conversation that proves to your prospects that you value them, their feelings, and their needs. If your prospects know you value them, the tension they almost certainly felt before you conducted the Meet phase will be significantly reduced.

Alignment between you and your marketing department is also crucial at this stage. It is difficult to build trust now if what you say differs greatly from what the prospect has garnered about your company, product, or service from your company's marketing efforts. It is much easier for your prospects to trust you if what you say aligns with what they already know about your company. Any incongruity creates doubt, apprehension, and resistance in your prospects—particularly in a prospect who knows that he or she has a multitude of choices among the many competitors in your crowded market.

Now, recall the Value equation that I introduced in the Leverage chapter. Its basic principle is that to get prospects to reach a buying decision you must make their perceived benefit greater than their perceived price. However, before a prospect will believe that you can bring him or her benefits, he or she must first trust you. The Meet phase is where you build that trust, which you take with you into the Probe phase when you search for specific ways to maximize our Value equation.

Lowering natural barriers, reducing tension, and building trust and rapport are all part of the crucial Meeting phase of the IMPACT Selling plan. The completion of the Meeting phase moves you naturally to a sales dialogue in which you will begin the next IMPACT Selling phase. We call that next step the Probe phase. In the Probe chapter, we will explore how to

1. Tune in to your prospects' perceptions of their needs.
2. Make them aware of some unrecognized needs.
3. Let your questions do the selling for you.
4. Allow the prospect to focus on his or her greatest needs and to tell you what those needs are.

ACTION STEPS

Set personal goals for boosting your effectiveness in the Meeting phase by taking time to list an answer in each of the following areas. Think of specific answers that apply uniquely to you, your company, your marketing or sales strategies, your market niche, or your customers.

1. Get your prospects to lower their mental/emotional defenses so you can become personally acquainted.

   Goal: _____

2. Eliminate tension and establish a strong trust bond between you and your prospect.

   Goal: _____

3. Build a warm and cordial rapport with each other.

   Goal: _____

4. Make a natural transition to a successful sales dialogue.

   Goal: _____

KEY TIPS

☑ Gain your prospects' attention by getting them actively involved in what you want to happen. The quickest way to get people involved with you is to get involved with them first.

☑ Establish eye contact and use your intuition to plug into the emotions of your prospect. Try to connect with everything that person is feeling.

☑ Ask your prospects questions to get them involved in talking about themselves or what interests them most. Nothing gets prospects involved in the selling process more quickly or effectively than inviting them to talk about themselves or their deepest interests.

☑ Reduce tension by winning the inner game. You have only a matter of minutes—possible only seconds—to establish your credibility and convince a prospect that time spent with you might be productive.

☑ Eliminate unnecessary tension inducers before you make the sales call. Have a neat appearance and dress in a way that will make your prospects feel you are a highly qualified professional.

☑ Look for tangible ways to help your clients relax. A quiet manner, a mild sense of humor, and a warm smile can go a long way toward breaking down barriers between you and your prospects.

☑ Be a good guest; receive graciously any hospitality your hosts offer. Allow them to like you.

☑ Build a bridge across the chasm of mistrust. The best way to move prospects from friendly chitchat to a business sales talk is to give then something firm to walk across. Make it easy for them to cross over by quickly getting to the point of your visit, by avoiding being abrupt, and by making them comfortable so that meeting you feels natural.

☑ Test your bridge before you invite the client to cross it. Enter into your sales talk by subtly introducing it, then watch the prospect's reactions carefully to see if he or she trusts you enough to proceed across.

CHAPTER 7

PROBE

PROBE

Helping people discover what they need and want most. Finding out what people will buy, when they will buy, and under what conditions they will buy, then listening them into buying. Enabling prospects to focus on and verbalize their needs and wants.

Better to ask ten times than to go astray once.
Yiddish Proverb

The Probe phase is the core of the IMPACT Selling system. To illustrate why this is so, I will again present the greatest secret in IMPACT Selling:

Show people what they want most, and they will move heaven and earth to get it!

In this chapter I present an easy-to-follow plan that will put the greatest secret in selling to work for you. After learning the Probe phase of the IMPACT Selling plan, you will know how to

- *Listen* people into buying instead of talking your way out of the sale.
- Discover what they will buy, why they will buy it, and under what conditions they will buy it.
- Get your prospects to focus their needs and wants in their own minds and get them to verbalize what those needs and wants are.

Each of those three is covered in order as I lead you through the concepts of customer-centered probing. Note that the last item on the list above goes well beyond the common sales strategies.

Based on the IMPACT Selling concept that says one of your primary functions is to deliver value to your clients, its premise is that many of your prospects may not even recognize what they want or need even if you show them. Your latest hot product may do something for them that they do not realize is even possible. To bring your prospects the most beneficial value you can, you may need to make them aware of emerging technologies. Therefore, one of your roles is to train your prospects and customers to recognize and understand their own real needs in today's rapidly changing business world.

MEASURE YOUR PROSPECTS— DON'T JUST SIZE THEM UP

One of the best ways to leverage your time is to avoid wasting it by "peddling" something that your customer does not want or need. You can avoid chasing such a dead end only if you listen to your customer talk about his or her needs. In other words, listen your way to a sale. I will use one of my favorite personal stories as an example.

Imagine that your investigation has turned up a prospect who needs medical help. Then, in the Meeting phase with that client, you build a solid trust relationship with him or her. If you then switch to a traditional sales demonstration for your best deal on your company's latest hot product, the scenario may be like that in this story I often tell.

Doctors are great examples of service providers who are expert at probing—sometimes more so than anybody likes. Nonetheless, picture what could happen if doctors acted in the role of old-school salespeople. If your doctor did not probe, you might walk into an office one day and be greeted with a scenario like this.

"Boy, are you in luck today!" he says.

"I don't feel so lucky . . . my head hurts like crazy!" you respond.

"Know why you're so lucky?" he asks, ignoring your comment. "We're running a blockbusting closeout sale on artificial hearts . . . getting ready for the new models!"

"But, Doc," you protest, "it's my head that hurts, not my heart."

"Yes, sir! I can fix you up with this *Super Pumper* model that's loaded with options for an unbelievably low price. In fact, it's a 40 percent savings. Besides, it's all covered by your insurance. Could I schedule you for installation Tuesday, or would Thursday be more convenient for you?"

If you are like most of us you would run—not walk—to the nearest exit.

Sometimes it helps to look at a ludicrous example like this one to detect a fatal flaw in out-dated selling patterns. Many salespeople trained in traditional selling techniques are just that insensitive. Retold at one of your sales meetings, this story may serve to illustrate to your staff the importance of probing for your customers' needs. Skillful listening is an excellent way to avoid seeming insensitive toward your customers' needs.

THE FATAL FLAW IN SELLING

As sales consultants, we train literally thousands of salespeople every year. Our observations repeatedly show that most salespeople talk their way out of more sales than they talk their way into. Salespeople who subscribe to the "jawbone theory" of selling lose many sales they could make if they focused more on what their *prospects* want or need. Pushing the latest advances in their company's product line will never reveal a customer's need and always runs the risk of sounding like the pushy doctor in my story.

PROBING GIVES YOU MORE SELLING POWER

The Probe step must be at the very core of *any* customer-centered, value-based selling system. When you probe, you look beneath the surface to discover and reveal what is really going on in the prospect's mind and heart.

The dictionary defines a probe as an instrument used to penetrate, usually for investigating or measuring. As an action verb, *to probe* means to interview, to ask questions and listen, to observe, and to study. In the IMPACT Selling plan, the two key words in the Probe definition are investigation and measuring.

Investigation enables you to discover what the prospect wants and the conditions under which the person will buy what you are selling. It keeps you from wasting time on prospects who will not buy what you are selling under any condition. More importantly, it uncovers needs you can meet and ways to suggest how to meet them.

Measuring means identifying, clarifying, and expressing your customers' wants or needs. Many people have only a vague feeling that they want *something* but haven't the foggiest idea what that something is. Others may have a deep desire that they have never even admitted to themselves. Some may think they want one thing, when what they really want is something entirely different. Still others know exactly what they want but do not know how to get it.

Skillful and sensitive probing benefits both you and your customers. It leverages your selling time, making you more productive, and it helps the customer get something that everyone needs: value. Probing allows you to avoid the amateurish technique of holding up one product after another and asking, "Is this it?" Also, probing will make you a highly respected professional rendering a valuable service to your clients—a service for which you can expect to be paid very well. Finally, probing will separate you from your competitors who are guaranteed to be pitching price and features instead of value and benefits.

Probing will also improve your leverage. The scenario above—holding up product after product—not only makes you look amateurish, but wastes your time. You do not have enough hours in a week to travel through today's crowded marketplaces without a clue as to what prospects need. Careful probing leverages your precious prime-time selling hours.

Now that I have clearly established the need for probing as a step to move you beyond the ineffective old-school techniques, I will show you how to integrate it into a sales presentation.

MASTERING THE MASTER KEYS

In the Probe step, the master keys to "listening your customer into buying" are *asking* and *listening*. They are your most effective implements for opening up the mind and heart of your prospect. Unfortunately, many salespeople have serious misconceptions about the meanings of those two key words, asking and listening.

Let us look twice at what I mean, first as the words are defined in typical sales jargon, then through the perspective of the IMPACT Selling plan.

In old-school selling jargon, *to ask* means one thing—to ask for the order. Often, asking people to sign an order blank is the first question some salespeople use. It is so common that most of us cannot remember the last time a salesperson asked us a question such as, "How will you use it?" or "What do you like most about it?" Without such personal interest questions the buyer may well feel cheated.

Now I will reexamine those two words—asking and listening—this time with the IMPACT Selling philosophy in mind. You will see different meanings for those two words when viewed in terms of customer focus.

Asking means that if you ask enough of the right questions throughout the interview you will most likely get an order.

Listening means that the most important task of the salesperson is to pay careful attention to what the prospect truly says.

In the next section of this chapter we will explore in detail how to use the master keys of asking questions. First, I will ask two vital questions about listening, then examine their answers:

- Why do most salespeople find it so hard to listen to what their prospects say?
- How can you improve your listening skills?

Most salespeople have been conditioned to ignore the prospect's needs and desires. What is uppermost in our minds as we walk onto a prospect's turf? Never be ashamed to say it: The number one thought in our minds is *to close a sale*. Most salespeople focus on what they will get out of the sale—not what the prospect will get out of it.

The selfish streak in most of us is reinforced by our traditional sales training. Unfortunately, much of today's selling stresses our needs and interests. We go out looking for prospects to buy what we are "selling," try to "warm them up" so we can lay our "pitch" on them, then "hit 'em with the close." If we do it well, we can make big money . . . for a short while.

Countless salespeople have been trained to use their listening time to think up what to say after—and sometimes *before*—the prospect finishes speaking. To improve your listening skills, that traditional focus must change. To survive in a crowded marketplace, we must lay aside our own interests so that we may discover and satisfy the needs and desires of our customers. This new focus is different and your customers will notice the difference. It will make your sales efforts successful even where others repeatedly fail—even where you may have previously failed yourself.

SELF-CENTEREDNESS IS NOT IN YOUR BEST INTEREST

Please do not misunderstand. I have never suggested that anyone adopt a martyr attitude and lay oneself down at the feet of every prospect, caring nothing about one's own needs. What we have discovered is that there exists vast difference between self-centeredness and serving your own best interest. Fortunately, serving your own best interest usually serves your customers' best interest. Here is that concept, expressed in this simple principle:

PROBE PRINCIPLE #1:
The best way to serve your own interest is to put the needs and desires of your customer first!

If you only want to talk about *your* interests, *your* products, *your* product's features, or *your* company, then do not be surprised if you encounter strong sales resistance at the outset. If you focus instead on the *prospect's* interests and the *prospect's* needs and desires, and on what the *prospect* values, then you will notice a remarkable difference in that person's openness to you.

In the Meeting phase, you laid the foundation for a bridge between you and your customer. A properly targeted probe will overcome sales resistance because your sales presentation will center on delivering value to every customer. Now the care you took in laying that foundation will pay dividends: Your customers will trust you enough to open up in the Probe phase.

PROBE PRINCIPLE #2:
To deliver value to the prospect, you must see yourself primarily as a value resource for the prospect!

What separates you from a vending machine is that you have an opportunity to meet your customers and to respond to the widely varied and specific needs of each customer you serve. The most helpful attitude a salesperson can have is to see himself or herself as a resource for meeting the needs and fulfilling the desires of customers.

If the primary focus of your sales approach is to create value for the individuals you meet, you will not only become an effective IMPACT salesperson but a very well-paid salesperson. To focus primarily on creating value, you must know what your clients consider to be valuable. The only way to do that is by probing.

PROBE PRINCIPLE #3:
To be a value resource for the prospect, you must first discover what the prospect perceives as value!

To paraphrase a familiar adage, "Value is in the eye of the beholder." That a product comes in 47 colors might be of little value to a person who is color-blind. Something that is lightweight and easy to carry might be a real turnoff to a weight lifter. And the story of a "40 percent savings" on that artificial heart showed how much value was created for a patient who merely had a headache!

The significance of creating value in the eye of your prospect can easily be seen by remembering the Value equation, which is composed of *perceived* benefit over *perceived* price. The old adage "perception is reality" is true for your prospects.

Your selling success will rise in direct proportion to your understanding of the value systems of your prospects. And that comes from the first of the master keys of selling—asking. We are now led naturally into the second vital component of listening—improving your concrete listening skills.

HOW YOU CAN IMPROVE YOUR LISTENING SKILLS

In IMPACT Selling, skillful listening is a highly professional undertaking. First, you must look like a professional listener. Get a top-quality leather binder with a legal pad and pen loop. This will be your primary listening aid. Treat it as if it were the most valuable piece of equipment you have, for it may very well prove to be just that.

Once you are ready to start the Probe step, open the leather binder as the prospect watches, take out the pen, and say, "In order for us to see how we may best serve you, do you mind if I ask you a few questions?"

Then *stop!*

Do not say another word until the customer gives you permission to ask those questions. I cannot emphasize enough how important this waiting interval is; it sets a pattern for everything that follows throughout the course of your sales interview. Use the same caution with each question you ask after the customer has agreed to answer. Always wait for an answer.

HOW TO LISTEN PEOPLE INTO BUYING

People who talk themselves out of sales do the vast majority of the talking and very little of the listening. People who use their mental skills instead of their verbal skills do most of the listening and very little of the talking during the Probe step. The first step toward improving your listening skills is simply to begin listening. Keep a mental stopwatch for yourself and your prospect. How much time are you each logging?

Once you've started listening instead of talking, you will be able to enhance your listening skills. Listening is a skill that can be learned and continually improved, but most of us have never been trained to listen. For example, which do we do most during the day, read or listen? Most of us generally listen more than we read, yet how many listening lessons did we get in school? It is not surprising that most people need help in becoming skillful listeners. The many evaluations we have conducted in our consulting work consistently show salespeople with miserable scores in the areas of listening skills.

Sales managers need to be especially mindful of the listening skill levels of their youngest salespeople who have grown up in today's fast-paced world of rock videos and Music Television (MTV). Their ears may have been deluged with more messages in their young lives than many sales managers have heard. To survive mentally under a barrage of hyped-up verbiage, many young people have nearly turned off their listening skills. They have certainly had little motivation to develop them. After the IMPACT Selling system is in place, I urge sales managers to use their intuitive skills to monitor their sales force's progress. A staff will listen no better to a client than to their sales manager.

Here are 10 great pointers that can help sharpen listening skills in any situation:

- Open your eyes, mind, and ears to be truly receptive to the messages the other person presents.
- Begin listening from the very first word and give the person your undivided attention.
- Focus on what the prospect says. Avoid trying to anticipate what the person is going to say; you may miss what he or she actually says.
- Do not try to read meaning into what you think the other person is saying. Actively help the person to accurately convey his or her meaning to you.
- Never interrupt! Interrupting is offensive and rude and may possibly cut off the dialogue flow. It also sends the subtle message that you are not serious about listening.
- Control outside interruptions and distractions.
- Use questions to encourage people to talk and to clarify your understanding of what they mean.
- Make notes of important points. Look for connections between apparently isolated remarks.
- Get your whole body involved in listening and show that you are paying attention. Look the person squarely in the eye, using facial expressions and other nonverbal clues to show that you hear and understand what he or she says.
- Remain calm. Never overreact to highly charged words and tones. Hear the person out, then respond. Most people will cool down and begin to talk calmly once they vent their anger and frustration.

Remember, your objective is to listen your prospect into buying. You do not need to remind yourself of what *you* think; you must find out what your *prospect* thinks. When listening, continually remind yourself that this is the Probe phase. There is not one Probe principle that requires you to "get your two cents worth in."

Many salespeople have asked me how long they need to continue probing once a prospect becomes a customer, often saying something like, "I call on the same people on a regular basis; some have been my customers for years. Do I really need to probe every time? That would seem ridiculous when I already know them well." My answer to questions like that is always, "Yes, every time!" Our world today is changing very rapidly, and the wants and needs of your long-time customers are constantly changing, too.

Continually probing even your well-established accounts may reveal surprise selling opportunities. If you are not probing to keep up with their ever changing needs, someone else may be. If that someone else is the one to whom your loyal customer expresses a newfound need, they are the ones who will make the sale. The secret to successful selling is to be in front of qualified buyers when they need to buy, not when you need to sell something to them.

HOW *NOT* TO DISCOVER WHAT PEOPLE WILL BUY

The second of the three objectives in the Probe phase is to discover what your prospects will buy, why they will buy it, and under what conditions they will buy it. Of course, the master key for determining those answers is in asking the right questions. Often, though, salespeople have no idea what to ask.

"Oh, I ask a lot of questions," a young furniture salesman once said, very confidently. Yet his sales manager had relayed to us that the man was working on his last chance because his sales had been so few and far between.

"What kinds of questions do you ask?" we probed.

"When people walk into the store, I usually ask, 'Can I help you?'," he replied. "Usually, they want to look around a little, so I just back off. When I see that they've found something they seem to like, I go right up and ask, 'Can I fix you up with that bedroom suite today?' "

After seeing how often salespeople ask questions like that, we began to develop techniques to introduce them to a much more effective line of questioning.

"What do you learn by asking 'Can I help you?'," we asked him.

"I learn whether they want to buy something, or if they are just looking around," he responded.

"How many people have told you they wanted to buy something when you asked them that opening question during the last week?" I pressed.

"Oh, let's see . . . I think there have been two, but we didn't have what one of them was looking for," he said sadly.

ASK AND YE SHALL LEARN
(IF YE ASK THE RIGHT QUESTIONS)

Can you see how little information that young salesman learned by asking his two unfocused questions? Let us list what he learned:

- He learned his prospects could talk.
- He learned they were not going to take his furniture away from him.
- He learned (by prematurely asking a bad closing question) that they were not ready to make a buying decision.

Now we will examine the difference between what this salesman's questions taught him and what negative effects they had:

- He was presenting himself as a servant instead of a skilled professional. "Can I help you?" is the type of question people expect from the Salvation Army after a natural disaster, not from a sales professional!
- His questions set up a high probability for a negative response. Questions that call for a "yes" or "no" response produce about 10 times as many "no" responses as "yes" answers.

- His line of questioning gained him no insights into *what* his prospects wanted. They told him nothing of what needs they were seeking to satisfy, what they would buy, or under what conditions they would buy it.
- He was trying to close before he sold anything. He was asking for a buying decision before he built any value for his prospects.

Listing the positive and negative effects of the salesman's questions enables you to see that they did more harm than good. We saw that this salesman would soon be out of a job unless he learned how to ask the right questions. We had to help this guy and we had to help him fast.

HOW TO DISCOVER WHAT PEOPLE WILL BUY

Here are some tips we gave him about how to ask the right kinds of questions during the Probe phase. We've developed a set of 10 powerful questioning pointers:

PROBING TIP #1:
Prepare the questions you will ask in advance.

Although every prospect is unique and every selling situation requires some variation, certain basic questions that come up in every interview can be planned and practiced. Through careful planning, you can make sure that you uncover the essential information and that your wording is precise. Since you will most likely get a great deal of practice with these questions, here is a note of caution: Be careful never to allow your questions to sound canned. Rephrase or refine them regularly to ensure originality and vitality.

One tip for making sure your questions sound fresh is to follow the example of television journalists. These professionals will open an interview with things like: "Tell me about..." or "What are your feelings concerning..." This approach generates a unique response every time because no two people will feel exactly the same way about anything. If your questioning always begins instead with the same curt, canned question, you may begin hearing a lot of the same curt, canned answers.

PROBING TIP #2:
Ask open-ended and indirect questions.

Sales questions that require only a "yes" or "no" answer tend to discourage people from talking. They also give you only limited information and set a negative tone. During the Probe step, ask open-ended questions that require prospects to tell you how they feel, what they want, or what they think.

For example, the young furniture salesman mentioned earlier might have asked: "Let me ask you this: How would you describe your decorating motif?" That is a nonthreatening question that does not require the customer to make a buying decision. It also opens the door for an in-depth conversation during which the salesman might have learned much about the customer's wants and needs. He may have heard the customer express a need that he could easily fill. With enough knowledge of the customer's needs, the salesman could probably have led him or her to some corner of the store, merely pointed and said, "Would this serve your needs?" Then he could have stood back, listening for more information, or watched while the customer closed the sale for him.

PROBING TIP #3:
Ask need-development questions.

In the Probe step, you must do more than get your prospects to talk. You must get prospects to tell you what they need. Therefore, ask questions that will give you insights into how each prospect perceives his or her needs.

Our troubled furniture salesman might have given himself a big raise by asking walk-in customers, "What kinds of entertaining do you enjoy?" or "What activities does your family enjoy in the den?"

PROBING TIP #4:
Ask questions that help you identify dominant needs.

There is usually one overriding need in the prospect's mind. Knowing that will help you to ask the right question. Ask questions that will probe for that single, dominant need.

"What do you like least about your present car?" a car sales-person could ask. An attentive, skillful listener, willing to let the customer tell all about the old jalopy out front, could get enough information from that one question to close a sale. If five cus-tomers could answer that same question about the same car, you might hear

"We need something much larger. We've got a two-year-old and we just had twins!"

"I need something much smaller. It gets lousy mileage and it's too hard to park."

"It's been the best car I've ever owned, but I just got a big promotion at work and I'm ready now for my dream car."

"It's been the best car I've ever owned, but the dealer has the worst service department I've ever dealt with. Though the car is reliable, it's often out of service for days awaiting simple, routine maintenance checkups. I need speedy service."

"It's a real clunker. I really can't afford a new car, but I've got to get something more reliable."

Many customers do not look at that which they are really seeking when they first walk in. The guy with the growing family may have stopped first at the Corvette convertible in the front of the showroom. Then, when an old-school salesperson asks, "If the deal is right, would you drive that home tonight?" the customer may laugh inside, shake his head, and steer clear of that salesperson. True IMPACT Selling probe questions would reveal the customer's dominant need, allowing the salesperson to continue to probe.

PROBING TIP #5:
Ask questions that help you pinpoint the dominant buying motivations.

Buying motivations and needs are not always the same. Buy-ing motivations address desires, feelings, tastes, and so on. I will illustrate the difference between buying motivations and buying needs with another of my own anecdotes.

I regularly sell my professional speaking services over the phone. When prospective clients say that they are considering booking me, I will often ask: "Whom have you had in the past?" Their answers reveal what kinds of speakers they like. If all they give me is a list of names, at least I learn what kinds of speeches they like. I can then probe, getting them to talk specifically about one or two who were particularly well-received by their audiences, and about why they were popular. That way I will know exactly which of the benefits that I offer to emphasize most.

You might discover the same sort of information by asking, "Whom are you buying from now?"

PROBING TIP #6:
Avoid asking offensive questions or asking questions in an insensitive way.

Some questions can offend prospects and cause them to back off from you. This is more important than ever before in our country's history. There is a very strong push to be "politically correct" in everything we say and do today. Many people are hypersensitive and can easily be offended. Those who are hypersensitive may respond more strongly to a "politically incorrect" statement than by merely throwing you out of their office. People have become targets of legal action for saying things that only a few years ago would have gone unnoticed or at the very most would have produced only a brief awkward moment. In a closely networked, crowded market, a reputation for offending buyers can spread rapidly and severely limit your sales potential.

Some examples of pitfalls to avoid are

- Never use leading or "set-up" questions such as, "You do want your employees to share in the success of the company, don't you?" What is the prospect going to say? "No! Let the ungrateful fools tough it out!" Then again, maybe that will be the prospect's answer. Either way, you lose.
- Nosy questions can be a real turnoff, or worse. Asking a woman, "What time will your husband be home?" might be asking her for information she does not wish to give out to strangers.
- Sometimes your manner can be threatening. Instead of asking, "How much can you afford to spend?", why not phrase it, "How much had you planned to invest?" or "What sort of budget level do you have in mind?"

Planning your most often asked questions in advance will help you dissect them for offensive overtones. You should also try them out on noncustomers. A sales manager could organize workshops in which the sales force could assume the roles of sensitive customers, allowing other staff members the opportunity to get feedback in a safe environment.

PROBING TIP #7:
Start with broad questions, then move steadily toward questions with a narrower focus.

Broad questions are usually less threatening and yield general information. Thus, they can help you get things rolling and steer you in the right direction. An example of a broad question might be: "What kind of future do you see for your firm?"

As your probing becomes more comfortable and picks up speed, you will need to get more specific with your questions.

"How many employees do you plan to add in the next 24 months?" is a good example of a narrowing question.

PROBING TIP #8:
Ask questions that are easy to answer.

Questions that require knowledge the prospect does not have can often make him or her feel stupid. For example, asking a customer who is buying stereo speakers, "What's the maximum continuous RMS wattage per channel on your amplifier?" might get you a dumb look for an answer. The smarter you make your prospects feel, the smarter they will think you are and the better they will like you.

A better opening, one that most people could answer, might be, "Do you have a large, powerful amplifier?" People who know the exact RMS continuous wattage per channel of their amplifiers will give you that for their answer, just to show you how much they know. If not, then you will not have risked intimidating a less savvy customer.

PROBING TIP #9:
Use questions to guide the interview and keep it positive in tone.

Some people love to ramble on and on. When the sales talk takes such a nonproductive turn, you are no longer in the Probe phase, but have begun a conversation. By skillfully using questions you can keep the interview focused and control its direction so it continues to produce useful information for your probe. Be especially alert for those people who have a tendency to drift into explosive subject areas like religion, politics, race, and deep personal problems. You must keep the talk on track.

Phrase your questions so that people can easily respond positively. Studies have shown that most people prefer to agree than to assert themselves and disagree. Agreement is easy. Disagreement takes energy, diverting energy away from the subject at hand: meeting your customer's needs. Always try to structure your questions so that the easiest response is agreement.

PROBING TIP #10:
Ask. Then shut up and listen.

The prospect cannot talk while you are talking and you cannot learn while you are talking. Never use your listening time to think up a witty comeback. Instead, have your leather binder and pen in hand and listen attentively, analyzing every word that your prospect says. People who see you take notes won't expect a hasty answer, but will be favorably impressed as they watch you refer to your notes as you formulate a carefully tailored response.

Questions are your greatest selling tool, but they only further the Probe phase if you use them properly to gather information about the prospect's needs. You are going to need all the information you can possibly glean in the next phase of IMPACT Selling, the Apply phase. The better you become at asking questions, the easier it will become for you to sell as you move through the remaining phases of the IMPACT Selling plan. Remember

You cannot talk people into buying, but you can listen them into it.

HELP PEOPLE CLARIFY FOR THEMSELVES WHAT THEY NEED AND WANT

The third major objective in the Probe phase is to enable prospects to discover, and in turn verbalize, their needs or desires. During talks with thousands of salespeople at seminars, we have discovered that most of them simply do not know how to help their prospects clarify their feelings and desires. In the remaining pages of this chapter, I will give you four pointers to help you learn how. As you read the pointers and the discussions, keep in mind this selling truism: A buying decision is ultimately an emotional response.

The way you present facts and focus relative values can either reinforce or cancel the emotions that lie behind a sale. In preparation for the pointers that will come next, read this illustration of a typical selling blunder, in which our young furniture salesman is once again featured as an example. A couple has walked into his store and are looking at recliners. The husband sits down in one, so the eager salesman rushes forward to ask a question.

"Can I fix you up with that new recliner today?" he asks.

"No thanks. We're just looking," comes the cool reply.

The salesman quickly sizes up the prospects and decides that they are merely time wasters. He turns to something else, like complaining to other salespeople about how bad business is.

That is not selling—it's peddling! Jumping straight to a close may get you a "no" that would have been a "yes" if the prospect but knew how well you could provide value to fulfill his or her needs.

The first of the two things a salesperson can do is to focus relative values. Again, this salesman's one-line opener and speedy exit did nothing at all in that area. He jumped right over the Meeting, Probing, Applying, and Convincing steps and tried to close the sale. He tried to collect money without showing the customer any value.

That salesman's second task was to reinforce a buyer's emotions and to present the facts. Did he do that? About the only fact he presented to that couple was that he was a salesman in that store and could write up a sale on that chair if they wanted it today.

Let us now cover those four pointers that will help you to present facts and focus relative values in a way that will produce a positive emotional response.

FOCUS POINTER #1:
Seek to understand the prospect's deepest feelings.

A prospect is not an adversary. Still, some things a prospect feels or thinks can be a hindrance to or can even work against your closing the sale. Some common things that produce negative feelings in prospects are confusion, misinformation, and false conclusions. If you are a skillful listener, your intuitive insight will tell you whether your prospect's emotions are hindered by any negative feelings. If you understand what your prospects are thinking and feeling, you will be at a distinct advantage.

Attentive listening during the Probe phase involves being alert, perceptive, and creative in searching out what your prospects feel or think about their needs and desires. Another of my true stories shows how attentive listening can be applied so that the close of a sale becomes automatic. It is about a real estate salesperson whom I regard as one of my sharpest acquaintances.

A husband and wife came to her in response to an ad for a house she had just listed. The wife did all the talking at first and was enthusiastic about everything the salesperson told her about the house. But the husband began finding fault with the house the moment they drove up. Soon the wife loved the house and her husband rejected it completely.

After the same thing happened at two more houses, the salesperson sensed what was going on and began to probe more deeply into the husband's unexpressed feelings. She found that the husband felt they could not afford the houses they were looking at but did not want to admit it to his wife. So his game was to find something wrong with every house they were shown.

The salesperson soon realized that she could show them a dozen houses in the price range the wife wanted to see and still not close a sale. Tactfully, she steered them to a house she believed the husband would feel they could afford.

Upon seeing the house he felt was in his budget range, the husband quickly became the ally of the salesperson. He began talking about all "the great possibilities" he saw for the house. When his wife gave up some of her demands, a sale was quickly closed.

Sometimes there is a conflict of values between multiple parties who have to agree before a deal can be completed. Most of the time, some conflict exists within almost every prospect we see. The better you have listened, the better you will be at spotting those internal conflicts. Uncovering the deepest feelings can alleviate the internal conflicts and enable you to focus relative values. This will help your prospects work through what they are thinking and feeling, and help you close more sales.

FOCUS POINTER #2:
Assure prospects you want to help them meet their needs.

Scores of scientific studies into human nature have repeatedly shown that most people approach buying decisions with some anxiety and often have very mixed emotions. Yet, those same studies also reveal that many prospects regularly look to salespeople to help them make up their minds. For example, if a prospect asks you, "How much is it?" as an opening question, he or she may be looking for an excuse not to satisfy a strongly felt need or desire. Such a question often indicates mixed emotions based on confusion or anxiety.

The question "How much is it?" often scares salespeople. Don't be intimidated. Although that question is usually a sign that you are selling in a crowded market with many competitors, you should not see it as an indication that you must also deal on price alone or lose the sale. Instead, view that question as a welcome relief that most of your competitors are stuck in the old, traditional modes and that your niche is a ripe plum, ready for your value-based application selling skills. As a skilled, value-based selling professional, you have to help prospects sort through their confusion and buying anxieties by helping them to focus on value instead of on pure dollar cost.

In the Probe phase, the best way for you to assure prospects that you want to help them meet their needs is to ask, "In order for us to see how we many best serve you, do you mind if I ask you a few questions?" Then proceed only if they say "yes." If they give you permission to ask questions, then focus questions so that you can figure out how to be of service. End your questioning by assuring the prospects that you want to help them meet their needs. With that solid foundation laid, you are ready to proceed with a productive sales interview.

FOCUS POINTER #3:
Ask questions to focus on the true issues.

Before concluding the Probe phase and moving on to the Apply phase, it is important to clear up any issues that may be unresolved. A common mistake made by many salespeople is to believe that an issue has been settled once the prospect has voiced an opinion. By talking instead of listening, the salesperson may have left the issues lingering in the prospect's mind. Your only clue may be a "no" at closing time. You may then leave the sales interview wondering what happened, when the true reason for the refusal lies in open issues lingering from a Probe phase that was not brought to completion.

Let us look to the life insurance field for an illustration of how much more successful a salesperson might be if he or she persists in focusing on the true issues.

The salesperson who answers, "You can never have too much life insurance" when a prospect says that he or she is already overinsured is leaving a crucial issue unresolved. Even worse, perhaps, is that the salesperson may set up a war of wills that will benefit no one.

The IMPACT Selling approach always involves asking questions instead of stating opinions or platitudes like that in the illustration above. The follow-up question, "May I ask why you feel you already have too much life insurance?" enables the salesperson to discover what the prospect is thinking and feeling.

"Because I'm already spending a fortune on premiums!" he or she may answer. That statement just revealed the true issue. This prospect may not feel overinsured at all, just overburdened with insurance premiums. Unveiling the true issue paves the way for a reflective question such as, "So you do agree that providing adequately for your family's security needs is a priority?" In keeping with guidelines I have laid out earlier, that question makes it easy for the prospect to agree with you. You would then be ready to move to the Apply phase and show the client how a policy with your company might reduce payments and increase coverage.

To reinforce your application-based presentations, you should regularly ask your prospects how they perceive the values you have shown them so far. Then, repeat the answer they give, turning it into a *summary statement*. For example, you might say, "You told me that you want a telephone system that is expandable and flexible, that will fit into your current budget, and that will include on-site training. Is that correct?" Rephrasing the answers to your questions as a summary statement is of paramount importance. This final questioning segment accomplishes several key objectives:

- It proves you are interested in correctly understanding not only what your prospects said, but what they truly meant.

- It provides the prospect with an opportunity to agree with or to correct your interpretation of what he or she said.
- It gives you the opportunity to ensure that you are on the right track as you begin the transition to the coming Apply phase.
- It helps you and your prospect begin to make the mental jump from probing into thinking of how to tie what you have learned together with your product knowledge to create value-based applications that fulfill your prospect's deepest wants and needs.

FOCUS POINTER #4:
All values are considered equal in the absence of a values interpreter.

The best tactic for focusing a prospect's needs and feelings is to keep weighing one value against another. If there is no obvious standard against which to measure the value you offer, you must provide some yardstick. Referring again to the life insurance example, you might use carefully chosen questions to balance "a little sacrifice now" with "the peace of mind that comes from knowing your children's education will be paid for if you are not around to provide for it."

A key goal of your Probe questions is to focus and interpret relative values for your prospects. By focusing on value for the client, you end the Probe phase as a respected consultant who has a proven interest in serving the client's needs. The clients will trust you and be at ease with you because you never treated them as adversaries. If you handle the Probe phase well and use the answers you've been given to reveal ways to offer your clients a valuable benefit, they will reward you.

TO SUM IT ALL UP . . .

The Probe phase is the very core of the IMPACT Selling plan. It enables you to accomplish three important objectives:

1. To listen your prospects into buying from you instead of talking your way out of sales.
2. To discover what they will buy, why they will buy it, and under what conditions they will buy it.

3. To enable your prospects to focus on and verbalize their wants and needs, and to interpret the relative values of the different ways in which they can get what they want.

The better you become at asking questions and actively listening, the more often you can accomplish those three vital objectives. This kind of approach separates the IMPACT Selling professional from the amateurs and the out-dated old school adherents. The Probe phase is truly the key to success in selling in a crowded market because it is where you differentiate yourself from your competitors.

ACTION STEPS

Mentally reconstruct a recent sales call in which you felt you could have closed the sale but did not get the prospect's name on the dotted line. Ask yourself if one of the following happened as you worked with that prospect:

1. Did you talk yourself out of the sale, or did you try to listen the prospect into buying?
2. Did you find out what or under what conditions the prospect would buy?
3. Did you help the prospect focus his or her wants and needs? Did you measure the relative values of the different methods of fulfilling those wants and needs?

KEY TIPS

☑ The three key objectives of your Probe phase are to *listen* people into buying, instead of talking your way out of the sale; to discover what they will buy, why they will buy it, and under what conditions they will buy it; and to get your prospects to focus their needs and wants in their own minds and verbalize them.

☑ The Fatal Flaw in Selling: Most salespeople talk their way out of more sales than they talk their way into.

☑ The Master Keys of Selling: *asking* enough of the right questions throughout the interview to get an order, and *listening* by paying careful attention to what the prospect truly says.

☑ The best way to serve your own interests is to always put the needs and desires of your customer first by seeing yourself primarily as a value resource for him or her.

☑ The best way to discover what people will buy is to follow a questioning sequence, moving steadily closer to the true buying motivations and needs of your prospects. Begin with open-ended and indirect questions that you prepared in advance. Create need-development questions that will pinpoint your prospect's dominant needs and buying motivations. Use broad questions initially, then steadily narrow your focus. Avoid asking offensive or insensitive questions and keep the interview positive in tone. Ask questions that are easy to answer, then *listen* to the answers.

☑ Since a buying decision is ultimately an emotional response, you have to seek to understand the prospects' deepest feelings, assuring them you want to help meet their needs. Always be alert for questions that hint at problems beyond what the prospects are actually saying and focus on the true issues.

CHAPTER 8

APPLY

APPLY

Assuring prospects that you understand their needs and then showing how a product or service will meet those needs. Unlike traditional demonstration selling, this is the process of meeting the stated or implied needs of the prospect. Showing and telling with power, continually building value and finding out how prospects feel about what they see, hear, and experience.

The skilled archer shoots one arrow at a time.
Anonymous

It takes a wise doctor to know when not to prescribe.
Baltasar Gracian

In the old-school method of selling, the traditional term *demonstrating* meant showing how your products work, what they look like, and all they will do. But in today's crowded marketplace, the hard facts presented in a standard, product-focused demonstration are often minor considerations to most consumers. Doing a *data dump* on a prospect merely adds your name to the long list of sources that continually deluge today's confused buyers. Demonstrating is no longer enough, in fact; it can work against you in making sales.

In IMPACT Selling, demonstrating your product is essentially a process of applying what you sell to the needs and wants of your prospects; it is application selling defined. That is why we call this the Apply phase instead of the Demonstrate phase. Applying describes more accurately what needs to happen for you to consistently make sales. Applying means that you show prospects how they can get value by buying from you.

There is a key IMPACT Selling point to remember, which we found from the results of a study into how people retain information. Here is a listing of the principal findings that affect your sales presentations. The study found that we retain:

- 10% of what we *read*
- 20% of what we *hear*
- 30% of what we *see*
- 50% of what we *see* and *hear*
- 70% of what we *say*
- 90% of what we *say* and *apply*

When your prospects both physically and mentally apply what you show them and you ask questions designed to get them to say what they think and feel about that application, they will retain 90 percent of what you show them. In this chapter, you will discover the power of transforming your old demonstrating techniques into IMPACT Applying. Here are some specific examples of what you will learn how to do:

- Show and tell with the power to sell.
- Answer the prospect's biggest question to get the action you want.
- Add to your sales punch by using leverage to build more value.
- Target your prospect's key benefit to heighten desire.
- Ask for the prospects' reactions and feelings about what they have seen and heard.

Here's an aphorism I've developed from my observations of value-based selling at work:

To a prospect, any price is too high until he or she truly understands the value of the application of a product or service.

Product knowledge is not how much data you have memorized about your products or services. Rather, it is how you apply what you know to fulfill the wants and needs of your prospects. You combine your application knowledge with what you learned in the Probe phase so that you can now present meaningful, valuable benefits for your prospects.

Now for an anecdotal story from our files to illustrate the difference between IMPACT Applying and old-school demonstrating.

An audiovisual production studio near our headquarters was struggling against tremendous apathy in selling its multimedia presentation services. Its sales department had put together fabulous sample tapes that would knock your eyes out. They were very powerful, had dramatic soundtracks, and would have been highly effective . . . if anyone would have bought them. But nobody seemed interested in buying multimedia presentations and dramatic soundtracks—especially not at the prices the studio charged.

The studio's first approach to its prospects' objections was to cut prices. It also offered special deals and threw in bonuses. None of these tactics worked. The studio had an excellent sales staff demonstrating an impressive product that was now priced very reasonably. Sales, however, still languished.

Finally, the company's sales manager had a brilliant idea. He suggested that the studio make a sample product-training film designed to help furniture reps train retail floor salespeople in how to sell their company's products. The sales manager took the sample film to a large furniture manufacturer and showed the company's president how his reps could increase their sales by helping retailers move more of their furniture.

He hit the jackpot. The manufacturer was thrilled. The furniture firm immediately bought projectors for each of its 270 salespeople, ordered several product-training films, and contracted with the studio to teach its salespeople how to use the films in training.

The studio was still selling the same powerful films it had been demonstrating for months, but now it no longer focused on selling its own products. By showing a furniture company how to apply the studio's films in a way that added value, the studio's multimedia film sales took off. Soon other companies picked up on the idea, calling the studio to enhance their sales in the same way. Within a year the struggling multimedia studio was expanding like crazy.

What was the difference between failure and success? The sales staff stopped demonstrating their impressive presentations and started applying what they could do to meet their prospects' needs. Additionally, they showed prospects how to apply their products to bring value greater than product cost. Remember, your prospects need leverage in their business, too. Show them how to leverage their own time, talent, and resources just as you have learned.

DISCOVERING HOW TO APPLY

Of course, the idea of applying what you sell to what your prospect wants and needs most may not be all that new. Many sales trainers, however, tell their students they *ought* to do it, but never say *how* to do it.

I now want to move beyond the "ought to" and focus on the "how to." At the beginning of this chapter I listed five specific *how to's*. Throughout the remainder of this chapter, I will cover each in detail, adding specific pointers along the way to help you move easily into the Apply phase.

HOW TO SHOW AND TELL WITH THE POWER TO SELL

How you use what you know about your products and services determines whether that knowledge will be an asset or a liability in selling.

For example, say you know absolutely nothing about personal computers, but you are considering buying one. You go into your friendly neighborhood computer store and start looking around. Typically, what will happen is that some computer jock will pounce upon you: "Can I fix you up with a PC today?"

"No, what I'd really like to see is a personal computer," you respond timidly. When you see the "Oh, brother!" look in his eyes, it dawns on you that PC stands for personal computer.

"We're running a special on this model all this week and it's a real bargain," he volunteers. "It comes with 640K RAM, one five and a quarter floppy drive, and a twenty megabyte hard disk... and you can add a tape backup for only $500 extra. Is that going to be big enough for you, or do you need something larger?"

"Uhhh, I think that's plenty big," you stammer. "I don't have too much room on my desk."

He winces and says that what he really meant was whether it would provide enough capacity to meet your needs. You admit that you did not even know that capacity was a factor, and that you have no idea how much of it you need.

Personal computers are a great example of Application selling because very few people truly want to own a computer. Do you really want to own a computer? Who cares? If a wet sponge would serve your needs, wouldn't you buy it? What you really need from a computer salesperson is information about how to apply a personal computer to fulfill your needs. If a computer salesperson probed deeply into your office needs, you would both learn a lot.

Once you both understood what you needed and wanted, you would probably like for the salesperson to recommend the system that would most adequately meet your needs for the amount of money you were willing to invest. You would probably then consider that salesperson a trusted friend. You would probably come back if you again found needs that could be filled by computer equipment. If some of this sounds familiar, it should. It is a natural customer response to the first three phases (IMP) of IMPACT Selling.

That is why IMPACT Selling must be followed in sequence: Each step leads naturally to the rest. Once you have completed the first three phases, you are ready to apply your products to fill known needs. We call that "putting more sell in your show and tell." Here are some specific pointers on how to apply what you have learned from your prospects during the Probe phase.

APPLY POINTER #1:
Choose the most appropriate product or service.

As simple as that sounds, it is also one of the most troublesome of our pointers. Yet, choosing the right product to show is a vital part of the Application step. It is troublesome for two primary reasons.

First, salespeople often skip the Probe step and jump right into a traditional demonstration. After all, they reason, there is no need to waste time. The prospect generally knows what he or she wants, and other products up or down the line can be shown later, right? Wrong! The true time-waster shows products that are inappropriate for your prospects' needs.

Here is an example, taken from our files, of what can happen when you attempt to jump straight to the Apply stage. I say attempt because if you do jump here, the Apply phase is reduced to nothing more than a traditional demonstration. You do not yet know enough to apply.

Our story is from a photocopier sales professional who confessed that she once learned a valuable lesson by blowing a sale she could have made.

A prospect's secretary called her and said that her boss, the president of a small company, wanted to see a copier that day. The salesperson made an appointment for late that afternoon.

She threw the top-of-the-line model into her station wagon and drove 50 miles to make the demo. She allowed plenty of time to set up because that machine could run colors, collate thousands of pages, automatically staple, and do just about everything else but make the coffee.

After delivering her canned demonstration, the company president said, "I don't need all that stuff. We never do colors and we do not have any use for collating and stapling. What I want is a machine that will give me top quality prints of single pages and spit them out in a hurry." He did not even ask the price.

When the salesperson promised to be back the next morning with the right machine, the man said he was going out of town that night and suggested she call for an appointment "next week." You can guess what happened. When she called back to make an appointment, she discovered that her prospect had bought a competitor's inferior product at a higher price than her deluxe job would have cost.

This is not an unusual story in today's highly competitive, tightly niched markets. Very often you get only one shot at showing your product or service. Anything you present after that is anticlimactic, even if you get a second chance. Downgrading can be embarrassing for the client, and upgrading can be tough for you. The only way to be really sure what to show is to probe thoroughly until you are certain about your prospects' wants and needs.

The second reason why choosing the right product is often troublesome is that salespeople often show the products they are most interested in. They may not have a clue about the prospect's desires. This is one area where a skilled IMPACT Selling sales manager can dramatically improve the success ratio of an entire sales force. You must be careful never to give your salespeople a reason to focus on products that only meet their own needs.

One warning we regularly deliver to sales managers is to carefully evaluate the structure of sales contests. The problem with most contests is that they encourage salespeople to push only the products being rewarded in the contest. The needs of the prospect become secondary, and a salesperson who honestly met the true needs of a prospect with a product not on the contest list might even suffer financially or appear low in the contest standings. Worse yet, others who steadfastly push the contest products might walk out of office after office with no orders at all. Many salespeople will lose interest in filling your customers' needs with an order that does not give them points in the contest.

Contests, therefore, are generally useful only in the short-term. They might temporarily mask your true problems, but in the long run you must focus on the needs of your customers. Contests have even been found to harm the long-term reputation of an organization when customers suspect that its salespeople are pushing products merely to win a contest. Such an attitude can be viewed by buyers as an insulting display of a lack of consideration for their needs.

Highly successful value-based salespeople know that the most appropriate products or services to show are always those that the prospect needs most and is most likely to buy. One well-known truism in sales is: *Give people too many choices and they will make no choice.* In today's crowded markets, your prospects face a dizzying glut of choices in products and services. Your value-based selling, however, will cut through the confusion by limiting the choices you give your prospects to those that fulfill their dominant need.

APPLY POINTER #2:
Tailor the presentation to the prospect's needs and wants.

Have you ever noticed how motion picture directors use cameras to show you what they want to emphasize? They open with a broad shot of a huge crowd of people, then they narrow the field of vision, zooming in ever closer. Eventually, they may focus on one person, moving in for a close-up to capture the nonverbal language of facial expression.

What a director does in zooming in for a close-up is to call your attention to what he or she believes to be the focal point. A successful director will understand what you most want to see. During the Apply phase of IMPACT Selling, you must do the same. In the earlier stages, you learned what to focus on. Then, when most salespeople are demonstration selling, you are application selling, zooming in on what the prospect wants to see.

Here are four possible focal points for your demonstrations. Which one will keep you on track, transforming your demonstrations into IMPACT Applying?

- You can focus on the *product* itself, which is what most salespeople do. They love to talk about all the gadgets, features, and variations of their product.

- You can focus on the *company* you represent and talk about their reputation for service, dependability, and fair prices.

- You can focus on *yourself* by saying, "I want to tell you why I believe so strongly in this product," or by noting that if you sell 200 widgets this week you will win a free trip to Bermuda.

- You can focus on the *prospect*—what he or she wants or needs and what value he or she will gain by ownership.

Right! You remember from Chapter One, *Focus*, to never outnumber your prospects. Our research clearly shows that customer focus is of paramount importance in the Apply phase because most prospects are not interested in having you focus solely on your product, on your company, or on yourself. If, however, you really focus all of your time, energy, and attention on the prospect, you have a high probability of closing a sale. To add more sell to your show and tell, get very personal with it.

APPLY POINTER #3:
Give 'em a show they'll never forget.

Canned demonstrations are like a straitjacket, limiting your ability to tailor your presentation to the prospect's needs and desires. Yet, that does not mean you need to go to the opposite extreme and struggle through a completely spontaneous demonstration.

Application selling calls for much harder work than does making a canned demonstration-based presentation. What it means is that you have to know everything about every product in your lineup—and you have to know it so well you can present it with equal enthusiasm and force in any sequence. That is a tall order!

Most truly successful salespeople we encounter are so well-versed in demonstrating every feature and benefit they have to sell that they can easily adjust to application selling. To give you incentive to always present a customer-focused, value-based application, remember this adage:

> *People won't long remember what you said, but they'll never forget how you made them feel.*

In the crowded marketplaces of the 1990s, people have to forget most of what they hear just to survive mentally. After meeting and listening to a line of salespeople all pitching similar products, most prospects have difficulty in distinguishing one company's products from another. What will stand out, then? Pushy, data-dumping, hard-pitching salespeople who made them squirm? Yes. The one salesperson who had the leather binder and the legal pad and wrote down everything the prospect said after asking probing questions and listening attentively? Yes, they will remember him or her, also. The real question is: Which one will leave a favorable impression? To "give 'em a show they'll never forget," make them feel better than they have ever felt during a sales demonstration.

APPLY POINTER #4:
Involve your prospect from the word go.

Consider this pointer in light of two things I have said before: (1) Ultimately, buying is an emotional response and (2) You do not get a second chance to make a first impression. You cannot afford to delay getting your prospects emotionally involved. A story from my personal file will help illustrate.

A friend of mine told me he had decided to buy a certain expensive brand of medium-duty truck and went to a dealer's showroom to take a test drive.

"The salesman acted as if I were going to hurt his truck," my friend recalled. "Every time I tried to touch anything on the instrument panel, he'd almost slap my hands. His attitude seemed to be, 'You do the paying, and leave the driving to us.' "

"Did you buy it?" I asked.

"Sure I bought a truck just like the one I'd been shown, but not from him," he said wryly. "I went to another dealership and bought it from a salesman who put me in the driver's seat all the way."

The treatment my friend suffered at the first dealer's created an emotional response that overrode his purely logical buying decision. He never even tried to find out if that first dealer had the better price. The salesman there made a lasting—and very poor—first impression. Getting prospects involved emotionally in the process is a much more powerful way to help them experience the transfer of ownership than by simply relying on a contractual agreement to make the sale.

The most successful real estate sales professionals we have met actively involve their prospects in planning what they will do to change the decor, and even where they will put their furniture. This technique helps the prospects to see themselves living in the house and strengthens the emotional attachment to it.

For example, many successful real estate salespeople know that clients must experience psychological ownership of a property before they will sign a purchase agreement. Thus, they usually insist that the selling family not be home when they show the property to a prospective buyer. They know that few families will come in and "take over" psychological ownership of a home from another family.

This principle of emotional attachment works in any selling situation, whether it be consumer goods or multimillion dollar leasing services. As a principle, it can be expressed in the following way.

APPLYING PRINCIPLE #1:
The transfer of ownership must occur in a prospect's mind before he or she will sign on the dotted line!

That mental transfer of ownership can only occur when you actively involve your prospects and enable them to see themselves using whatever you are selling. Selling is definitely a hands-on activity—especially when it comes to the prospect's hands. The best time to begin getting your prospects emotionally involved is right from the beginning.

HOW TO GET THE ACTION YOU WANT BY ANSWERING THE PROSPECT'S BIGGEST QUESTION

"What is every prospect's *most important* question?" When we pose that question in our sales seminars, the answer we most often hear is "How much does it cost?" That answer is wrong! Though "How much does it cost?" is the most *frequent* question prospects ask, it is only a mask for the real question behind it.

The prospect's most important question is always, "What's in it for me?" In other words, "What am I going to get for my money?"

When your prospects say, "It costs too much!", what they are really saying is, "It doesn't have more value to me than the money I would have to spend to get it." (Remember that I covered this topic in the Leverage chapter.)

The question of value versus price translates into another very important principle:

APPLYING PRINCIPLE #2:
Without a values interpreter, all sales degenerate into a struggle over price.

When you satisfactorily answer the prospect's most important question—What do I get for my money?—things like price and financial terms will be minor considerations when you ask for the order. Be a value interpreter for your prospects. If your sales career has been dominated by prospects who always seem to haggle over dollars, this may sound too good to be true. It is not always easy to steer your prospects to a correct value interpretation, but haggling over price is not always easy, either.

To make it easier for you to be a value interpreter for your prospects, we have identified four tested and proven tips on how to keep price from becoming the major issue in a sales interview. I will present all four before completing the discussion of the second element of applying. As you read each Value Focus tip, recall the Value equation in the Leverage chapter (Value = Perceived Benefit over Perceived Price):

$$V = \frac{PB}{PP}$$

VALUE FOCUS TIP #1:
Avoid making price an issue yourself.

Interestingly, studies show that the typical salesperson is much more concerned about price than is the typical customer. To find an amateur salesperson, just look for the first one who seems to love to talk about price. Here are some of his or her typical strategies:

- He or she compares one product with another purely on the basis of cost.
- He or she talks incessantly about how big a discount you can get.
- He or she boasts about having a lower price than the company's competitors do.

Those strategies merely remind the prospect of how much the product is going to cost. Even if the prospect is not too concerned about price at the beginning of the sales interview, he or she will become more and more concerned about it the more you talk about it.

The most successful IMPACT Selling professionals handle price as if it were a minor consideration. Naturally, when the prospect makes it an issue, they deal with it honestly, openly, and effectively. Even then, they minimize its importance, tactfully moving the money issue back to the Values equation. Your major focus in the Apply phase is value—never price.

The next three tips explain how professional salespersons minimize the cost factor.

VALUE FOCUS TIP #2:
Focus on benefits—not features or price.

Make certain that you understand the difference between a feature and a benefit. That may sound like an elementary statement, but even experienced salespeople sometimes do not appreciate the significance of the difference. This difference highlights a basic and critical philosophical principle of IMPACT Selling:

A *feature* is a product or service attribute. It is something built into the product or service, or some quality that makes it attractive.

A *benefit* is an advantage that a particular feature provides. Benefits are what a given customer will derive from a particular feature.

By talking about features, we focus on product. By talking about benefits, we focus on building value for the customer. Understanding the significance of the difference between those two words—feature and benefit—will form the basis of your transformation from demonstration selling to application selling.

Here are some examples that clearly show the distinction:

- A handle on the top is a feature, but ease of handling is a benefit.
- Availability of service nationwide is a feature, but convenience to the customer is a benefit.
- One-stop shopping is a feature, but saving time and minimizing confusion is a benefit.

The best way to answer your prospect's most important question is to focus all your attention on what benefits the person will derive from using your product or service. The discussion on this Value tip provides the perfect opportunity to pass along the third principle that we have discovered.

APPLYING PRINCIPLE #3:
All values are considered equal until someone points out the difference!

A skilled IMPACT salesperson would never assume that any fool knows a handle on the top makes a product easier to carry. Using the value-focused approach to selling, you show *how much* easier the handle makes carrying the product. The logical extension of this is to let the prospect *feel* how much easier it is to carry, thereby getting the prospect involved.

Never assume that a prospect understands the benefits a feature offers. Your job is to point out the benefits. Always sell every benefit as if it were the greatest thing since sliced bread. The more benefits you apply to the prospect's needs or wants, the more often you show the prospect "what's in it for me."

VALUE FOCUS TIP #3:
Focus on value and work to deliver it.

Showing your prospect the benefits of ownership is your key to creating value. It is the only way you have to create value. The more value you create, the more desirable the product or service becomes to the prospect, and the less important price becomes. Of course, the definition of value depends on the individual buyer. Remember that the key is to create value that exceeds price, then deliver it consistently and on time.

You must go beyond simply verbalizing value, making certain that prospects *feel* what you present. Remember that your prospects will not long remember *what* you said. Your job is to work hard to make the prospect *feel* the value. With a little ingenuity, you can usually get the prospect to express what they value most in their own words. Only then will you know that the prospect has turned the value you have offered into feelings.

In my seminars, I often suggest that salespeople think of a sales interview as an old-fashioned set of balancing scales. Here is how I often put the Value equation in graphic terms.

One one side, the prospect puts all of his or her negative feelings about what I'm selling, and I put all my benefits of ownership on the other side. When value outweighs the prospect's negative feelings and objections, I've got myself a sale.

It works fantastically well!

VALUE FOCUS TIP #4:
Relate every benefit in terms of a value.

One way you can focus attention on value is to relate every benefit in terms of a value.

The dictionary says that value is "worth in money" and that what gives something its value is its *desirability* to the person who values it. Your task, therefore, is to translate every feature and benefit into a tangible value—something the prospect desires. Create enough desirability and the prospect will close the sale for you.

We have heard many salespeople debate the difference between selling *tangible* and *intangible* values. A tangible value is one you can see, hear, touch, taste, or smell and is considered easier to sell. An intangible value has more to do with emotions, logic, or some unseen factor. The ultimate answer to that oft-heard confusion over tangible and intangible values can be expressed in the following principle.

APPLYING PRINCIPLE #4:
All values are intangible until someone makes them tangible, and all intangible values can be made tangible with a little creativity!

Travel agencies are especially good at using this principle. With vivid pictures, videos, and brochures of exotic places, they make the intangible value of "getting away from it all" tangible for their prospects. Whatever you are selling, every effort to translate benefits into tangible values your prospects can "get their teeth into" is worth its weight in gold.

That brings us to the third basic element of Apply.

ADD TO YOUR SALES PUNCH
BY BUILDING MORE VALUE

Notice how value keeps showing up in every aspect of the Apply phase of IMPACT Selling. That's because there are many ways to convey value. Here is another analogy that helps many salespeople.

Building a sale can be likened to building a house. The building blocks are features and benefits translated into values for the prospect. The building blocks of value are the essential ingredients of the Apply wing of the house.

What I have presented up to now has given you the building blocks by clearly stressing the significance of value. Now, I want to help you learn how to build value with the materials you have.

When to Build Added Value

Timing is important, too. You need to know when it is time to stack up your building blocks. Obviously, you build value every time you enable the prospect to connect with a benefit of ownership. We will now look at other opportunities you have to build value.

First, *build value every time the prospect expresses approval.* If the prospect says, "Oh, I like that!" take advantage of the opportunity to talk about what a great value "that" is. "That" may be a feature you had not yet seen as a benefit for this prospect. Never brush aside such a comment, but always seize it as a chance to let the prospect become more deeply involved with whatever you are selling.

Second, *build value as you answer each objection.* Often an objection is nothing more than a request for more information or a greater reassurance of value. Keep in mind that objections do not just go away. Unanswered objections will remain as barriers you must surmount in order to get your message across to the prospect. Face them forthrightly, and push them out of your way by adding value.

Third, *build value each time the prospect asks a question.* A question is nearly always a request for a reason to buy, and, of course, the number one reason to buy is always value. Never back away from questions. Instead, view every question as an expression of interest, treating it as an invitation to pour on more value.

How to Build Added Value

Now let us look at some ways you can build value.

First, *turn the prospect's questions and objections into questions.* If the prospect asks, "How much does it cost?" ask, "What range of investment did you have in mind?" If the prospect says, "We can buy one a lot cheaper!" ask, "But can you get one your employees would learn to use as quickly for that smaller investment?"

Second, *summarize and review benefits frequently.* What you know so well, your prospects may not know at all. You may remember every minute feature and benefit you have covered, but do not expect that from the prospect. At best, the average prospect will remember less than one out of five benefits you mention only once. However, since people learn by repetition, continually review the benefits you cover—especially those the prospect seems to like most.

Third, *keep focusing relative values.* Remember, one of your most vital tasks in selling is to be a values interpreter. Interpreting relative values is a permanent part of reality in competitive, price-sensitive markets in which buyers are swamped with countless choices that *seem* to fulfill their needs. Here are two important techniques that may help you:

1. A values interpreter *relates* each value to the prospect's needs and wants. Among the most fruitful sentences in the salesperson's vocabulary is, "What you get out of it, Mr. Smith, is . . . "

2. A values interpreter constantly weighs one value against others. For example, if you are selling tires and a prospect says, "I like a wider stripe than that," you might say, "I'm sure looks are important to you, but don't you agree that your family's safety is what truly matters?"

Always bear in mind that the more value you build, the greater your chances of making a sale.

Fourth, *continually emphasize the value that most directly satisfies the prospect's chief dominant need.* If you have laid a good foundation in the Probe phase, you will know the prospect's chief dominant need. Focus on the value that satisfies that need and keep hammering away at it until the prospect feels assured that buying what you are selling is the best way he or she can have that need met.

Going back to the balancing scales analogy, the fastest way to tip the scales on the value side is to pile in more and more value that relates directly to the prospect's most compelling need. Values weigh more and you will need fewer of them to tip the scales. A value that satisfies a client's chief dominant need is worth at least ten values that matter only marginally.

Here is our fourth method to boost your customer impact by applying instead of merely demonstrating.

TARGET THE *KEY BENEFIT* TO HEIGHTEN DESIRE

In a classic story of key benefit selling, the principal characters are a real estate salesman, a woman, and a cherry tree in full blossom.

"Oh! Look at that cherry tree . . . I've never seen so many blossoms," the woman shouted as they drove up to look at a house.

"Do you like cherry blossoms?" the salesman asked. Any fool could see the answer to that one, but he wanted her to tell him how much she liked them.

"I've always wanted a cherry tree in my yard!" she said.

"The yard's too small!" her husband quickly grunted.

Guess where that salesman took them first. You guessed it—right to the back yard to look at that tree! He even picked a blossom and gave it to her.

"The patio door needs to be replaced," noted the husband once they were in the dining room.

"Yes, but look at the view of that cherry tree!" said the salesman.

"The kitchen window is mighty small," said the woman.

"It is small, but you can see that cherry tree while you're washing dishes," the guy said.

"This is a crazy shape for a master bedroom," complained the man when they went upstairs.

"Wow! You can smell those blossoms from here!" the salesman said as he threw open a window.

He tapped their key benefit and sold the cherry tree to that couple, throwing in the house as a bonus.

That is what targeting the key benefit is all about. It is finding the one dominant benefit—related to the most significant feature—that the prospect gets most excited about and constantly bringing everything back to it. Used creatively, it is a powerful sales technique.

How to Find the Key Benefit

Granted, it is not always easy to find the single most critical benefit that most excites your prospect about your product or service. Many prospects are so guarded in their reactions that they will deliberately try to conceal any warm feelings they have about any benefit. We have found this to be especially true of seasoned, professional buyers. Even if you have trouble uncovering the key benefit, it is crucial that you keep trying.

Here are some suggestions that can help you spot the key benefit for your prospect.

First, *stay alert for strong reactions during the Probe phase.* For example, if prospects say they need a follow-up for their sales training program, ask, "Would you say that investing in a program that has ongoing reinforcement and repetitive involvement is what you most need?" If the answer is "yes," make a note of it, show your prospects every bit of reinforcement material and systems you have, and ask, "Don't you agree that this system has all the follow-up you need?"

Second, *look and listen for the slightest clue to a strongly emotional response.* This can require all your intuitive insight skills, for it may show up in the way the prospect caresses the texture of a product, or the client may keep coming back to some feature or may ask many questions about something you have mentioned. For example, a prospect may tell you that he or she is looking for a very basic computer system, but keeps wandering off to a more advanced, sophisticated system. If you see something like that, at least explore what it means. Professional IMPACT Selling requires total concentration on every available source of information.

Third, *if you don't know, ask.* That's right; just come right out and ask, "What do you like most about what I've shown you?" Once you ask, quietly listen and watch carefully. Nine times out of ten you will find out exactly what you want to know.

Whatever method you use to uncover your prospect's real, underlying desires, zero in on that key benefit and use it as the foundation for *everything* that follows in making the sale. Now, on to the last of the five elements of applying.

ASK FOR A PROSPECT'S FEELINGS AND REACTIONS

The last stage of the Apply step is to ask prospects to share openly with you how they feel about what they have seen and heard. That idea scares high-pressure salespeople to death. They would rather assume they are making the sale until the prospect beats them over the head and runs them out. But there is no need to fear asking the prospect such a question—particularly if you have been asking the right questions all along.

Asking for the prospect's reactions and feelings does three very important things for you.

First, *it lets you know where you stand.* You might discover that you can close the sale if you can clear up one or two issues. You also might discover many unresolved conditions to be met before you can tie it up. Or you might discover that you cannot make the sale under any condition. At least you will know what you need to do—even if that is to pack up and move on.

Second, *by asking, you enable prospects to admit to themselves how they feel and comment to you on how they will act.* By verbalizing their feelings, they can often clarify things in their own minds. You will probably have smoother sailing once your clients can hear themselves saying, "I like it!"

Third, *asking enables you to reinforce positive feelings and clear up any misconceptions prospects may have.* By carefully interpreting their reactions, you can test to see if you have communicated what you had intended. If your prospects understand what you have said and feel positive about it, you can reinforce the values you have created and help your prospects toward psychological ownership. On the other hand, you might discover that they have misunderstood some point you have made. If so, you can clear it up before you move on.

TO SUM IT ALL UP...

In the Apply phase, we have seen that to sell you must do far more than merely demonstrate what you are selling—you must apply the most appropriate product or service to the needs and wants you discovered during the Probe step. There is a world of difference between traditional demonstration selling and application selling and a world of difference in the results they will bring you.

Your chief objectives during the Apply phase are to

- Show and tell with the power to sell.
- Answer the prospect's biggest question.
- Add more sales punch by building value.
- Target your prospect's key benefit to heighten desire.
- Ask for prospects' reactions and feelings about what they have seen and heard.

In the next chapter, you will see how important it is to assure your prospect of the accuracy of every claim you have made in the Apply phase.

ACTION STEPS

You could develop a workshop where you reaffirm the principles of application selling with your staff. Review your current sales presentations to see how you might put more power in them by using the following suggestions:

- Think application, not demonstration.
- Answer the *What's in it for me?* question for your prospects.
- Build more value by tuning in to your prospects' needs/desires.
- Target the prospect's key benefit.
- Talk openly with your clients about their feelings and reactions to what you have shown them.

KEY TIPS

☑ You must *show* your prospects how to apply your products or services because we retain only 20 percent of what we *hear* and 50 percent of what we *see* and *hear*, but fully 90 percent of what we *say* and *apply!*

☑ Apply what you learned from your prospects in the previous phases of IMPACT Selling by choosing the most appropriate product or service and tailoring your sales presentation to the prospect's specific needs and wants. Give 'em a show they'll never forget by getting them involved from the word go.

☑ With any product and any prospect, particularly in a crowded market, the transfer of ownership must first occur in a prospect's mind before he or she will sign on the dotted line!

☑ Without a values interpreter, all sales degenerate into a struggle over price. Three tips to maximize the Value equation during the Apply phase are (1) to avoid making price an issue yourself, (2) to always focus on customer-based benefits and value, and (3) to work to deliver both.

☑ Develop a good sense of timing about *when* to add value during your sales presentation by building value every time the prospect expresses approval, every time you clarify an objection, and every time the prospect asks you a question.

☑ To create maximum value, tap into your prospects' emotions. Stay alert at every phase for the slightest clues to their key benefits; you will use those clues again and again.

☑ Get your prospects to openly share how they feel about what they have seen and heard so you will always know where you stand. Expressing their feelings enables prospects to admit to themselves how they feel, and hearing their comments gives you a chance to reinforce your prospects' positive feelings, while alerting you to any misconceptions they may still have.

CHAPTER 9

CONVINCE

CONVINCE

Proving your claims, creating additional value to further justify price, relieving prospects' fears, and making prospects believe enough to act.

Some things have to be believed to be seen.
Ralph Hodgson

In the Convince phase of IMPACT Selling, your primary task is to provide support to all the claims you have made about your product or service. You will need the trust and rapport you built in the Meet, Probe, and Apply phases to make your clients believe enough to act on your business proposal. Many salespeople try to begin their sales approach at the Convince phase, typically by explaining to the prospect why they chose to work for their company or represent the product or service they sell. If the other phases have been bypassed, you will encounter the same barrier to selling that salespeople have battled perpetually: Most prospects are skeptical of salespeople's claims.

YOU'VE GOTTA MAKE 'EM BELIEVE

The results of a recent Gallup poll revealed that salespeople rank among the lowest of *all* professionals in credibility.

There is an old joke that asks, "Do you know how you can always tell when a salesperson is lying?"

"No, how?"

"If he waves both arms in the air, he may be telling you the truth. If he jumps up and down and won't look you in the eye, he still may be telling you the truth. But if he ever opens his mouth, he's lying!"

How deserved is the reputation for dishonesty among salespeople? Our feelings on this do not matter because it is a perception we must all face. You knew it before you entered the sales profession. What makes this fact so crucial to each of us is that our livelihoods depend upon the extent to which people believe what we say and that there is a strong predisposition to disbelieving salespeople among most prospects you will meet.

Another important reality is that each prospect has his or her own value system by which all values are measured. Prospects will do what they want to do, or at least what they believe is best for them. Before most people will take action based on a belief, the belief must be strongly held.

That people must have strong beliefs is such a universal truth that I have incorporated the challenge it presents to salespeople into a quotation, which I often cite at seminars:

What people believe strongly enough, they act upon!

If people believe strongly enough that what you are selling will be worth more to them than the money you are asking for it, they will buy it. If they do not, then they will not buy. It is just that simple. Therefore, the true challenge in selling lies not in closing a sale, but in building enough trust and value for a prospect so that the close becomes organic. To survive in the crowded markets of the 1990s, you must find ways to cut through all the mistrust and conflicting values to convince your prospects of two things:

- That what you say is true.
- That the value of the benefits you offer outweighs the price you are asking.

That is a tall order, but thousands of successful IMPACT salespeople do it every day, and you and your sales force can, too. In this chapter, I demonstrate how you can *consistently* convince prospects of the value of your product or service—time after time, day after day. It boils down to four basic actions that will convince your prospects and set the stage for them to buy:

- Prove your claims.
- Bring your own witnesses.

- Justify your price.
- Relieve the prospect's fear of buying.

Each of these four items has been used to form the basis of our four Convince principles. Those principles will be introduced in order throughout the rest of this chapter. Under each Convince principle are specific actions to show you how to implement that principle in your everyday selling endeavors. I will now explore them one at a time, introducing the first basic topic of the Convince stage as a lead-in to its Convince principle.

YOU HAVE TO PROVE YOUR CLAIMS

It might damage your ego, but it will certainly help your bank account to assume that most prospects will not believe anything you say unless you prove it to them. We have researched the old-school selling methods, surveying hundreds of buyers. The unmistakable messages in the responses force us to admit that most buyers have excellent reasons to be skeptical about the claims of salespeople. We identified three principal reasons why most prospects are skeptical.

First, *we stand to gain something if they believe us.* Former Secretary of State Henry Kissinger recently told about a reaction he once got from the late Chairman Mao Tse-tung of China.

"What do you want from us?" Chairman Mao asked bluntly.

"We don't want anything but your friendship," Mr. Kissinger replied.

"If you want nothing, you shouldn't be here, and if I wanted nothing, I wouldn't have invited you here," said the crafty old chairman.

Today's inundated buyers feel the same way. They know that you stand to gain something if they buy, so they balance everything you say against that knowledge.

Second, *they have been lied to before.* A seasoned veteran salesman recently attended one of our seminars because of a question his son had asked him. After a statement the salesman made at home, his son responded, "Dad, are you telling me the truth or is that just sales talk?" That question made the salesman aware of how his sales tactics were affecting his whole life and led him to seek a new, and more honest, way of doing business.

Think about your experiences as a buyer; salespeople lie to you, too. The Federal Trade Commission's "truth in advertising" rules have made it difficult to get away with misrepresentation, but anyone who wants to stretch the truth may easily do so while remaining within legal bounds. That, however, remains essentially a lie.

Third, *people have become jaded by oversell.* By the time the average person in the country reaches adulthood, he or she will have seen more than a million television commercials and heard nearly as many radio spots. This deluge has promised everything from robust health and instant wealth to perpetual happiness. To survive, most people have developed highly effective mental tune-out devices that filter out any dubious-sounding promise.

These and other factors make the Convince step absolutely crucial to your selling success. You have to prove every claim you make about your product or service, about your company, and about yourself. Once you establish rapport and credibility with your prospects and present the truth, you will shift the burden of truthfulness over to them. This adage is at the core of that concept:

A truth ignored is no better than a lie accepted.

When your prospects know the truth about how much value your products or services will add to their lives, they reach a decisive moment. If they are honest with themselves, they will not be able to accept anything less than the truth you have presented.

Throughout my sales career, I have steadfastly maintained that personal and professional integrity are essential to successful selling. In today's marketplace, absolute honesty is vital. So vital, in fact, that we have consistently found that false claims cost more sales than they will ever gain. It is not enough for you to believe that a claim is true; you must back it up with proof the prospect will accept.

This concept is so central to building credibility that we have turned it into the first of our four Convince principles:

CONVINCE PRINCIPLE #1:
It makes little difference what you believe is true, unless you can prove it to your prospect.

Our research has shown us that a single claim, proven to a customer's satisfaction, is worth 100 unsubstantiated claims. Yet, one false claim uncovered by a prospect can do more damage than a truckload of claims you have proven to him or her. The damage done by false claims is compounded in a tight niche market because such news will travel fast with today's instant communications. Be certain you can back every claim you make with irrefutable facts. To make that task simpler for you, we have developed four one-sentence aids we call *Claim Provers*. Here's the first of the four.

CLAIM PROVER #1:
If you can prove it, show your evidence.

It is important that you actively back every claim you make, especially those that sound too good to be true.

The successful IMPACT salesperson frequently offers supporting data, verifying documents and tangible evidence to prove every claim made. Obviously, not every prospect will doubt every claim you make, unless you look like Al Capone. Nonetheless, you can never know which prospects will doubt which claims. Therefore, the safest strategy is to have proof for them all.

Here are a couple of pointers to help you with Claim Prover #1.

The more dramatic and remarkable the claim, the more proof it usually requires. If you claim your service can reduce a corporate expense by 20 percent, you had better plan to show a lot of evidence to back it up. Be cautious with each prospect by beginning with modest claims, keeping in mind this second pointer.

Constantly test to make sure you have given enough evidence for each claim. For example, if a prospect says, "Oh, I know that's true!" it is safe to move on to the next point. But first, make sure you get confirmation through feedback from the prospect.

CLAIM PROVER #2:
Reinforce all claims visually.

The ancient Orientals brought us that familiar adage, "A picture is worth a thousand words." What that means to you is that prospects will believe and remember what you *show* them much more easily than what you simply *tell* them. At the beginning of the last chapter, I showed the results of a study revealing that people remember only 20 percent of what they hear, but 50 percent of what they see and hear. Bringing along simple graphic evidence will serve to

- Speed up your proof.
- Make your claim easier to grasp and believe.
- Enable your prospects to remember it longer.

We are a visually oriented society. In the 1990s, people have come to expect to have what they hear enhanced by what they see. From office memos embellished with the flair of desktop publishing to fast-paced graphics on the nightly news, high-quality visual reinforcement is a permanent part of our lives.

As powerful as visual aids are, there is no substitute for hands-on experience. Recall another revelation from the study we cited in the last chapter that showed people remember 90 percent of what they say and apply!

CLAIM PROVER #3:
Let prospects experience it themselves.

Another time-proven adage is, "The proof of the pudding is in the eating." If you claim that your product is easy to carry, let the person pick it up and carry it around. If you claim that your product is simple and easy to use, let clients use it themselves to experience just how simple and easy it is.

The hands-on evidence concept can be a tough assignment with some products or services (such as life insurance) and with some types of selling (especially telemarketing). That is one reason why so many companies make "free trial offers." Still, no matter how tough it is, every bit of creative effort you put into helping people experience for themselves the claims you make will be richly rewarded by increased credibility.

CLAIM PROVER #4:
Repeat important claims and proofs again and again.

Have you ever wondered why major advertisers keep repeating the *same* commercials over and over? A logical answer might be that they cost so much to produce. Yet, a typical advertiser will spend more money on air time to run a commercial just once than it spends on actual production.

Companies run the same commercial repeatedly ad infinitum (sometimes ad nauseam) because studies show it is the best way to get people to believe them, remember them, and act upon them. When you are selling, the more often you repeat something, the better your chance of having it accepted and remembered. Your equivalent of a studio's repeating commercials is to repeat the statements that you know represent value to your prospects. Unlike television ads, however, you will not repeat your statements exactly the same way. Instead, you will make your value statements in the Probe phase by asking the right questions, in the Apply stage when you show prospects how your product benefits them, and again in the Convince phase when you present your evidence.

BRING YOUR OWN WITNESSES

The second element of convincing your prospects consists of enhancing your evidence with the backing of testimony from witnesses. What do the courts view as the most compelling evidence in a trial? You guessed it—an eyewitness! What is the strongest theme in advertising? Word-of-mouth! Word-of-mouth advertising has a high credibility level among buyers for one simple reason: The claim is made by someone who will not profit from his or her buying decision.

Never before has word-of-mouth advertising been more important than in today's highly niched, volatile markets. Since there is less room for error, third-party testimony has become a significant tool that buyers use to reduce their risks. We have turned these truisms about eyewitnesses and word-of-mouth advertising into a principle in the convince phase of IMPACT Selling:

CONVINCE PRINCIPLE #2:
Prospects expect salespeople to make claims for what they are selling, but they are impressed when someone else makes or endorses those claims.

An important corollary of this principle is never to make a claim for yourself or your product that you can get someone else to make for you.

The eyewitness concept will never work as an endorsement for your products or services if you merely try to turn it into your own word-of-mouth advertising. Telling a prospect, "Why, just last week I was visiting one of the biggest buyers of our latest super deluxe software package and the person went on and on about how it improved efficiency in the department and increased profits enough to earn bonuses for everyone." Real word-of-mouth advertising flows around you and does not involve your mouth! So, what can you do to corral that glowing praise every customer gives you? We have developed four powerful techniques, entitled "Witness Pointers," that show you how to bring your own witnesses to boost your sales.

Here is a creative example of getting others to speak for you.

A major corporation for which we consulted was holding a roll-out of a new product, as the previous model had been notorious for its poor reliability. The company had made significant improvements in its new model but still had a serious image problem to overcome. The company knew very well that its low credibility would not allow its salesforce to make unfounded claims about the new improvements.

The corporation's clever solution was to make *before and after* videos in which its sales distributors talked openly about the problems of the old model. The company then showed the distributors the new, improved model and taped discussion in which the distributors raved about the great improvements. This showed, *using other people's words,* how much better the new product was.

In the Convince phase, it is important to show concrete evidence rather than tout your own advertising claims.

WITNESS POINTER #1:
Try to get a written endorsement from every customer.

The best way to get endorsements is to ask for them—it is that simple! Yet you would be surprised at how many salespeople either neglect to get endorsements or are apprehensive about asking for them. To make you more comfortable when asking, consider the following technique.

Remind your customers that their names are widely respected in the business and that you would appreciate an opportunity to mention them as satisfied customers. At that point, many of them will volunteer immediately to write a letter. It is highly likely that you'll get a positive response, because in today's tightly niched markets many, if not most, of the major players know the others in their focused market. Most people will see a benefit in having their names circulated among others in their own market.

If your customers agree to allow you to use their names but do not volunteer to write a letter, simply make a courteous request. Very few will turn you down if you have successfully built a solid trust bond, and even if they do it is usually because of personal or professional reasons. Most customers will feel flattered that you believe a letter from them will have significance.

When a customer has agreed to write an endorsement letter, you should offer to return a few days later to pick it up personally, ostensibly because you would like to save him or her the trouble of mailing it. In actuality, your return subtly places a deadline that will help get the letter written as promised. Further, it enables you to see the customer again and thank them personally. Moreover, if you have truly built value for your customer, those second trips around often produce leads on other prospects whom your customer wants to help by sending them your highly respected talents!

A note of caution: Make absolutely certain that your satisfied customer understands you plan to use his or her letter as a promotional device. If he or she does not want you to use it that way and finds out later you did, you might lose that valued customer. Even when customers understand how you will use their letters, reassure them that you will use their signs of good will with discretion and integrity.

WITNESS POINTER #2:
Carefully select the endorsements you use with each prospect.

We all are imitators. We imitate the people we respect and admire, and sometimes those whom we wish to impress. This supposition can be turned into a powerful buying motivation, one that has worked on you many times. Have you ever tried a new restaurant, store, or product, or seen a movie because a friend recommended it? Of course you have.

Through our research, we have uncovered a gem of a sales motivator for our car dealer clients. Naturally, all customer-focused sales professionals want to find out *why* the prospect is out looking at cars. One of the most frequent responses their prospects give for buying a new car is: "My neighbor (or co-worker or friend) bought a new car, and I started thinking maybe it was time I looked into replacing mine." This response is often rooted in that old idea of "keeping up with the Joneses." If you get a similar answer, you have a perfect Apply technique; just dig up every "Jones" you can think of who has your product. The benefit you will deliver is that your prospect will not have to lust after "the Joneses' " new car anymore because you will sell them a better model.

The more recognizable a name is, the more convincing it will be to your prospect. In other words, if you can do better than "the Joneses," then make it specific. That is one good reason to discover during the Investigate and Probe phases all you can about every prospect you call upon. Handing a prospect an endorsement from a respected golfing or bridge partner, an esteemed business associate, or a friend can be a marketing gold mine.

If you cannot find an endorsement from someone the prospect knows, think of satisfied customers to whom the prospect can most closely relate. You might choose endorsements from people of similar ages with similar interests and a similar social status. Even in giant, multinational corporations an endorsement from an individual unknown to your prospect can establish a link if the prospect at least respects the company represented by the endorsee.

I will finish the discussion of this pointer by tying it in with the first one: Try to get a written endorsement from every customer. The more endorsements you have in your file, the more likely you will be to present an endorsement that carries weight with your future prospects.

WITNESS POINTER #3:
Treat endorsements with dignity and respect.

An endorsement letter is worth many times its weight in pure gold—so treat it with dignity and respect. Here are several specific ways you can do that.

Speak of the customers who have endorsed you as if you believe they are the greatest people in the world. Remember that in your profession, they are.

Protect your endorsements. You should carry them in plastic sleeves or file folders to keep them looking fresh and new. Never present a dog-eared or soiled endorsement. The best impression can be made by maintaining them in a separate binder worthy of their value.

Show your endorsements as if you feel you are granting the prospect a special privilege by showing them. If, for example, you carefully present each one across a table to your prospect, you create several significant advantages:

- You allow your client time to read them, which assures him or her you have nothing to hide.
- You show respect both for this prospect and the customer who gave you the endorsement.
- You exhibit a good reason for the prospect to give you an endorsement when you ask him or her for one later because your actions demonstrate the careful consideration his or her letter will get.

People who give you endorsements show a great deal of trust, and prospects notice the respect you give your customers. If you recall the body language lessons from the Meet phase of IMPACT Selling, you will be compelled to treat endorsement letters with dignity and respect. We have repeatedly proved that prospects remember small things like how you handle endorsement letters, because such things relate more to how you made them feel than does what you said. And prospects will always remember how you made them feel.

For your own benefit, you should also have a backup file of duplicate letters in a cross-referenced system keyed by industry, topic of the endorsement, and the level of the endorsing executive.

WITNESS POINTER #4:
Try to involve satisfied customers with prospects.

Sometimes you can get a prospect to make an appointment for you with a friend, neighbor, or associate. If so, the appointment itself becomes a highly convincing piece of evidence.

We want to distinguish this practice as being vastly different from the old-school, high-pressure tactic of giving discounts or premiums to customers who furnish you with leads or set up appointments for you. Sophisticated buyers in today's crowded marketplace will react very negatively to that sort of tactic, which leaves customers feeling like one of your employees because you have offered them a payment for work performed. It also tells them very clearly that there was more bargaining room in your final price; they could have struck a better deal. Having such a reputation can quickly ruin your sales effectiveness in a highly competitive niche market.

Here is an illustration from the actual experience of a furniture rep who works in North Carolina near the headquarters of The Brooks Group.

This particular rep—I will call her Sheryl—has developed an extensive, mutual sharing network among the furniture retailers who buy from her. When a store gets a large response from an ad for a sale on her products, she contacts that store's manager. She then raves about the dynamite ad she just saw and asks the manager for permission to share the ad with other retailers in her territory, promising that none will be in his town. Since Sheryl is well-known for her network of winning ads, store managers are glad to cooperate and know they will be on the inside track to get the best ads from other stores.

Sheryl then takes that ad to other stores, suggesting they run a similar sale—featuring her products, of course. "And if you have any questions about how well the ad works, call Joe at Smith's Furniture and ask him," she will say. Often, she suggests they call him "right now." When they do, they simultaneously polish Joe's ego and convince one of Sheryl's prospects for her. The prospect is thrilled to have a proven, successful ad; Sheryl writes up a large order as she scores big points by complimenting a previous customer. Now *that* is a win-win situation! Sheryl has sold as many as five boxcar loads of furniture in one week by circulating a single ad.

It may take creativity and finesse to pull it off, but Sheryl's system is an incredibly powerful Convince tool. Get your sales force together to brainstorm for ways to involve satisfied customers in selling for you just as this sharp furniture rep has done.

We are ready to move on to the third challenge for you in the steps that were listed at the beginning of this chapter.

JUSTIFY YOUR PRICE BY PROVING VALUE

Before prospects will buy what you are selling, you must prove that it is worth more to them than it will cost. Before you can do that, you must believe it yourself. If you frankly do not believe that your product or service is a bargain to your customers, you will have a tough time justifying your price. Besides, if you are selling only to make a quick buck, you will find it a difficult way to earn a living. Today, long-term success requires a deep-rooted belief in the virtue of your profession and in what you sell. That thought leads us to

CONVINCE PRINCIPLE #3:
You must believe that what you sell represents real value to your prospects.

Before you can convince your prospects that you are giving them value, rephrase this principle as a question and ask yourself, "Do I believe that what I'm selling represents a real value to this prospect?" If you cannot answer that with a resounding "yes," you have only three options: Either convince yourself of your product's value, quit selling it, or abandon the IMPACT Selling concept and rely on outdated, old-school methods.

Despite how firmly we may each believe in our products or how excited we may get over them, the Convince phase will always be a challenge because we are not the ones who need convincing. In crowded and competitive markets, price is a very critical issue that must be dealt with professionally and capably because careful buyers try to squeeze every penny from each purchase. In order to ease your efforts in facing that challenge, we have developed four *Price Justifiers*, which are explained below.

APPEALING TO A JURY OF ONE

Besides yours, the only opinion that truly matters is that of your current prospect. If that person believes that he or she will get enough value to justify the cost, you have a sale; otherwise, you do not. It is that simple! As we have seen before, however, what is simple is not always easy. Let us explore some ways in which you can justify your price in the prospect's mind.

PRICE JUSTIFIER #1:
Imagine a value meter.

You have seen hokey versions of price justifiers in those fast-paced television commercials that peddle overpriced merchandise as a bargain. The announcer will say, "You get this complete 12-piece set of super-sharp knives, plus this handy butcher's guide, plus this European chef's cookbook... all for the unbelievably low price of $19.95. But wait, that is not all. Act now and we will include the Brooklyn Bridge... that is a whopping $3 million value! And it's all yours for this special TV-offer price of $19.95."

While this TV huckster's application is executed poorly, the basic idea is sound. It is one of the most effective techniques for justifying your price. You simply stack up value in the minds of your prospects until they are convinced that price is no longer an issue.

To measure the value you build during your presentations, picture an imaginary value meter in your prospect's mind. Form a graphical, mental depiction of a meter needle that you move up every time you increase value. However you track value, it is vital that you make the prospect keenly aware of how much value he or she will receive for the money spent. To help the prospect keep track of the value needle's position, you should frequently conduct value reviews that summarize all the value you have demonstrated.

Sell every benefit as if it were the greatest of all values, and just keep adding more of them.

Never rely on the assumption that a benefit is understood. Check the value meter through feedback from the prospect.

PRICE JUSTIFIER #2:
Interpret relative values, again!

As stated in the last chapter in Applying Principle #3, "All values are considered equal until someone points out the difference." Although you made your first thrust at interpreting relative values in the Apply phase, it will be an ongoing process that will need careful attention in the Convince phase, as well. You may well find it to be an issue even in the final phase, Tie-It-Up.

We found another example of interpretation of relative values when we recently conducted some sales consulting for a sales professional whose products are highly sophisticated home security systems that can cost more than $10,000.

He told us that "It's not worth that to me" is a common response from the prospect who hears his quoted dollar price.

That is when the alarm salesperson must become a values interpreter. One technique that has proven to be highly successful is for the salesperson to turn to the prospect's wife and say, "Mrs. Brown, your husband has told me he travels a great deal, right? Would it be worth that much money to know you are safe from possible intruders, and that you can sleep comfortably when your husband is not home?" Suddenly a different interpretation of values has significantly raised the value of the product.

"It sure is!" she will usually say.

"Uhhh! Where do I sign?" the husband quickly asks.

When someone says, "Your price is too high, " start asking yourself "Compared to what? Compared to peace of mind? Compared to being the best dressed person you know? Compared to convenience? Compared to an inferior product?" Once you find the value (or combination of values) that the prospect considers to be higher than the price, interpret that as a benefit to the prospect.

One cautionary note here is that if you regularly hear the objection, "Your price is too high," it is a sign that you have not made a solid application-based sales presentation. Rather than forging bravely ahead, hoping the customer will forget about price if you talk fast enough, you should drop back into some Probing questions to discover how to add more value.

PRICE JUSTIFIER #3:
Personalize all values.

The most significant question you must help your prospect answer will be "Is this worth what it will cost me?" Endorsements from other customers will not answer this question. Neither will a top rating from *Consumer's Guide*. Nor will being widely acclaimed by experts as the best bargain in the industry. The ultimate test will always be the answer to the very personal question, "Is it worth it to *me*?"

That is why the Probe phase is so crucial to the IMPACT Selling system. Probing is that critical phase during which you identify the personal values that matter enough to your prospect to justify paying whatever you charge for your product or services. If you offer enough benefits, tailoring those benefits to meet personal desires and interests, you will easily convince your prospect that your price is not too high.

For example, we have worked with many furniture manufacturers who sell expensive luxury furniture. If the value they present to their prospects were merely functional furniture, few people would pay. If, however, they focus on the prospect's personal value agenda that includes prestige, comfort, reliability, styling, or luxury, the salespeople can easily move the needle on the value meter high enough to justify the price in such a prospect's mind. The key to their success has come when they readjust their sales force's perceptions so that it understands what benefits move the value meter needle up in the mind of a "high-end" furniture buyer.

Recall from the last chapter Applying Principle #2, which stated, "In the absence of a values interpreter, all sales degenerate into a struggle over price." In the Apply phase, you interpreted values; in the Convince phase, you pile those interpreted values onto the prospect's mental balance scale. Use everything you gained from the Meet and Probe phases to personalize the values you present. The higher a value ranks in the prospect's value system, the greater the weight it will carry on those unseen "justify-the-price" balance scales. Speaking of scales, here's a great way to tip them quickly.

PRICE JUSTIFIER #4:
Sell the key benefit.

Remember the story about the cherry tree in the Apply chapter? The key benefit that lies at the core of a dominant need is the greatest justification you have for the price your prospect must pay to get whatever you are selling.

Marketing consultants often ask their clients, "What is your unique selling proposition?" In other words, what is there about your product or service that sets it apart as superior to all other products or services on the market? In IMPACT

Selling, the answer to that question is always personalized to be *the single benefit this prospect finds most attractive*. To the real estate sales professional in the Apply chapter, it was a cherry tree in the backyard. It may be a certain look, a convenience, a texture or feel, a sense of security, or anything else that the prospect becomes most deeply emotional about.

Whatever the prospect's dominant need, you must identify and isolate the key benefit related to that need because it is the one that will literally open the door to the sale. The greatest justification for paying any price is, "I like it!" Your task is to help your prospects like what you are selling enough to pay the price for it.

To conclude my discussion of the Convince phase of IMPACT Selling, I will cover the final challenge for you in the four basic actions of the Convince phase.

RELIEVE THE PROSPECT'S FEAR OF BUYING

Fear can be among the strongest motivations for buying a product or service, yet fear can also be one of the greatest deterrents to making a positive buying decision. Fear of buying often proves to be the toughest challenge a salesperson faces. It may be founded in the prospect's fear of failure, fear of loss, fear of ridicule or rejection, or fear of the unknown. You must help prospects overcome their fears so they are comfortable enough to buy.

How can you overcome your prospect's fears? Since it is such a universal challenge, we have developed four "Buying Fear Relievers" that I will soon introduce. As a prelude to their introduction, I will present the final principle of the Convince phase. Then we will explore these specific techniques you can use to make it work for you.

CONVINCE PRINCIPLE #4:
Fear of buying disappears as trust in you, and in the values you offer, rises.

The greatest fear busters are trust and value. Let us look at some ways you can make them work for you as you seek to convince your prospects to buy.

BUYING FEAR RELIEVER #1:
Reconcile the buying decision with the prospect's value system.

Any time we act in a manner that is inconsistent with the way we see ourselves, we can expect to feel some fear. That is true even if what we are doing has the highest motivation.

For example, many people who leave a "secure" job with a steady salary and set out to work in sales on a straight commission basis are scared that they will fail and be humiliated. Years later, they may look back on it as one of the greatest steps they ever took, but at the beginning it threatens their value system.

That same dynamic situation often evolves when a person looks to buy something—especially if the purchase costs a great deal or if it represents a significant change to one's existing pattern. For example, people who have lived in rental houses for years may feel as if they are taking on the national debt when they sign a mortgage contract for a house. That buying decision may be a very sound one for them, but initially they will feel as if it violates the values they have lived by for so long.

One of the most valuable services you can render is to help your prospects reconcile their buying options with their value system. Ignoring fears rarely conquers them. Thus, it is usually helpful to explore openly the fears that prospects feel so they can become aware of their own value systems and limitations. This may be a time in their lives when they are ready for personal growth, and your services will help them move toward it. With that in mind, I present

BUYING FEAR RELIEVER #2:
Help prospects expand their own self-belief.

We each have our own self-belief system—that imaginary world inside where we feel safe, comfortable, and satisfied. Any time we start to do something that violates that world, we feel that we are on dangerous ground. As a result, we become afraid to try things that our emotions have not allowed us to experience before.

You can help your prospects overcome such fears by helping them to reevaluate their self-belief systems. One way to do that is to focus for them how great the benefits of ownership will make them feel. Another method is to help them gradually experience the feelings that ownership will bring. Yet another method for helping prospects to overcome fears is to make them feel wise for being smart enough to buy from you.

BUYING FEAR RELIEVER #3:
Assure them of the wisdom of their choices.

Rarely will you find people who are so self-confident that they do not feel hesitant about buying what they want or need. Most people find buying an unsettling experience. A thousand questions may be rushing through a prospect's mind as he or she contemplates a decision to buy, such as "It this the right thing for me to do? What will happen to me if I make a serious buying mistake? What will so-and-so think about my decision? Can I pay for this thing? It is really me? Do we really need it?" These questions result from doubts prospects have about themselves; in other words, they are questioning their own self-confidence.

You can do your prospects a big favor and simultaneously boost your chances for closing a sale when you reassure them of the wisdom of their decisions. There are some excellent techniques to help you offer this reassurance. For example, you cannot tell a prospect that his or her decision is the "right thing" for him or her, nor can you tell the prospect that a "no" is the wrong thing, either. You are not a judge, yet you can reassure your prospects that they are making a wise decision—at least from a values perspective. Follow these helpful tips and you will help your prospects have faith in their buying decision.

You Must Believe It Yourself

In the past, if you knew intuitively that a buying decision was not a wise one for a buyer, old-school selling techniques would have said that you could demonstrate a high level of professionalism by trying to convince the prospect otherwise. If you have had a difficult time selling certain things to some people because you knew the products were wrong for the buyers, you have seen for yourself the resistance that today's buyers have toward old-school techniques. Such an experience should be a signal to you that it is time to reconsider your own values. However, when you clearly know that a prospect is making a wise buying decision, reassure them with every bit of persuasive power you have.

Recap the Benefits

You will be amazed at how often a major benefit only dawns on a person the fifth or sixth time you repeat it. Do not assume he or she understands each benefit; make the extra effort to be certain he or she does. Even if the person previously recognized the benefit as more valuable than its price, he or she may not have seen himself or herself as wise for understanding the value. When you recap benefits, it may provide a major source of comfort for your prospect.

Reinforce Your Prospects' Positive Feelings

If your prospects express a liking for some benefit, get them to talk more about it. If they are silent, ask them what they like most about what they have seen. Give them an opportunity to take psychological possession by asking them to tell you what they most look forward to about owning it. The more they talk positively about the benefits you have shown, the more they sell themselves. You may enjoy the luxury of listening to them do the convincing for you as they describe their feelings about owning your product.

Answer Any Lingering Questions

Honesty will always be a top priority, and both honesty and complete openness are essential during the Convince phase. Stop periodically, taking time to ask if prospects have any unanswered questions. Before you attempt to move to the last phase of IMPACT Selling, you must uncover and eliminate any objections. Never brush off a prospect's honest objections lightly. Deal with each objection as it comes up, or they will later function as earmuffs to block out everything you say. Never hedge on an answer. Doing so can negate all the convincing you have done up to that point.

In the final phase of IMPACT Selling, entitled "Tie-It-Up," we will return to the topic of lingering doubts with a discussion of some specific insights on how to handle objections.

TO SUM IT ALL UP...

The Convince phase is where you make your prospects believe enough to act on your business proposal. It is where you back up all the valuable benefits you have promised.

As a review of the four basic elements necessary to best complete the process of convincing prospects to go ahead with a buying decision, you have to

- Prove your claims.
- Bring your own witnesses.
- Justify your price.
- Relieve the fear of buying.

Once the first five IMPACT phases have been thoroughly and professionally completed, you will easily make the transition to the final Tie-It-Up phase during which you will complete a highly effective, IMPACT Selling close. By the end of the Convince phase, you will have used focus, leverage, and alignment to build up to the close of a sale organically. At this point, the Value equation—*Perceived Benefit over Perceived Price*—has been maximized and your prospect is becoming your next customer.

ACTION STEPS

With your specific products and services in mind, list at least one way you will use each of the four Convince actions we covered in this chapter:

1. Prove your claims.

    ACTION PLAN: _____

2. Bring your own witnesses.

ACTION PLAN: _____

3. Justify your price.

ACTION PLAN: _____

4. Relieve the fear of buying.

ACTION PLAN: _____

KEY TIPS

☑ To convince your prospects to buy, you have to cut through their natural mistrust of salespeople and get them to believe strongly enough in you to act.

☑ You must be able to back every claim you make with hard evidence, clarified with visual aids. Then repeat your claims again and again.

☑ You must bring your own witnesses to the prospect through endorsement letters or other irrefutable testimony from someone other than yourself. Carefully choose the endorsements that will have maximum weight with each individual prospect. Get your satisfied customers involved with your new prospects.

☑ Continue to build value to justify your price. Picture an imaginary value meter in your prospect's mind and keep piling on benefits to move the meter up. The needle jumps the highest when you hit the prospect's dominant need and pinpoint the key benefit that your product or service will provide them.

☑ Recap the benefits you have listed to relieve the natural fear of buying. Help your prospects reconcile their buying decisions with their current values and remain alert for opportunities to expand the limits of their current values.

☑ Reinforce every positive feeling you hear the prospect express.

☑ Clear up every lingering doubt; never just *assume* that you have. Rely only on positive feedback from your prospect as proof that his or her doubts have been dispelled.

CHAPTER 10

TIE-IT-UP

Tie-It-Up

Wrapping up the sale and allowing prospects to take ownership. Negotiating terms and conditions of the sale, clearing away objections to the sale, and asking for the order. Reinforcing the sale after it is complete.

Men who have lost heart never yet won a trophy
Greek Proverb

In this chapter, you will discover how to complete the sales transaction while keeping the emphasis focused where it has been throughout each of the first five phases: on the prospect! As with each preceding phase, I have identified certain tested and proven procedures for the Tie-It-Up phase. In this chapter, I present the four basic elements of the final phase of IMPACT Selling:

- Negotiate the conditions of the sale.
- Clear away objections.
- Ask for the order.
- Reinforce the sale.

TIE UP THE SALE, NEVER YOUR CUSTOMER

We have traded in the old expression *closing the sale* for *tying up the sale* because closing has become sales jargon for tying up the prospect. The traditional closing approach will never deliver long-term growth and success in today's value-hungry markets. Today's buyers have been so heavily inundated with clichéd sales pitches that they have heard all the tired tricks before. The concepts in this chapter will help accelerate you to the forefront of today's value-based selling environment.

IMPACT Selling does not rely on clever closing gimmicks to trick people into buying something they really do not want to buy. Nor is closing the centerpiece of a sale, around which all other elements are built. Remember that the Investigate and Probe phases are the core of IMPACT Selling. Tying up the sale is a natural outgrowth of performing the other five steps successfully; it is an orderly and simple step taken deliberately after the other steps have been completed. It can even be both an enjoyable and exciting time–both for you and for the prospect.

Remember that your prospects want what you are selling, or they would not buy it. They probably wanted it before you walked in. Perhaps they only wanted a need fulfilled and you showed them how to apply your products or services to fulfill that need. The underlying theme in this final phase is that you have already accurately identified what your prospects want and they understand that they need it. With that knowledge, all that remains is the simple process of tying up the loose ends of the transaction so that you both get what you want. The first basic element is to nail down the detailed conditions of the sale.

Negotiate the Conditions of the Sale

Negotiation entails working out a mutually satisfactory agreement between two or more people for something both want to do. Successful negotiation requires handling the details so that all parties involved feel they have won.

In a way, everything you have done up to this point has been a part of negotiating the sale. By adhering to the IMPACT Selling plan, you have already:

1. *Investigated* to discover who was interested in your business proposal.
2. *Met* with prospects to enter into dialogue about your proposal.
3. *Probed* to find out what prospects wanted most, how much they planned to invest, and under what conditions they would buy.

4. *Applied* your most appropriate solution to your prospects' most compelling needs and desires.

5. *Convinced* your prospects that they can meet their needs and fulfill their wishes by buying from you.

The first five phases of IMPACT Selling are the prelude to formal negotiating, and without this prelude you cannot enter into formal negotiations. Skipping over any one of the five steps will sabotage even your best efforts to tie up the sale. Without first laying down the full IMPACT Selling groundwork, the final phase will reduce you to employing unprofessional and out-dated—although well-known and traditional—closing tricks.

Though the final phase should flow organically out of the first five, your success in negotiations will improve as you strengthen your negotiating skills. To enhance the success of your negotiations, I will give you four winning strategies that have helped thousands of customer-focused sales professionals become effective negotiators.

NEGOTIATION STRATEGY #1:
Open the negotiations on a positive note.

The most powerful time to open formal negotiations is right after your prospect has expressed approval or delight over some feature or benefit. Read that last sentence again; the key phrase is *your prospect has expressed*. Now relate that to the principles and strategies I presented in the previous two chapters. In the Apply phase, I said that you must regularly ask about the prospects' feelings and listen as they express them. In the Convince phase, I said that you must move their value meter by listening to what they express about the value you have presented. When you hear the prospect express approval or delight, simply ask, "Is there anything that would keep you from going ahead with this?"

Then STOP!

Extensive research has proven that question to be the most effective for opening negotiations. It is a sincere and honest question, it cuts right to the heart of the matter, and it is not in any way offensive. To use it properly you must stop after you have asked, wait for the prospect to respond, then listen attentively to the answer. If the answer is "I do not see any reason not to go ahead," you then know you have just entered the Tie-It-Up phase and can begin writing up the sale.

If the only responses you ever hear to that question prompt you to move ahead, then you do not need the rest of this chapter. However, as a seasoned sales veteran in highly competitive markets, you know many prospects will still show hesitancy and offer some reason for not going ahead. If so, do not panic; simply continue with more of our strategies.

NEGOTIATION STRATEGY #2:
Get all the conditions on the table.

The prospect will almost never be so direct as to give you information by saying, "I'll buy it under the following conditions." More often, prospects take a more brusque approach, responding only to the specific conditions you have presented. Some responses you might hear are "I don't know! That's a lot of money!" or "I wish you had a more advanced model." To those answers, many salespeople begin hammering away at all the reasons why the prospect's objection should not veto the sale. Such tactics from a salesperson are rude, inconsiderate of the prospect's desires, and insulting to his or her intelligence; they are a major diversion from customer focus.

Most of the conditions brought up by the prospect are merely smoke screens to cover up deeper feelings of uncertainty. You cannot negotiate with a smoke screen—when you satisfy one condition, the prospect will raise another. You must answer the deeper question, settle the deeper uncertainties. Here is where your intuitive insight will tell you that you need to return to the Probe phase.

Probing again is the only way you can get all the conditions on the negotiating table so you can deal with them. Ask questions such as, "Is that the only reason you'd be hesitant to go ahead?" or "If I could show how to solve that problem, would you be ready to go ahead?" Pursuing this line of questioning will eventually bring all the conditions out into the open.

Do not attempt to avoid this process. Although it may seem like a backward step to return to probing, it is far better for negative feelings and thoughts to come out at this stage than when you are trying to wrap up the sale. Before attempting to move on, you have to guarantee that you have addressed all the required conditions. Once you feel you have all the conditions on the table, you can go on to the next strategy.

NEGOTIATION STRATEGY #3:
Make sure you understand the conditions.

Make sure you understand all the conditions your prospect has listed. An excellent aid to correctly understanding all conditions is to list them and read them off to your prospect. Restate each in your own words and ask the prospect if he or she believes you truly understand what he or she is feeling.

To begin moving toward negotiations, you might say, "Let me see if I understand what you've told me. You feel uncertain about being able to handle the timing of an expenditure of this size right now, and you would prefer a modified implementation schedule. Is that right?" It is important that you clearly understand what the prospect feels.

Equally important is ensuring that the prospect also understands what he or she feels. For example, you may surmise that a prospect is feeling, "We can't afford this," whereas what he or she is actually feeling may be, "We can't justify spending that much money for such an item to our boss." The only way you can reach that kind of understanding is through dialogue. There is a big difference between those two positions. Stay with the dialogue process until you are confident that you and the prospect agree on what the stated conditions mean.

NEGOTIATION STRATEGY #4:
Offer to try to work out any problems.

At this point, you want to make it clear to your prospect that both of you are sitting on the same side of the negotiating table. In effect, you must convey your feelings by saying, "I know you'd like to have the benefits I've shown you, and I know you have some concerns. I want to help you eliminate those concerns so you can have the value I've created and the benefits you want." To do this, agree with your client that you both want the same thing and offer to help eliminate any problems that might prohibit the prospect from getting what he or she wants.

Abraham Lincoln probably did this better than anyone in history, as both a lawyer and a statesman. As a lawyer, he would sit and listen carefully to everything his opponent said. Afterward he would slowly rise and address the jury. He then began telling the panel what a fine person and how brilliant his opponent was, and how he had brought out some very valid points for the jurors to consider.

"However," he would gently add, "there are other facts that need to be considered before you make a decision." Then he would skillfully list all the reasons the jury should decide the case in his client's favor. Jurors who sat before Mr. Lincoln have said they felt that old Abe was just helping them to reach an honest verdict. That was precisely his approach. He made them feel as if they were on the same side of the issue because he stressed that the prime issue for them both was to reach an honest verdict.

The important thing is that both you and your prospect reach this stage of the sale with (1) a clear understanding of the conditions under which the prospect will buy and (2) a strong bond of trust between you and the prospect. With both of those firmly established, your prospects will trust in you when they see that your interest lies in helping them get what they want.

Clear Away Objections

To ensure your long-range success, always view objections as conditions that must be met before a satisfactory sale can be consummated. The way you handle objections will often determine whether you make the sale. In other words, it can determine whether you provide your prospect with a satisfactory deal.

Most objections raised by prospects emanate from feelings rather than from a factual standpoint. The salesperson must deal with objections forthrightly by addressing the feelings behind them. A traditionally flippant response to a price objection, such as, "Sure it's a lot of money, but just look at all you're getting!" is asking for trouble. A canned response like that cannot possibly deal with the true feelings of today's sophisticated and demanding prospects. As an IMPACT Selling professional, you must rise far above the old price-oriented mentality, always focusing on value and trust.

The real reason why most salespeople deal so poorly with objections is that they do not know how to deal with them properly. All their training has focused on memorizing canned responses to every objection that could possibly come up. They sound like playbacks of recorded messages: "If a prospect gives Objection Number Four, you counter it with Response Number 67." You should forget all of them you ever learned.

A successful IMPACT salesperson never responds to objections with canned answers. The key to eliminating objections with a customer-focused orientation will be treating each objection uniquely, as it relates to specific needs. Instead of offering canned responses, we have developed four general tactics to show you how to face prospects' objections with candid confidence.

OBJECTION TACTIC #1:
Simplify the objection.

At least half the work of solving any problem is to state it clearly and succinctly. Often, when an objection is verbalized so that a prospect can really understand how he or she feels, the objection disappears. A long-time friend of mine once closed a large real estate transaction simply by pointing out the true objection. What followed—what always follows in all properly conducted IMPACT Selling transactions—was that his prospect closed the deal for him. Here is his story as he tells it.

"Once when I was selling a huge land development program, a wealthy widow had objected to the large amount of money involved in the deal. I gave her a moment to reflect, then said, 'What I hear you saying is that you can't justify investing that much money on a project like this. Is that right?' "

" 'That's right,' she said thoughtfully. 'Wait a minute! My husband is dead! Whom do I have to justify it to?' she said, with a big grin. She then grabbed the pen out of my hand and said, 'Where do I sign?' "

"At that point, I couldn't have stopped the deal if I had wanted to."

Of course, not all objections will be answered quite that easily, but none will ever be answered if you do not know exactly what that prospect is feeling and, in turn, do not help him or her to understand what he or she is feeling. When you break an objection down to its simplest form and state it as a question, you demonstrate to your prospect that you have truly been listening. Naturally, the best way to show the prospect that you truly have been listening was described back in the Probe phase when you opened your leather binder, took out your pen, and looked the prospect in the eye while waiting for answers. If you have maintained that professional listening pattern, you may well overcome all objections as easily as the salesperson in the last example did.

OBJECTION TACTIC #2:
Use the feel, felt, found formula.

Although this technique has been around for years, it is still a powerful strategy to eliminate objections from prospects. I will take you through each of the three keys words: "feel," "felt," and "found."

First, you say, "*I understand how you feel about...*" Many sales-people find their clients actually look relieved and say, "You do?" It was as if they had expected the salesperson to say how silly it was for them to feel as they did.

You can say, "I understand how you feel," without the slightest fear of being dishonest. Even if you have never had precisely the same feelings, you may still empathize. We all know what it feels like to have some misgivings about a decision. If you could not empathize with your prospects, you probably would not have persevered so far with the IMPACT Selling plan.

When you say you understand how your prospects feel, that does not mean you necessarily agree with their reasons, though they will often believe that is what you said. In truth, you may think their feelings are totally unfounded. Nonetheless, you should be able to empathize with the person's having them. Saying you do will ease the tension of the moment, leading the prospect to believe that you will deal with the bad feelings they are having. That is precisely what you do next.

Next, you say, "*Many of my clients have felt the same way.*" It's like saying, "You're not an oddball," or "It's not unusual for someone to feel as you do." That takes yet more pressure off clients, now relieving them of any need to defend their feelings. The net result is that they can now look at their feelings more objectively. You have given your prospects positive reassurance and have complimented them on their sagacity in finding an objection that many others have also found.

Once you show them you understand, you become their ally. Also, since they trust you and know you have helped others who felt as they do, they will accept your suggestions on how to deal with their feelings. The most effective way to give people advice is to lay it out in the open so that they can discover it for themselves instead of having it rammed down their throats.

Finally, you say, *"But they found . . . "* That allows you to show your prospects how others have dealt with their feelings. You are not playing amateur psychologist, but merely suggesting that others have found such feelings to be groundless. Here is an example of how it can work.

"I understand how you feel about investing that much in an advertising program. Many of my other clients have also felt it was a large investment. But later they found that they began making many more sales as a result of the new campaign and that the new program produced a positive increase in cash flow."

This three-step approach gives you a powerful method to eliminate objections that are based mainly on feelings. When you use the three words *feel, felt,* and *found,* you show your prospects that you:

- Accept their feelings.
- Assure them that those feelings are valid and shared by others.
- Show them that others have found those feelings to be groundless because of one or more benefits of ownership.

Some objections will indicate that your prospect does not yet fully understand the value of all the benefits you have presented. When that happens, you should use the following objection tactic.

OBJECTION TACTIC #3:
Make sure prospects understand all the benefits.

Do not assume a prospect understands all the benefits you have explained just because you have repeated them several times. Make sure the person understands them. Even highly successful IMPACT salespeople can lose a deal by not ensuring that their clients truly *understand* all the benefits offered.

At a recent seminar, we heard this story from a well-known speaker, who is a veteran of the IMPACT Selling plan. It illustrates just how essential it is to *be sure!*

"I once learned the benefits lesson the hard way. I had received a call from an officer of the Hanes Corporation who was considering booking me to speak at an upcoming training seminar.

I had used the IMPACT Selling principles you taught me and felt I had a good chance of getting what I considered a great booking.

"In one contact with the Hanes executive, he said, 'I'm sure you'll do a good job for us, and your fee is about what others have quoted us.' I thanked him for his time and he closed with, 'I'll get back with you after I've talked with my boss.'

"Some time later, I hadn't heard from him, so I called. 'Oh, we went ahead and engaged _____.' They had scheduled a speaker whom I know and whose fee is identical with mine.

"I asked, 'Do you mind if I ask what I did wrong? It will help me know how to do a better job with other people.'

" 'Oh, you didn't do anything wrong,' he assured me. 'It's just that his fee included a pre-meeting survey to determine our needs.'

"I could have kicked myself! I always do a pre-meeting survey—at no extra cost—and I know I had mentioned it to him, but I *assumed* he understood it. The other guy outsold me because he *made sure* the prospect understood the benefit."

Always make sure *your* prospects know and understand *all* the benefits. In a crowded marketplace, you should expect that if you do not, someone else will.

OBJECTION TACTIC #4:
Test to see that the objection is gone.

Sales amateurs often brush aside objections with a canned response. Believing such objections have been swept under the rug, the salesperson proceeds as if there were no conflicts in the client's mind. When the potential customer walks out without a purchase order, the salesperson wonders why the prospect did not buy.

In contrast to the amateurs, value-based selling professionals always face every objection honestly. Unfortunately, honesty alone will not ensure that the prospect is *satisfied* with your response. To find out, you must check to see if each objection has been handled to the prospect's satisfaction. Make sure each objection is gone and will not come back to haunt you.

After you have used the Feel, Felt, Found formula, you should ask for the prospect's reaction. You will have taken him or her through the three-step process, but you have to determine if your approach made sense. Try a question like, "Can you see how you might find the same thing to be true for you?" It is a simple test but it does two important things for you.

First, knowing your prospect agrees tells you that the objection is gone. If it is still there, you can use the Feel, Felt, Found formula again and get more specific.

Second, letting the client speak provides an opportunity for the prospect to verbalize his or her way of dealing with the objection. You will be surprised how often prospects will pick right up on it. "Sure, I remember some office furniture I once bought that I thought would never wear out...and I always thought it made my office look great!"

To proceed to the next step, we will assume that you are with a prospect and that you have dealt with him or her as a model IMPACT salesperson. You have investigated, met, probed, applied, and convinced. The prospect trusts and likes you. The prospect believes you know what he or she wants. Now, halfway through the Tie-It-Up phase, you have negotiated the conditions of the sale and cleared away every objection and are ready for the final step before signing the order.

Ask for the Order

Everything you have done up to this point is wasted motion unless you ask for the order. However, asking for an order is not nearly as major an activity for an IMPACT sales professional as many salespeople and trainers have traditionally made it out to be. If you have successfully completed the first five steps—finding out what your prospects want most and showing them how they can get it—asking for the order is a natural final step.

You cannot make the buying decision for your prospects, but you can ease the decision-making process for them. We have developed five tested and proven techniques for making the buying decision easier for you and for your prospects. You must choose which one is best for you based on your own style and on the circumstances of each situation.

CLOSING TECHNIQUE #1:
Use trial closes throughout the interview.

This simple concept involves beginning to move toward the close before you actually get there. By moving slowly forward, the final jump may be a small step. Here is a great illustration of the concept.

Sailors use what they call a *monkeyfist* to simplify what could be a tough task. The big ropes they use to tie a giant ocean liner to a pier are often four to five inches thick and may weigh hundreds of pounds. Can you imagine how hard it would be to throw one of those massive ropes from the ship to the pier? Even if a team of big stevedores could do it, how would you like to be the poor guy on the other end who had to catch it?

So, sailors have developed a special technique in which they tie a little ball—a monkeyfist—to one end of a small rope and toss that over. The guy on the pier easily catches that, ties the small rope securely and starts pulling it in. The huge line is tied to the other end and comes right along with it. Mission accomplished!

Trial closes work just like the monkeyfist. Throughout the negotiation step, you use small test questions that will not throw your client off balance. If the prospect grabs one and starts pulling on it, hook the close to it and allow the prospect to wrap up the sale for you.

You may have noticed that earlier questions I discussed in this chapter are trial closes. "Is there anything that would keep you from going ahead with this?" is a trial close. "Can you see how it might work the same way for you?" is another good one.

This trial close technique is about as close to a canned approach as IMPACT Selling ever gets; however, you should always think about each prospect individually and find a trial close that feels natural in each situation. A trial close is a good way to ease into asking for a buying decision, and it may tell you that the decision to buy has already been made.

CLOSING TECHNIQUE #2:
Ask them to buy now.

When you feel the time is right, simply ask your prospect for the order. Be cautious, though; the way you ask for an order can make it easier or more difficult for the prospect to make a buying decision. We have found a question that has a high success rate for thousands of salespeople: "Is there anything that would keep you from buying now?"

There is nothing tricky about it. If you have successfully used IMPACT Selling, asking for the order is merely a matter of tying up the loose ends of the sale. You look your prospect straight in the eye, ask him or her to buy, and then do not say another word until the prospect has responded.

Many salespeople are so afraid of rejection that they feel they must break any silence that lasts more than a few seconds. They may even jump in and say something damaging like, "Maybe you need more time to think about this" or "Now, I don't want to make you feel pressured." Interrupting will only delay the decision at best and it may sabotage it permanently. Remember that some people simply need a little space when they are making a decision.

We have found some salespeople who are reluctant to use such direct closes as those we have recommended. For those salespeople, we offer two other techniques that also work well.

CLOSING TECHNIQUE #3:
Assume the sale.

Many excellent salespeople are more comfortable assuming that the prospect has bought and immediately start handling the paperwork, all the while asking the prospect questions about details. When they finish writing up the order, they might ask, "Is there anything else we should include before we finalize the agreement?" If not, write the final terms on the agreement, mark a big "X" where the prospect should sign, then hand the agreement and your pen to the new customer.

This approach is a variation of the first one where we recommend using trial closes throughout the process to move gradually toward finalizing the deal. With this technique, prospects never have to make one big decision to buy—just a series of smaller decisions—and many prospects feel much more comfortable with that gradual process.

One drawback to assuming the sale is that some people feel pressured when you hand them the agreement if they are not ready to make a decision. Therefore, when you use this technique, keep your intuitive insight in high gear for signs that your move makes the prospect uncomfortable. If you sense any uneasiness, lay the agreement aside and drop back to some more Probe questions to uncover the true reasons he or she is feeling hesitant.

CLOSING TECHNIQUE #4:
Use the either/or close.

Some salespeople do not feel comfortable with any of the first three closes because each boils down to a "yes" or "no" answer. Another method that makes it easy for prospects to decide to buy is to use closing questions that give them a range of answers. One of the most effective alternative closes is commonly known as the *either/or* close. Here is how to give your prospects more options than "yes" or "no."

In the either/or close, ask a question that lets the prospect choose between having it one way or another. "Do you like it best in the conventional style, or would you rather have the newer model?" "Should we schedule delivery Wednesday, or do you prefer that we schedule it for next Monday?" "Do you prefer to make a single payment, or would you rather use our convenient easy payment plan?"

One good way to lead into an either/or close is to summarize the benefits and state the price just before you ask the question. It is best to ask the question immediately after the prospect has made a positive statement about some feature or benefit he or she particularly likes.

The greatest advantage in using the assumptive close is that it shields people from having to make a straightforward buying decision. Instead, you give them an option that is far less threatening and implies that they have made a positive buying decision. With this close, there is less pressure than in asking them to choose which model they want or the conditions under which they will buy. However, both the assumptive close and the either/or closing technique put very little direct pressure on prospects. Neither one is heavy handed, high pressure, or pushy.

CLOSING TECHNIQUE #5:
Deal with fear of making a decision.

Often you will find that a prospect is sold on the product, feels comfortable with all the conditions of the purchase, yet remains hesitant about making a buying decision. In such cases, it is vital that you allow the prospect to proceed according to his or her own internal time clock. Never make a thinking prospect feel rushed.

We had a young graduate of one of our seminars report a case to us where this had happened to her. This is the story she passed on to us.

"In a recent sales interview, I had become excited about how much I was going to earn from a huge deal I was just about to close. However, the prospect just kept hedging and I got impatient, and probably a little too pushy. The woman stopped me and said, 'Look! If you can give me a few minutes to think about this, I might say yes. If you have to know right now, the answer is NO!' "

"I instantly recovered by saying, 'Take as much time as you like!' then leaned back with a big, friendly smile after laying the agreement aside. Next, we talked for 20 minutes about her family, then she signed the order without a moment's hesitation.

"That's one mistake I'll never make again!"

It will not always be that easy. Still, if you sense that a prospect's request for a little time or space is a cover for a deeper barrier to making a decision, probe into exactly why the person is hesitant. If you discover there is some key issue that remains to be settled, handle it in stride and get back on track with the close. If you do not find the true reason for the prospect's hesitancy, keep probing until you are able to pin down the dominant factor.

Once you uncover a key issue this late in the process, focus on the issue as precisely as possible. Use very straightforward, honest Probe questions, such as, "If it were not for the balloon note at the end of the lease agreement, would you be ready to go ahead with this?" If the prospect says yes, you know exactly what you are dealing with. With an answer that clear, you would then end your reversion to the Probe phase and negotiate a new set of conditions that are acceptable.

Reinforce the Sale

Once a prospect makes a decision to buy, many salespeople pack up and get out as fast as they can. We have found that prospects often gain much intuitive insight from the body language of a hit-and-run salesperson. It seems as if the salesperson is silently saying that they should make a speedy exit before the prospect changes his or her mind.

Never rush for the door before the ink dries on an agreement. You are experienced enough to know that if a customer truly wants to back out, he or she will find a way to back out no matter what has been signed. Moreover, your haste to depart can damage the trust bond you have worked so hard to create. Besides, if you have successfully completed a deal through proper IMPACT Selling, you will have full confidence that the customer has no desire to back out.

To recall my earlier quotation, after a long sales interview "People will not long remember all you said, but they will never forget how you made them feel." Don't make them feel they've been victims of a quick-hit artist. Instead of running off, take time to let the glue dry on this new bond you have just created. It is better to take a few minutes to tie up any loose ends before you leave. By lingering a few minutes, you can help reinforce the positive aspects of the sale for the customer. Remember that you are selling trust and value and that a few extra minutes can reinforce those perceptions for your prospect.

SALE REINFORCEMENT #1:
Compliment prospects on their choices.

Saying "I think you've made a wise choice" is a simple, yet very effective way to reinforce every sale. Its value to you is leveraged because it not only congratulates purchasers, but opens the door for them to express their positive feelings about their purchases. Expression serves as reinforcement. The more your prospects talk about it, the more comfortable they will become with their decisions.

This self-acknowledgement can help to head off future problems. For example, if clients' decisions are called into question, their positive statements to themselves may now have provided a dress rehearsal for how to answer potential critics later. The better they look, the better you look.

SALE REINFORCEMENT #2:
Invite them to buy more.

Often the best prospect for a sale is the very client to whom you have just sold your product or service. Many salespeople question this because they assume their new customer cannot afford another purchase just after making one. Some miraculous results can come your way by asking your most recent customer for repeat business. Here is a terrific story that we picked up from a business colleague. It came from a sales manager (we'll call him Mel) who had bought his first Mercedes automobile a few years ago.

Mel bought his car from a very young salesman, whom I will call Brad. After Mel had given Brad a check for about $40,000 for a sedan, he was standing in the lobby chatting with the young salesman and his sales manager.

Brad was evidently still in training, but strangely it was his sales manager's anxiety that was in evidence. He kept trying to hurry Mel out the door.

As the door was about to close, Brad said, "You've made a wise investment, and I think you are in for a real treat when you discover what's so special about owning a Mercedes."

"Thanks, I'm sure I'll enjoy it!" Mel replied.

"In fact, there's only one way you can make a better decision than the one you've just made," Brad mused.

At this, the sales manager rolled his eyes toward the ceiling as if to say, "What am I going to do with this kid!"

"How's that?" Mel asked.

"Go ahead and let me deliver that 450SL sports coupe we talked about for your wife, too!" Then Brad just stood there, quietly grinning, waiting for Mel to sell himself another car.

"I'll tell you what!" Mel said after thinking for a minute. "You find me a metallic gray one with a blue top and you've just sold yourself another car!"

Chuckling about it later, Mel said, "I suspect that young salesman almost wet his pants right there in the lobby."

Mel knew exactly what the kid had done, but it worked nonetheless. As Mel handed the sales manager a second $40,000 check, he said, "When was the last time you sold two cars, worth $80,000, in only 15 minutes?"

"Never!"

It was only because he had never dared to ask anyone to buy a second car.

You will never know until you ask. A person who is sold on a product might add to the sale, might upgrade his or her choice, or might even duplicate it. Think about the logic of it. If you have honestly just given a prospect what he or she wants most, wouldn't he or she naturally be interested in even more of the same?

SALE REINFORCEMENT #3:
Assure your new customer of satisfaction.

You should always reassure your new customers that you are not leaving them alone with their new products. You cannot afford to have them feeling as though they have just signed on with a bunch of strangers with whom they can hardly make contact. A simple "I'll check back with you next week to make sure you got everything okay," can reassure them that they are not dealing with an impersonal organization. You might want to add, "If you have any problems with delivery, feel free to call me." Then make it easy for them to get in touch with you.

Most importantly, if you promise to check back with them, make sure you do. If there is a problem, and you do not check back, you will only compound the anger they feel. Finally, if they do call you, you must return their calls immediately. You are likely to be at a crucial crossroads with that person and you want to make sure you turn up the road leading to long-range success with them.

TO SUM IT ALL UP...

Remember, there are four basic parts to the Tie-It-Up phase of IMPACT Selling. The first three actually consummate the sale, and the fourth is an important follow-up step to ensure your continued future success.

- *Negotiate the conditions of the sale.* Successful negotiation requires handling the details so that all parties involved feel they have won.
- *Clear away objections.* The key to eliminating objections in the 1990s will be in treating each uniquely, relating to specific needs.

- *Ask for the order.* If you have successfully completed the first five steps—finding out what your prospects want most and showing them how they can get it—asking for the order is a natural final step.
- *Reinforce the sale.* Compliment prospects on their choices. Invite them to buy more. Assure them of satisfaction.

You cannot take the final step until you have completed each of the preceding five. Successful completion of the "I" through "C" phases earns you the right to move to the "T" phase. When the process is complete, you will then have

- *Investigated* to discover who was interested in your business proposal.
- *Met* with prospects to enter into dialogue on your proposal.
- *Probed* to find out what they wanted most and under what conditions they would buy it.
- *Applied* (not demonstrated) your most appropriate solution to their most compelling needs and desires.
- *Convinced* them that they can meet their needs and fulfill their wishes by buying whatever you are selling.
- *Tied-It-Up* by negotiating the conditions of the sale, clearing away objections, signing the order, and reinforcing the sale.

These six steps will ensure that you follow a customer-focused, value-based track to selling, making you an IMPACT Selling professional. IMPACT is the most powerful selling system ever devised.

Once you fully embody a needs-based system, you can mobilize and arm your entire sales force with this powerful plan. When you, your sales force, and your marketing department are aligned with IMPACT Selling, you will be able to join that exclusive club in the top 5 percent that accounts for 60 percent of all sales. And, even as your sales climb, you will find yourselves working shorter hours than ever. In short, you will come to see why I like to call IMPACT Selling: *Working smart in a crazy world!*

ACTION STEPS

Set a goal for each of the four Tie-It-Up steps that will improve your closing skills by listing a specific answer designed to serve your own personal selling style and circumstances:

1. Negotiate the conditions of the sale.

   GOAL _____

   _____

2. Clear away objections.

   GOAL _____

   _____

3. Ask for the order.

   GOAL _____

   _____

4. Reinforce the sale.

   GOAL _____

   _____

KEY TIPS

☑ Closing is not the centerpiece of a sale, around which all other elements are built—the Investigate and Probe phases are the core of IMPACT Selling. Tying up the sale is a natural outgrowth of performing the other five steps successfully; it is an orderly and simple step taken deliberately after the other steps have been completed. Think of the process as enjoyable and exciting—both for you and for the prospect.

☑ Strive to make it clear to your prospect that both of you are sitting on the same side of the negotiating table. Two key factors in this are (1) a clear understanding of the conditions under which the prospect will buy and (2) a strong bond of trust between you and the prospect. With both of those firmly established, your prospects will trust that your interest lies in helping them get what they want.

☑ Use the "Feel, Felt, Found" formula to clear away last-minute objections. "I understand how you feel about..." "Many of my clients have felt the same way..." "But they found that..."

☑ Use trial closes throughout the interview by moving toward the close before you actually get there. Remember to toss them a monkeyfist and see if they tie the close up for you.

☑ Never rush out of the door after the order is signed. Take time to reinforce the wisdom of new customers choices with compliments and by inviting them to buy more.

PART III

KNOWING YOURSELF

CHAPTER 11

VALUES AND SALES SUCCESS

It is harder to hide feelings we have than to feign those we lack.
Francis de LaRochefoucauld

Value systems in our society have shifted dramatically during the last two decades. The new values demand a totally different approach to selling than those that were in favor under the preceding value systems. These value shifts have occurred not only for buyers, but for sellers as well. IMPACT Selling demands a new value structure. As Bob Dylan sang, *The Times They Are A–Changin'!*

Unfortunately, when I first entered the sales profession, I was taught that the way to sell was through manipulation, intimidation, and domination. Our training back then stressed that the best way to get appointments was to stretch the truth about the real purpose of our calls, that the only real way to sell was to pressure our customers, and that selling was "only a numbers game." The old game plan was to hit an area quickly, talk fast, and set people up for the "power close." The Golden Rule took on a new twist, rephrased to say, "Do unto others, then get out!"

Sadly, that once popular approach to sales is still taught by some trainers and corporations today. Only a short time ago, one of the most popular sales-training books was *Selling Through Intimidation*. High-pressure tactics, trick closes, and speed-talking techniques continue as the foundation of far too many sales-training systems. Even today there are occasional releases of books guaranteed to teach you how to "power sell" your way to success through so-called hardball techniques.

Companies that trust their futures to those tired techniques will not survive in the competitive and tightly niched markets of the 1990s. Salespeople who trust their careers to those simple and out-dated methods will languish right along with the companies that espouse them. Salespeople and organizations who trust their careers and business success to their personal credibility will thrive.

This new idea also contrasts markedly with the old-school philosophy that sought out people who had the *personality* for sales. A good personality for sales may well produce short-range sales success, but today's demanding and busy customers are unlikely to place their faith solely in a winning sales personality. A reputation for honesty must be built on a level deeper than personality. Long-range sales success will rely on the credibility one has as a *person*.

More salespeople than ever before now recognize that personal credibility is the most vital ingredient for success in selling. Today's successful salesperson relies not on making single sales nor on tricking customers into buying, but on a multifaceted strategy of long-range, repeat business and customer referrals, grounded in a reputation as an honest and highly credible person.

CREDIBILITY UNLOCKS THE DOOR TO SUCCESS

Since we know that most people get tense in crowds, it follows that crowded marketplaces will also make buyers tense. The greatest personal challenge you face today is overcoming the tension that exists in a highly crowded selling environment.

Behavioral psychologists have a term known as *territorial imperative*. Most graphically evident in lower animals, it is nonetheless true with humans: Virtually every living creature marks out an area that he or she will defend against all intruders. When that personal space is invaded, its owner examines the intruder carefully to determine if it is *friend* or *foe*. Only when one trusts the intruder will he or she relax. Without credibility, you will remain an untrusted intruder.

If your credibility can transform this natural tension into trust, you will have a greater chance to break through its resistance and close the sale. Failure to establish credibility with your prospects will reduce you to merely another face in the bustling crowds of salespeople they see daily. Your credibility is the key to your prospects' view of you as an honorable person.

CREDIBILITY BEGINS WITH HIGH SELF-ESTEEM

Often, people with low credibility have no clue why their reputations suffer. They know that deep down inside they are honest people, yet they fail to convey that conviction to others. The reasons for that failure are usually based on the nonverbal communications they send out to people around them.

Communications experts have made it common knowledge that more than 80 percent of the signals we send to others are communicated nonverbally. That means that for every statement you make, you send four nonverbal signals to your prospect. Every contact you make with your prospects must be an action that tells them you are trustworthy. Always assume that your every action is under scrutiny to see whether you should be allowed into the prospect's personal space. See how much sense this idea makes in light of my earlier affirmation: "People won't long remember what you said, but they'll never forget how you made them feel." Most of the signals that determine how you make people feel are in that nonverbal 80 percent category.

More than any other single factor, the way you see yourself determines the way others see you. Your self-image shapes everything you say and do. It shows up in the way you dress, walk, talk, sit, laugh, and in what you do with your eyes and hands. People watch all these signals when they decide whether to trust you and believe what you say. Therefore, a salesperson with low self-esteem will transmit his or her internal struggle to prospects. The prospect senses that something is amiss and never trusts the salesperson enough to open up his or her personal space. Therefore, the most direct route to high credibility is through high self-esteem.

We have found a very clear and straightforward relationship between low self-esteem, low credibility, and low sales performance. Unfortunately, we have also discovered that many salespeople suffer from very low self-esteem. By the same token, many have almost no self-confidence. This may be evident in a reluctance to make eye contact, in an unkempt appearance, in a timid speaking voice, or in stilted gestures. Low self-esteem is sometimes also reflected in flamboyance, a loud voice, and boisterous laughter. (Paradoxically, our research further indicates that many people with low self-esteem often exhibit unusually high levels of achievement drive.)

The good news is that the converse is also true: High self-esteem leads to high credibility and high credibility with prospects results in increased sales performance. Therefore, a major step toward sales success is to eliminate low self-esteem.

ATTACKS ON YOUR SELF-ESTEEM

The selling profession often takes a toll on our self-esteem. There are three particular hazards inherent in selling that often create self-image problems:

- Value dilemmas.
- Cognitive dissonance.
- Fear of rejection.

Let's look at all three in depth.

Value Dilemmas

Being forced or asked to make a choice between sentiments or qualities that cause conflict between actual and ideal values places one in a value dilemma. As the selling world gets steadily more competitive, more salespeople will inevitably face these value dilemmas. They will see ever increasing demands by employers for more travel, higher quotas, and greater personal sacrifices to the company. Customers will also add to the increased pressures by demanding value-added extras that require much more of a salesperson's time than the old tactics of pure demonstration selling.

The increased demands on the personal lives of salespeople will force many to choose between social and family demands and professional demands. As today's crowded markets become even more crowded, selling will become more of a *call to duty* than a job, demanding more time and requiring more psychic energy than ever before. These value dilemmas for salespeople can be reduced if salespeople understand that selling today is a highly demanding *profession* and not merely a *job* to pick up some quick money. Understanding the new sales demands and accepting the new value structure of today's markets will be essential in order for new-entry salespeople to be able to remain in the *profession* for the long-term.

Cognitive Dissonance

This is a psychologist's way of saying that you feel you are acting in a way that is inconsistent with the way you see yourself. As a salesperson, cognitive dissonance may begin when you are trained to manipulate prospects or treat them abusively, or even unethically. Trouble may also develop when, under threat of losing your job, you are told to stretch the truth, hide certain facts, or cover up for poor quality or service. Maybe you have found yourself tempted to stretch the truth when dealing with prospects because you think it will help close a sale. Any of those occurrences can cause stress in an honest person who respects other people. Unethical selling techniques most often require you to act very differently than how you feel you should act.

Your personal reputation with your customers is one of your most valuable assets as a salesperson. In fact, in today's crowded marketplace, it could be *the* most valuable asset you have. In addition, you must be able to assure your customers of quality products or service. Never make claims you cannot back up. You do not have to work for any organization or individual who knowingly misleads customers. There are plenty of honest and reputable businesses that are looking for honest salespeople. You must never squander your reputation on the few who may operate unethically when faced with the challenges of a shrinking market share. When you honestly represent a reputable company, you eliminate cognitive dissonance. Your prospects will notice the difference and will feel comfortable with their sense of your inner peace.

Fear of Rejection

Get enough doors slammed in your face and you can begin to feel very low, even to the point of fearing your next sales call. Overcoming the fear of rejection is a simple matter of knowing that "No" is a normal part of the selling game. More importantly, if you do not hear "No" regularly, you are not talking to enough prospects. Fear of rejection becomes a problem only when it creates a reluctance to make sales calls or to ask for an order when it is time for the close. No one relishes rejection, but it is not a catastrophe. In fact, rejection is a key part of a sales professional's success cycle! In truth, it is only a minor stop along the road to hearing a lot of yes responses.

All buyers perceive values differently. If your product or service does not represent sufficient value to one prospect to get them to make a buying decision, that does not mean it lacks value for everyone. While your company determines the cost of a product or service, your buyers must figure their own perceived benefit and perceived price. Therefore, the Value equation—based on perceived benefit and perceived price—indirectly proves that rejection has nothing to do with you as a person. You are not responsible for the outcome of your prospects' value judgments unless you knowingly represent poor value.

Once you have eliminated those three major causes of low self-esteem, your body language will move you toward a new image in the eyes of your prospects. This new image will build credibility.

THE FOUNDATION OF YOUR SELF-ESTEEM

I have now shown that long-range success in IMPACT Selling requires credibility that in turn is based on high self-esteem. Yet, I have not discussed how your self-esteem is founded on your values and your deepest motivations. If you never ask yourself what your motivations are, you may be driven subconsciously only by the fastest buck you can pick up. This may put you into a state of cognitive dissonance. To avoid this threat to your self-esteem, you must be in touch with your own value structure.

To have confidence in your abilities in order to excel in sales, you must know that you operate on a higher value level than immediate monetary rewards. You need to be primarily motivated by a deep-seated desire to help people find what they want most and to help them get it.

As we have worked with tens of thousands of salespeople through our seminars and consulting experiences, we have been surprised to discover how many of them have only a vague idea of what their value structure truly is and how they formed it. It is also surprising how many people invest their lives in pursuits that do not reflect their own values. Failing to follow your own values will never lead you to true success or happiness, yet nearly everyone we work with says they are trying to become successful and happy.

It is one thing to say you want to be successful or happy in life, but it is often quite another to have a clear vision of precisely what success and happiness mean to you. What are your chances of finding something if you do not know what it looks like? Without a clear vision of your own definition of success and happiness, you are unlikely to find them no matter how long you search. Therefore, connecting with your own inner value structure is the key to success and happiness that will truly satisfy your deepest needs.

I will now complete this chapter with four basic topics on values. The first one concerns connecting with your own value structure and will help you see what individual values really drive you. In the next one, you will learn to evaluate whether you have found your actual values or your ideal values. After that, I present clues for setting a course toward success based upon your own value system and bring your actual values and ideal values into alignment. Finally, the last topic will tie everything together, giving you the peaceful inner harmony that results from your ideals matching reality.

Your value structure lies at the core of your sales success, representing the new order in selling in crowded niche markets. It is what truly drives human performance in the long-term after the hype of pop psychology and pep rallies has worn off.

DISCOVERING HOW YOUR VALUES ARE FORMED

Tell me about the subcultures you have lived and worked in and I can tell you a great deal about your values.

Our values are deeply intertwined with the subcultures where we have lived and worked. Our values concurrently shape and are shaped by our choice of subcultures. On the one hand, we surround ourselves with those subcultures that reflect our current values. On the other, our values are shaped by the subcultures that surround us. There is much truth to that old saying, "Birds of a feather flock together." It reflects our tendency to seek out those people and groups that value the same things we do. Here is one example.

If one of your highest values is physical fitness, you probably spend a lot of time around gymnasiums or other athletic establishments because you enjoy the company of other physical fitness enthusiasts.

"Oh, no!" you might protest, "I only go there for the equipment!"

"You could buy your own equipment."

You shake your head, "Can't afford it."

Yet you could buy a complete home gym system for the cost of only a few years of health club memberships. If you disliked contact with the physical fitness subculture, you would buy your own equipment and avoid people you dislike. Your choice to join a club instead shows how we choose subcultures that value the same things we value.

Though immersed in subcultures that we have chosen because of our shared values, we regularly rub elbows with people with whom we share only one—or at most a few—values.

Some people detest the values of people they work with everyday. While they may try to get along with their co-workers, when quitting time comes they escape like the place was on fire. Nonetheless, if we work around people long enough, we will find ourselves talking, thinking, and even acting somewhat as they do.

Let me illustrate from my experience as a football coach and college administrator.

I did not think of myself as an academic because, as a coach, I never felt I completely meshed in with the academic subculture. Yet, my role as a college administrator kept me feeling a little on the outside with the other coaches. Both of those subcultures had a lot to do with making my value system what it is today.

My exposure to the academic environment had a great deal to do with the high value I place on education, on the way I talk, and on the way I teach and conduct seminars. Similarly, the discipline I learned during my time in the athletic subculture strengthened my strong sense of teamwork and my high achievement ethic.

We all pick up both positive and negative values from all our subcultures as we go through life. The big question is, "Do your subcultures *determine* your values, or do they *reflect* your values?" On the surface that may appear to be an empty riddle, but if you examine it more deeply, you will see that it is a very crucial question.

ARE YOU AN AFFECTIVE OR AN EFFECTIVE PERSON?

A leading psychologist observed that all of us have both an *affective* and and *effective* side. Only one letter is different between the two words, yet the difference in their meanings is great. Our effective side is the part of us that *affects* other people. Our affective side has to do with how much *effect* other people have on us.

We all do both affecting and effecting but with some people one side is dominant. Problems arise when the affective side dominates. This takes place when we live according to the way our subcultures affect us instead of having an impact on the people who surround us. When this happens, we are allowing others to choose for us what matters, what we believe in, and how we spend our time. Life's real winners lean toward the effective side.

It is one thing to be influenced by your subculture in minor ways, such as picking up a local accent after living in a community for a long time. It is entirely different when the influence is pernicious, shaping our lives against our own deeper values and making us predominately affective. Effective people choose for themselves and influence others more than they are influenced by them. Thus the question, "Are you an affective or an effective person?" becomes one that you should answer for yourself.

HOW TO CONNECT WITH YOUR OWN VALUE SYSTEM

If I could inspire you to do but one thing, it would be to connect with your own deepest values and never settle to invest a moment in anything less. Though that sounds simple enough, you will recall that I have consistently stressed that many things that sound simple are not easy. There is a big difference between simple and easy. It is simple to run a marathon, but it is not easy. It is simple to break a negative habit, but it is not easy. It is simple to truly listen to a prospect, but it is not easy. It is simple to identify a prospect, but it is not easy to get him or her to sign an agreement. It is simple to follow IMPACT selling ... but it is not so easy to actually implement the process on a consistent and regular basis.

Connecting and staying in touch with your deepest personal values is a tough and unending challenge. It requires serious thought. You must ask yourself difficult questions and carefully analyze your actions and attitudes. Nevertheless, it is the only way you can truly know what values drive you. It is the only way to attain your highest sales potential.

Before dealing with specific techniques for connecting with one's deepest values, we must separate them into two categories: *Ideal Values* and *Actual Values*.

Ideal values are the ones we prefer to think of as the driving forces behind all our attitudes and actions. They represent our idealized principles. Our actual values are those values that make us do what we do all day, every day. There is often a significant difference between the two.

To separate your ideal values and your actual values and then connect with them both, you will need to ask yourself some frank questions. I have developed a list of questions to point you in the right direction. For now, just read through them. They are repeated at the end of this chapter so that you may examine them in depth after you have finished it. You should take time then to seriously consider how your answers affect your actions and attitudes, both in your personal life and in the world of professional selling.

- What is my personal definition of success? My personal definition of sales success? If I became very successful, what would my life be like? Ideal Value? Actual Value?
- What three principles most frequently guide my decisions and actions? Ideally? Actually?
- What three qualities do I consider most essential for reaching personal and professional success as I define it?
- What excites me more than anything else in the world?
- What is my greatest treasure?
- What is my greatest fear in life?
- What is my primary consideration in making decisions about Money? Career? Relationships? Time allocations?
- What percentage of my time is spent in direct and active pursuit of my ideal of success?
- What priority do I place on the following areas of life: Career? Family? Financial security? Recreation? Spiritual and mental growth?
- How would I most like to change my life?

* What will my life be like ten years from now if I continue in my present direction?

Those ten questions are relatively simple, but this is one case where simple happens to be easy. While each question requires some thought—and the more thought you put into them, the more productive they will become for you—you should be able to answer them easily. Your answers to these questions will direct your future actions, serving as a guide to your sales career.

Once you have answered those questions, you will be more strongly connected to your current value system. With the strength of that connection renewed, you will be ready to move on to understanding your knowledge of your current values.

UNDERSTANDING YOUR OWN VALUE STRUCTURE

Although answering the questions may be easy, understanding your answers is a different matter. Although understanding may be simple, it will not be easy. It may get confusing. Here are some examples of dilemmas that may be raised by answering the questions and understanding your answers:

If your personal definition of success deals only with your career or money, what does that imply about the rest of your life? Defining success only in financial terms cannot possibly meet all your needs as a total human being.

Also consider what it means if some of your answers conflict with one another. For instance, if you define success primarily in financial terms, then rank your family at a higher priority than your career in another question, you clearly have a conflict in ideal values and actual values. This is a classic value dilemma. Such a conflict should be reason for a significant assessment of your actions and attitudes. A failure to deal with this conflict could very easily lead to ultimate failure as a salesperson regardless of an individual's level of selling skills, product knowledge, best intentions, or level of motivation.

Fully understanding your values is complex because it is multifaceted; it is both an event and a process. It is an event because it involves doing something in a deliberate way at a specific moment. Yet, it is a process because it is never truly finished. Your life changes continually, thereby causing your values to evolve continually.

DECIDING WHICH VALUES TO KEEP
AND WHICH TO THROW OUT

A value is any principle, quality, or thing we make a priority in our lives. It is a quality that we rank higher or lower than another quality. Not all values are equal; some will be more important than others and some may be utterly destructive to us.

The priority we place on any one thing at any one time will change as we pass through the various stages of our lives. Our values will evolve depending on our circumstances. For example, a young adult with a growing family would place a high priority on developing a solid base of financial security. That high priority item will shift with age and will drive the young person's actions in vastly different ways as retirement approaches.

Achieving success can be a value. Working hard can also be a value—so can laziness. Success in a sales career (and in other areas of your life) relies on how you set your priorities. Your prioritization of values determines your *personal culture*. If a mismatch occurs between your personal culture and your corporate culture, your value structure will face a value dilemma. Success and happiness in your career therefore depend upon understanding your value structure.

One technique to use in studying your value structure is to see how your actions on the high priority items in your life affect and interact with the other lower priorities. Again, let us use physical fitness as an example. If you place a high priority on fitness, it will be one of your values. While that is an excellent value to hold, you must always season your values with good judgment. Whatever we set out to do, we need to be in good enough shape to do it. Yet if we get so caught up in building a strong, slim, healthy body that we leave no time for our families or our mental development, we can easily become so depressed that we do not have the drive even to keep our bodies fit—much less anything else.

Some values are so idealized that they can be detrimental to us. For instance, a person who places physical beauty at the top of his or her priority list will one day lose that highly valued item. Sooner or later age will catch up, resulting in a rude awakening. That discovery will impart a sense of failure. We can become terribly disheartened when we choose an ideal value that is impossible to control. Some people live in a constant state of frustration due to their inability to actualize their ideal values. One way to recognize those people is that they always seem to be at war with themselves. They are torn between their ideal values and the actual conditions in which they live. Your sense of inner peace can serve as a sentry to warn you if you have adopted a value that is too highly idealized.

One key to living peacefully with yourself, then, is to learn how to sort through your values to determine which ones to keep and which to throw out. When your value priority list is properly aligned with reality, your inner peace will tell you so. Therefore, if you do not have inner peace, the true question becomes that of how to select realistic values. The best guidance I can give you about how to do that is to concentrate on changing what you can and accepting those things that you can do nothing about—and to be perceptive enough to know the difference.

Always be aware of whether or not your most highly prized values are things you can change. If you do not have any control over those values, you will experience the negative emotion of unending frustration. Recall that in Chapter 4, I introduced the idea that buying is basically an emotional response. Since that is true, it is essential to your success that you do not exhibit negative emotions that will translate into negative emotions in your prospects. To achieve your highest selling potential, you must eliminate the negative emotions that value conflicts will generate within yourself. Though you may believe you can keep them inside, I can guarantee you they will be exhibited in your professional environment. It is clear that there will continue to be a great deal of anxiety and competitive pressure in the finely niched marketplaces of the 1990s. With this vast amount of environmentally imposed anxiety, the last thing a sales professional needs is a battle with internal feelings that can result in a diffused, confused, and weakened level of performance.

FORGING A VALUE SYSTEM

Once you complete the list of ten questions and evaluate your answers, you will see a set of values that guides your decisions and actions. Whether you recognize it or not, you are operating under that value structure right now. You may have carefully and consciously chosen this value system or you may have allowed the subculture and circumstances in which you live to choose it for you. One thing is certain, though: You would never have opened this book if you were not operating under some sort of existing value system.

Sadly, many sales and sales management people simply take life as it comes and allow their value judgments to be made for them. I compare these people to a flounder. A flounder will merely lie on the ocean floor and soak up whatever floats by it. What floats by may be richly nourishing food, or it may be poisoned with pollution. The flounder will just take it in and build its life around whatever drifts past. Flounders are affective. You most likely know lots of flounders.

Those who are not flounders, I liken to trout. These are people who have chosen to live their lives more actively. They know where they want to go and expend themselves in their efforts to get there. If they have to swim upstream against a strong spring current, they will do it to get where they want to go. Trout are the effective people around you.

While it is simple to define the differences between an affective salesperson and an effective salesperson, it is not easy to figure out who fits which category. This even applies to yourself. Unfortunately, many salespeople who are flounders incorrectly think of themselves as strong trout.

Flounders will not be able to survive in today's buyer-driven markets because their way will be to merely sit and wait for prospects to deliver success to them. Success will never drift down to the bottom on which they lie, however, because trout above them will be aggressively pursuing their market. To help ensure that you act like a trout and never like a flounder, I have developed two techniques to help you uncover your current value structure. You can then pursue an active role in turning your ideal values into your actual values.

First, make a list of those facets of your life you consider important, then prioritize those you list. You should include such things as family life, career development, social development, physical fitness, and spiritual and mental growth. Next, write out the two or three overriding principles that guide you in each area.

Keep your list with you and continually check your actions to make sure they are consistent with your value system. Any inconsistencies you discover with this technique will make the difference between your ideal values and actual values obvious.

Second, write out a simple, but complete, statement of the purpose of your life. It should be short enough to be memorized easily, yet complete enough to encompass every area of importance in your life. Then, unlike the flounders who are merely drifting around you, let your statement of purpose become the ultimate value system through which you filter life's pollution. Keeping your statement of purpose in mind will give you the strength to swim upstream against any current. The coming decade will bring swift currents of increasing demands and expectations that will require your very best efforts.

As review, so far in this chapter you have learned how to connect more deeply with your current value system and to use the knowledge from that renewed connection to understand your current values. Next, you learned techniques to modify your value structure so that your ideal values and actual values are more closely aligned with each other and with the current reality of the circumstances in your lives.

Now you need to learn to apply your freshly forged value system to your daily life to produce new results.

RESTRUCTURING YOUR LIFE AROUND YOUR VALUES

These are three things you must do to be your own salesperson amid all the subcultures that surround you.

- You must choose and live by your values.
- You must forge your own self-expectations.
- You must function in a manner consistent with the way you see yourself.

Recall that early in this chapter I told you how 80 percent of your communication signals are nonverbal. Failing to embody all three of the ideals above will frequently cause value dilemmas and cognitive dissonance in your life, which your prospects will sense. So, how do you transmit only positive nonverbal communication? The answer, again, is simple but not easy.

Naturally, you need a better answer than that. To help find the answers you need, we have developed five specific techniques, entitled *Restructuring Clues*. The key element in keeping your life in tune with your own values is to constantly restructure your attitudes and actions around your own continually evolving value system. These clues will help you in that quest.

RESTRUCTURING CLUE #1:
Ultimately, only you can decide.

As has been common knowledge for years, each of us has only one true freedom in life. It is a freedom no one can give to us and no one can take away. Each of us has the freedom to choose how we will react to whatever happens to us, whether it is rampant price-cutting by a financially troubled competitor or a tragedy in your personal life.

You cannot often choose everything that happens to you, but you can—and always do—choose how you will react to what comes along. Just as with most other freedoms in our lives, this freedom brings with it a responsibility. Here, it brings the responsibility of not allowing your choices about values, or your actions based on those values, to be controlled by some subculture.

Ultimately, only you can decide what values will guide you and what you will do about them, but the choices you make will determine the success of your sales career. Your choice may be to adopt the values and practices of one or more of your surrounding subcultures, but that is a choice, nevertheless. Always be aware that whatever your actions, you chose them. If your actions do not bring you external success and/or inner peace, you are free to choose new ones. Have the wisdom to see that this is something you can control.

RESTRUCTURING CLUE #2:
Your attitude determines your actions.

Tell me what you feel and I can tell you what you are most likely to do in almost any given situation. That is because our attitudes determine our actions. In selling, perhaps more than in any other profession, actions determine success. Everything you do and say is observed by your prospects and customers and filed away to help them decide whether to trust you or not.

After more than 2,500 years of philosophy, psychology, and motivational research, no one has come up with a better way to express the relationship between our actions and attitudes than the Hebrew king who said

As ye thinketh in thy heart, so shall ye be.

You are your own person. If you do not like the sort of person you are, or that you are becoming, the place to start changing yourself is in how you think about life and about yourself. You will never be any more than you think you are.

RESTRUCTURING CLUE #3:
Your own actions shape your life.

Scapegoating is one of America's favorite sports. It seems easier to blame our circumstances, our upbringing, or our sub-cultures for everything wrong in our lives than to face the fact that most of what is wrong is the result of our own actions.

Most people who take the flounder approach to life will complain bitterly about the poor quality of the junk that passes by them on life's ocean bottom. They will blame their poor quality of life on the pollution that settles down on them. Yet, they are responsible for their own quality of life because they chose to limit themselves to what drifts past.

If you are not living in harmony with your ideal values, do not waste time fixing blame. You are free to make the choice to be a flounder or a trout. If you expend your energies on positive actions to change your circumstances, you will take the trout's approach to life.

RESTRUCTURING CLUE #4:
Emotions are symptoms—not guides.

Here is an ironic truism: *People who only do what they feel like doing today are bound to spend the rest of their lives unable to do what they feel like doing.*

Part of your continual maturing process is realizing that emotions cannot ultimately be used as the guides for your actions. Emotions will, however, provide valuable signals to show how close to your ideals and values your actions are. Just as a doctor looks at symptoms, you can use your emotions to tell if something is wrong, and even to discover what is wrong. Yet, you must only use your emotions as symptoms, keeping in mind that a clear thought is always superior to an emotion as a guide for your actions.

RESTRUCTURING CLUE #5:
Restructuring is a life-long process.

Many people continue to base their actions on values they held when they were much younger. They are nearly always miserable in their present circumstances. Failure to adjust our values to suit our continually changing circumstances results in a serious disruption in our inner peace.

For example, take the successful college or professional athlete who remains a "jock" throughout his life, one who values the trophies from his past more than he values his future goals. This guy spends much of his time leaning over a beer and talking about the way his life was, instead of facing the way it is and can become. True happiness lies in working now to build hope for the future rather than excessively dwelling on past victories.

The happiest people I know are the ones who always keep their values in harmony with the circumstances and subcultures they find themselves in at any given moment. They concentrate on getting the most out of life now, and in the future, instead of on the ideals they prized when their circumstances were different.

TYING IT ALL TOGETHER

What does all this mean to you as a salesperson trying to identify prospects and convince them to buy your products or services in a progressively competitive environment? Again, the answer is simple but not easy. You can only become truly successful and happy in life when you stay in constant touch with your own ideal values and keep your daily actions in harmony with them. Once again, with all of the turmoil going on in our rapidly changing society—and in your rapidly changing markets—the last thing you need is to have internal turmoil as well.

Take some time to work through the exercise at the end of this chapter. There you will find the questions presented earlier under the subtopic entitled, *How To Connect With Your Own Value System.*

First, use these questions to connect with your value system. Then use the insights you have gained in this critical chapter to understand how your value system affects everything you do. Next, use the Restructuring clues to transform your life into one that embodies your updated value structure. Finally, stay in constant touch with your emotions, using the symptoms they reveal to tell you when your connection with your values is slipping. When you discover that your inner peace is upset, you will know it is time to reread this chapter and repeat the process. This should be an endless cycle for you.

You will not achieve success in today's crowded markets when your internal peace is disrupted or if you lack a solid commitment that is grounded on basic values. By following the techniques I have suggested, you can carefully plot a course for your life that will clarify your own values and bring *every* area of your life into harmony with your own definition of success.

THINK IT THROUGH AND FOLLOW IT THROUGH

Plan and take a definite course of action for the immediate future that will lead you closer to bringing your attitudes and actions into complete harmony with your definition of long-term success.

Don't let the moment pass. Follow through now by answering the ten questions we gave your earlier. Study your answers as a guide to connect with your own personal values:

1. What is my personal definition of success? If I became very successful, what would my life be like?

   Ideal Value? _____

   _____

   Actual Value? _____

   _____

2. What three principles most frequently guide my decision and actions?

   Ideally? 1. _____

   2. _____

   3. _____

Actually? 1. _____

2. _____

3. _____

3. What three qualities do I consider most essential for reaching success as I define it?

1. _____

2. _____

3. _____

4. What excites me more than anything else in the world?

_____

_____

What is my greatest treasure?

_____

_____

5. What is my greatest fear in life?

_____

6. What is my primary consideration in making decisions about

Money? _____

Career? _____

Relationships? _____

Time allocations? _____

7. What percentage of my time is spent in direct and active pursuit of my ideal of success? _____

_____

8. What priority do I place on the following areas of life:

Career? _____

Family? _____

Financial security? _____

Recreation? _____

Spiritual/Mental growth? _____

9. How would I like most to change my life? _____

_____

_____

10. What will my life be like ten years from now if I
continue in my present direction? _____

_____

_____

KEY TIPS

☑ The greatest personal challenge you face today is overcoming the tension that exists in the selling environment. Your credibility can transform this natural tension into trust. Failure to establish credibility with your prospects will reduce you to merely another face in the bustling crowd of salespeople they see daily.

☑ The shortest route to high credibility is through high self-esteem.

☑ Eliminate value dilemmas, cognitive dissonance, and fear of rejection so that your internal sense of peace creates a natural body language that sends out positive signals, instilling trust in your prospects.

☑ Connect with your own deepest values and never settle to invest a moment in anything less . . . *take the test!*

☑ Forge your new value system with these tools: 1) Carry a list that prioritizes the facets of your life you consider most important and 2) Write out a simple, complete statement of the purpose of your life and use it as the ultimate guide to filter out life's pollution that drifts your way.

☑ Emotions are symptoms—not guides. People who only do what they feel like doing today are bound to spend the rest of their lives unable to do what they feel like doing.

CHAPTER 12

PERSON VERSUS PERSONALITY

There is no substitute for talent. Industry and all virtues are of no avail.
Aldous Huxley

Clearly, success in value-based, customer-driven selling requires deeper personal qualities than merely having a good sales personality. Yet, personality has often been mistakenly used as the key issue by sales managers when hiring new salespeople. The common belief is that if a person meets a certain personality profile, he or she will be able to sell.

During the screening of new candidates, one basic question that should be asked is, "Can they sell?" The answer to that question is that almost everyone *can* sell. Mastering the mechanics of IMPACT Selling is easy for most people, and we have seen exceedingly successful salespeople with practically every personality type under the sun. In today's competitive marketplace, personality, by itself, has little to do with selling unless it represents some dreadfully repulsive or negative behavior.

Equipped with that knowledge, a far different and penetrating question needs to be asked about candidates than whether or not they can sell. A better question to ask is, "Will they sell?" This is where we start to see a significant distinction. While nearly everyone *can* sell, not everyone *will*. Many people simply have no interest in sales. Some may be too lazy or undisciplined to put forth the effort required to find and close sales, whereas others may lack the clarity of focus toward key values that is necessary for sales success. Some just do not value selling as a profession. Others may simply not enjoy the sales role and its complex demands.

Although it is possible to identify and hire candidates who will sell, even that is not the ultimate question that needs to be answered. The willingness to sell, by itself, may have been enough in the days when salespeople simply ventured forth armed with a smile, a strong handshake, and a case full of product samples and literature. Ironically, today's highly competitive markets have even moved beyond the penetrating question of, "Will they sell?"

INTELLIGENCE *AND* PERSONALITY

Today, the crucial question to answer in finding successful value-based, customer-oriented salespeople is, "Will they sell our products in this environment?" Now we have become very specific. Just because people can sell a low-priced, high-volume commodity item doesn't mean they can sell big-ticket, long-term, low volume items to a very high-level market.

By the same token, some people perform exceedingly well in a highly structured, bureaucratic, salary-based environment, while others perform peerlessly in an unstructured, independent contractor-oriented sales situation where everything (including pay) is based upon production and bottom line results. Our research has shown conclusively however, that intelligence, in addition to personality, has to be considered as a crucial quality when determining how someone will sell in a specific environment.

This research has revealed that in specific sales fields the intelligence level of successful salespeople fits into a relatively small band on the mental capacity scale. For example, among our clients who sell a demand product on a repetitive basis to relatively unsophisticated buyers, the top sales performers fall between the 40th to 60th percentile in our mental capacity scores. With our clients selling complex, highly expensive products— often exceeding several million dollars—the top performers regularly fall between the 70th and the 90th percentile level.

Though few selling environments require that one be a Mensa Society member to be able to sell successfully, for some, a high level of mental acuity can be an important attribute. For others, it is not nearly as critical a factor. However, one role of management is to properly match intelligence levels with the demands of the specific environment. For instance, in an environment in which very basic products are sold, an exceptionally bright salesperson might become easily and quickly bored while repeatedly making the same simple sales presentation to apprentice buyers. That same bright salesperson, however, could easily find long-term satisfaction and success selling complex products that require complicated transactions with highly alert and demanding executives.

While intelligence is an important factor to consider, personality does, nonetheless, play some role in sales success at all levels of selling. For example, a salesperson with a drab, negative, and introverted personality may find limited success in selling lavish vacation packages to the Mediterranean. By the same token, a salesperson with a superficial, glib personality may just as likely win the trust of very few prospects who were concerned with the detailed data of complex financial transactions.

KEY INTANGIBLE ATTRIBUTE FOR SALES SUCCESS

Though personality and intelligence are clearly important factors in sales success, it is my view and experience that the single personal attribute most essential in driving long-term sales performance is the value structure of the individual salesperson and how well that salesperson's "intangible personal culture" integrates into the cultural configuration of the sales environment in which he or she is functioning. How people perceive and establish priorities relates directly to their sales performance. Long-term success depends upon how salespeople see the world of selling, how they see themselves in that world, and how they prioritize the many demands made on them by today's highly crowded selling environments. And all of these factors must match the priority of activity as determined by the organization of which the salesperson is a part. The closer the fit, the better is the performance; the greater the disparity, the greater is the chance for failure.

How many times have organizations added someone to their sales force who had what appeared to be an outgoing, glittering, powerful personality, only to discover six months later that they person could not perform? What we see in those cases is the true person emerging from the personality. All things being equal, personality is driven by needs, whereas that true, inner person is driven by the all-powerful value structure.

Here's a good story that illustrates the power of value structure over intelligence and personality in sales success. Our firm was contacted by a collection services company that was in a panic over a saleswoman about to ruin its business. Here is the story in the words of our account representative, who was directly involved with the consulting assignment.

The collection company was terribly confused. Recruiting this woman had been a real coup. She had long been number one in sales for a copier company. After years at the top of this fast-paced market, she had tired of its tempo. When she began looking to switch to a more even-tempered market, her search did not take long. With her outstanding credentials, the collection company hired her immediately.

But nothing went right. This woman not only had a terrible sales performance, but the collection company's clients actually hated her. They were calling the office in droves, with comments like 'Get her out of our face, or lose our business forever!'

When they called me, I met with her to administer our battery of assessment instruments. After reviewing her results, I knew immediately that she was wrong for the job. The copier market is very hard-charging. In contrast, the collection agency dealt mostly with hospitals—a very soft, easy-going market. They like to take time to think. She was obviously driving them nuts.

While she apparently fit the classic mold of traditional salespeople, it was all based on personality. The person inside was not well-suited for connecting deeply with people who specialize in very personal, very human problems.

FORGET ABOUT "BORN" SALESPEOPLE

Never again can you hire someone who is reputed to be a "born salesperson." To build a sales force that will succeed in the 1990s, you must advance to the next level. The *sales personality* is just as out-dated as the old-school techniques we have continually warned you to forget.

The personality required for long-range sales success in today's crowded markets is highly variable; the person is not. How people set priorities, what they value most, and their empathy for their fellow human beings is what will ultimately drive sales performance. All reasonably intelligent people can master the IMPACT Selling plan. It is not the steps that trip them up; it is their attitude. While nearly anyone can learn the mechanical steps, achieving long-term success in sales requires the right person. Filling a sales force with the *kind* of people profiled in this chapter will answer the most important question for any sales manager: Will they sell our products in this environment?

The good news is that I have now given you what it takes to perform in today's crowded markets. IMPACT Selling and all its principles have equipped you for long-range, successful performance. Your remaining challenge is to fill your sales force with people whose value structures match what needs to be done. Throughout this book, I have shown you tangible skills that successful salespeople will need. This final chapter outlines intangible attributes necessary for sales success and presents detailed guidance—explained in each of the six IMPACT phases—that will enable managers to evaluate sales candidates and begin to focus on hiring IMPACT sales professionals.

PERSON VERSUS PERSONALITY

Before I get to the individual discussions on personal attributes, here is a story that shows the significance of person over personality.

I worked with a man (let's call him David) who was one of the first people I knew to use a fax machine to close sales. As a person, he was tremendous at building trust, a characteristic especially important in the Meet, Convince, and Tie-It-Up phases. David also had an exceptional sense of timing. He was the Smokey the Bear of sales in that he could sense a close before it even came. His uncanny sense of timing was also relevant in the Meet, Convince, and Tie-It-Up phases. The combination of the two attributes made him a powerful closer.

When David sensed the prospect was ready to buy, he acted as if the prospect had already told him yes and offered to fax his office right there on the spot to get confirmation of the order. His sense of timing was so perfect that he did not want to let the moment pass, so he would say, "Let's do this: Let me write this up now and fax it into our office; that way we'll have immediate confirmation." His prospects were so favorably impressed by the offer of an instant confirmation from the warehouse that they rarely resisted further.

This method would never work with the stereotyped, traditional sales personality. If a salesperson had not built trust and rapport, he or she could appear extremely pushy. If the prospect still had lingering doubts or was beginning to feel trapped, this tactic could easily make him or her feel like the lid was slamming down on "the kill." Instead, David made the customer feel significant by giving the order the high-priority instant attention the customer wanted. The key to David's success was that his value structure enabled him to *intuitively* know when and what to do.

Whatever someone sets as a priority, he or she will tend to do. Keep that truism in mind as you read these personal attributes while factoring in the special requirements of your specific market niche and products. Also, keep your own and your sales staff's individual attributes in mind, carefully noting crossover attributes that may help you identify an unusual strategy like David's

The actions that make a sales IMPACT are Investigate, Meet, Probe, Apply, Convince, and Tie it up. A discussion of seemingly intangible attributes necessary for mastering and implementing IMPACT follows.

INTANGIBLE ATTRIBUTES FOR INVESTIGATION

A carefully devised strategy for the identification of qualified prospects. The game plan where all success in sales begins. The physical activity of prospecting where tangible results are achieved: Prospects are found; appointments are made; and effective, well-presented sales presentations are planned.

Self-Discipline

The ability to marshal one's time and energies to push toward preset goals with minimal diversion.

Self-Starting Capacity

The ability of a person to initiate energies toward the achievement of a goal.

The identification and implementation of concrete, practical ideas and methods that a salesperson can use to identify and achieve goals certainly enhances self-discipline and self-starting abilities. By applying strong and accurate personal motivators, a salesperson can be encouraged to be a self-starter in active pursuit of goals and objectives.

It is essential for salespeople to see their abilities accurately, focusing on reality and not on the abilities others would like for them to have. The ability of a salesperson to exercise self-discipline depends upon that person's mastery of a set of personal evaluation techniques. Therefore, a high level of self-awareness will certainly serve a salesperson extremely well in this area.

To ensure consistently ambitious performance, a salesperson must maintain a positive focus toward achieving results while ensuring that he or she is in touch with his or her own deepest personal motivations.

Realistic Goal Setting

The capacity to set goals that can be achieved with current resources and the ability to perform within a specified time frame.

Realistic goal setting is crucial to the success of any sales performance and is intertwined with several personal characteristics of salespeople. Let us look at two different aspects of goal setting: long-range and short-range. Afterward I present two organizational abilities that will help with each type of planning.

Qualities that clearly aid salespeople in setting realistic long-range goals include role confidence, self-direction, and overall clarity of perception. Low confidence may result in the setting of goals that are aimed too low. One must have drive to achieve established goals. High clarity of perception enables a person to see what is actually happening clearly enough to have a realistic view of the situation. It is necessary to understand both of these to set realistic long-range goals.

Short-range goals, on the other hand, are more directly affected by a person's organizational ability and practical, results-oriented thinking. One commonly found shortcoming in this area is often called "analysis paralysis." This occurs when practical, results-oriented thinking takes a backseat to endless focusing on long-range planning.

Here is a good method to enable one to achieve short-range goals more easily: Establish good long-range goals, divide them up into smaller steps identified as short-range goals, then divide short-range goals into specific activities. Next, move backward through those steps with simple action plans to accomplish the activities that will complete the short-range goals, which in turn will fulfill long-range goals.

Notice that the next two topics, *Concrete Organization* and *Conceptual Organization*, are closely related to how long-range and short-range goal setting are handled.

Concrete Organization

The ability to identify and use resources in the accomplishment of short-range goals.

Good concrete organizational abilities rely on a salesperson's ability to properly allocating resources to accomplish the activities that are identified when long-range goals are divided into short-range goals and activities. Concrete organization is the ability to understand the immediate, concrete needs of a situation and to set an action plan for meeting those needs.

When allocating resources, a salesperson should not limit himself or herself to the readily identifiable physical resources. Success at concrete organization also includes evaluating and using human as well as time resources in achieving goals. Properly allocating resources requires a clear focus on structure and order, practical thinking, and empathy. When those three precepts are followed with proper balance, any salesperson can achieve a high level of concrete organization.

Here is one parting idea on balancing the third precept listed above, empathy. Many sales managers have traditionally felt very little empathy with those who work for them. Failure of a sales manager to consider personal capacities or problems often has a negative effect on the sales force. Yet, one must use caution when employing empathy. Concern for one's staff that goes beyond empathy may make a sales manager more vulnerable to manipulation by some staff members. The same is also true for salespeople who run the risk of being manipulated by prospects and customers.

Conceptual Organization

The ability to evaluate situations and understand long-term needs requirements.

This capacity is more abstract than concrete organizational skills, which may feature more readily observable results. One's abilities at conceptual organization depend on identifying and evaluating resources for long-range goals. Success requires the proper allocation of resources for the development of a plan and the accurate prediction of that plan's outcomes.

The qualities that serve best in this capacity are a focus on viewing structure and order and a person's overall clarity in viewing the world in general. If a salesperson is strong in those qualities, that person can turn long-range projections into reality and make accurate predictions of outcomes such as quotas or sales projections.

Long-Range Planning

The ability to develop strategies and tactics that may not bring immediate rewards yet will be essential in the accomplishment of long-range goals.

Salespeople will have to develop excellent long-range planning skills in order to survive in the crowded marketplaces of the 1990s. Anyone who sacrifices his or her long-range success for short-range, quick-hit sales will seriously undermine his or her ability to prosper in today's markets.

Long-range planning is easiest when it involves a well-known plan that is clearly defined and accepted as sound. Implementing IMPACT Selling gives a sales force the confidence it needs to bypass short-range conquests while allowing it to focus on long-range prosperity.

Once the IMPACT system is in use, salespeople can continue to focus on long-range planning by defining one or two goals that would be major factors in their success. They can then divide these long-range goals into a series of short-range goals, which in turn will be subdivided into identifiable activities. By having small activities to complete, a sales force will have a continual feeling of accomplishment, while moving steadily toward the completion of a larger long-range plan.

Goal Focus

The ability of an individual to maintain a sense of targeted direction in the face of obstacles.

In any endeavor, strong goal focus requires a worthy goal. Yet even clear goal focus alone is not enough. Staying on track toward the completion of long-range goals also requires a proven game plan that everyone believes in. This is another secret to the success of IMPACT Selling because it can serve to improve goal focus among members of any sales force.

When goals are clearly defined, understood, and well-known they can then serve as a rallying point to keep an entire staff on track. Despite short-range obstacles that may cause minor setbacks, the attainment of the long-range plan will always be clear when the IMPACT Selling philosophy is adapted.

Sales managers should never assume that a sales staff remembers the long-range goal. Such very basic tools as public bulletin boards and memos or newsletters can help to keep the target clearly in sight. It is much easier to focus on a goal that can be clearly seen.

Handling Rejection

Maintaining a positive self-image in the face of personal or professional rejection.

Americans are conditioned to admire winners. Nobody remembers who finished second unless the losers were defeated so soundly that it was particularly humiliating. Culturally, we all listen to the subtle programming we have grown up with and often see the true value in our lives only in those things we can measure as goals or performance.

In our hearts, we all know that we are valuable as human beings, yet we have been taught that we must logically justify our existence. Failure to *measure up* often makes us feel we have no value. On any given day, any salesperson can fail to measure up. Therefore, the selling profession often takes a toll on self-esteem. Sales managers must be continually alert to the feelings of their sales force when its members fail to close sales, especially if one person experiences a string of rejections.

A major task for salespeople is to learn to separate a professional refusal from a personal rejection. Each individual salesperson must clearly understand that his or her performance on the closing of a sale does not change his or her unique self-worth. Staying focused on the long-range success that IMPACT Selling promises is a very clear way to maintain that direction. Continual focus on a solid, proven plan will take the pain out of the inevitable daily rejections that all salespeople face. Quite frankly, if salespeople never hear "No," it is because they are not seeing enough prospects.

Persistence

The ability to maintain continuity in one's actions regardless of obstacles and diversions.

Persistence is the ability to have continuity in one's actions, and to remain on a predesigned course of action though encountering problems during the process of completing the action. Our research clearly shows that highly successful salespeople tend to be good at both goal focus and at results orientation.

Thinking on One's Feet

The ability to quickly identify the critical elements of a situation and to develop effective alternatives.

Intuitive Insight

The capacity to evaluation "gut" feelings and instincts and to make decisions based on those feelings.

It is difficult to think correctly on one's feet without the benefit of the subtle connections that intuitive insight brings. To best tap their intuitive insight, salespeople should make an effort to keep one personal item about each person they deal with in the back of their mind. It is also important to remember that they are only one element in the very full and busy life of every person they talk with. Having only limited personal information about a person, salespeople are probably not as sensitive as they ought and need to be. When one is sensitive to the personal side of the people one deals with, one can rely on hunches, feelings, and "gut" instincts when interacting with them. Having some personal information as background enables salespeople to channel those feelings into an accurate and powerful evaluation process, thereby improving the accuracy of their interpersonal agenda.

Effective salespeople are aware of the continual, nonverbal communication that occurs between people. There is much more to it than simply having an awareness of body language, although knowledge of the well-studied area of nonverbal communication will certainly be helpful in evaluating personal situations. The more a salesperson knows about a person and his or her circumstances, the better the salesperson can interpret and apply what he or she sees.

Salespeople must watch for warning flags in this area. Sales professionals who feel a tug at their heartstrings each time they deal with a prospect have become too close. Salespeople should strive to keep all interactions as objective as possible and regularly evaluate their interactions from a logical, does-this-make-sense point of view.

Self-Confidence

The belief in one's ability to effectively execute responsibilities.

People may clearly see their value as unique individuals, yet their cultural conditioning has taught them to value themselves more in terms of their ambitions or their roles in life. This causes many people to not regard themselves as unique, valuable entities apart from their goals or functions. For salespeople to maintain a high level of self-confidence, it is essential that they learn to value themselves as unique entities apart from their roles or ambitions.

At issue here are the problems encountered when a competent salesperson who constantly strives for the highest ideals finds rejection. Salespeople must learn that a professional refusal by a prospect is not a personal affront. Although there will certainly be isolated times when that may be true, that type of situation points to other problems. Even in cases where refusal or rejection is the result of sales incompetence, the salesperson's focus should be on improving a *skill level*, enriching product knowledge, or uncovering a better qualified prospect—not on internalizing rejection as a personal affront or as a negative measure of self-worth.

INTANGIBLE ATTRIBUTES FOR MEETING

Engaging prospects personally. Turning resisters into active participants. Breaking down mental barriers and involving prospects in the sales process. Reducing tension, establishing trust, and building rapport to lower mental and emotional barriers. Starting a successful sales presentation.

Initiative

The ability to take action and marshall one's energies toward the completion of a task. The power, ability, or instinct to begin or follow through with a plan or task.

One's initiative can have a dramatic impact on one's success in certain selling fields. Without sufficient initiative, a salesperson could end up sitting around watching the clock all day and wondering what happened to the time. Although a salesperson with low initiative might do well at selling in a retail store, most of today's crowded niche markets will offer little success to a salesperson who doesn't have initiative. No one can succeed in the Meet phase without the initiative to go out and actually meet prospects.

Attitude toward Others

The capacity to maintain an open and receptive feeling toward others.

One's attitude toward others is strongly connected to one's ability to benefit from intuitive insight. Maintaining a positive, open, and objective feeling toward others allows a salesperson to more fully tune in to their nonverbal communications.

An improper attitude, such as that based on prematurely judging others could cause a salesperson to miss the messages prospects send their way. Salespeople need to be careful not to judge a situation based on how they think it *ought* to be. With an improper attitude, it is easy to override the logical progression of a relationship, blocking normal interactions.

Also, an attitude of fear on a salesperson's part could equally sabotage their nonverbal communication link by causing him or her to exercise an unnecessary degree of caution early in the relationship. It is essential, therefore, to keep an open mind. Then, when evaluating a person or beginning a new relationship, be that relationship personal or professional, a salesperson will be prepared to maximize his or her understanding of that person based on a full range of communication.

Relating with Others

The ability to interact in a meaningful and productive way that enables one to develop rapport and trust.

The salespeople who are the absolute best at relating with others are those with a high degree of intuitive insight and a positive attitude toward other people. If one has very few preconceived ideas of what others should be and an honest concern for others, then his or her intuitive insight can work wonders toward relating to people he or she meets.

We have found that salespeople who relate poorly to others are often trying to present an image different from the image they have of themselves. Since few salespeople are accomplished con artists, they will rarely present a polished picture of their false image. When a business prospect senses any insincerity from a salesperson, he or she will no longer feel comfortable. Of course, it is well-known that buyers who are uneasy with a salesperson make few positive buying decisions. Those salespeople who relate well with others are good at establishing rapport and building the trust that is needed to put prospects at ease.

Objective Listening

The capacity to pay attention to another's point of view without bias.

The key word in this definition is *bias*. After reading the last two attributes, *attitude toward others* and *relating with others*, it should be clear that people who listen with bias or prejudice will have a filter on what they hear. Without objective listening, a salesperson will not be able to connect with a prospect's deepest values and find his or her chief dominant need.

Evaluating Others

Making realistic and accurate assessments about others.

A person's ability to evaluate others is based on intuitive insight and logical, practical thinking ability. Since you have just read how a person's attitude toward others can block intuitive insight, it is clear that one's attitude can aid or hinder that person's ability to evaluate other people correctly.

Once a salesperson can *accurately* evaluate another person's strengths and weaknesses, he or she can understand their actions, which can then lead to an understanding of the other person's thinking. Without an accurate evaluation a salesperson may miss a great opportunity. A good example would be a salesperson with a strong prejudice against explaining technical terms to female buyers. He may assume that women cannot understand technical information. Of course that absurdly prejudiced attitude is not based on any accurate data or objectivity. Without taking the time to discover the buyer's true talents, the salesman might never discover that she is the only person in the company who can accurately assess the need for his product.

A tip for achieving one's best in this area is to list the pros and cons about a person and then make an objective evaluation based on this objective listing. With a proper, open-minded attitude, this list will include things that the salesperson may have picked up through intuitive insight. Practice with this technique can improve one's ability to evaluate others objectively.

Sense of Timing

Knowing when to take appropriate action.

Having a good sense of timing enables salespeople to look at the whole picture and effectively evaluate how their immediate request or action fits into the current situation. Good timing will make a salesperson's actions and decisions effective, accurate, and timely.

Salespeople with the best sense of timing also have a high level of intuitive insight. Good timing is not just "being lucky"; it involves knowing how to say the right thing at the right time. There is no better way to ensure that than to have learned what a prospect wanted to hear and to be ready when the nonverbal communication tells the salesperson that the prospect is ready to hear it.

A salesperson's focus on getting results can also improve timing. In a meeting with a prospect, for instance, one should remain constantly focused on the single goal of discovering and meeting his or her needs. This level of connection with the prospect will give salespeople a better sense of timing than they would have had if they had focused merely on getting to the end of a canned pitch, because you will each be striving to achieve the same result. Good timing will tell a salesperson when to move from the Meet phase to the Probe phase.

INTANGIBLE ATTRIBUTES FOR PROBING

Helping people discover what they need and want most. Finding out what people will buy, when they will buy, and under what conditions they will buy, then listening them into buying. Enabling prospects to focus on and verbalize their needs and wants.

Self-Confidence

The belief in one's ability to execute responsibilities effectively.

The importance of self-confidence was discussed in the Investigate phase. In the Probe phase, it is an important attribute because here the IMPACT salesperson has a much larger responsibility than merely reciting a "canned sales pitch." Since the

Probe phase bears the burden of anchoring the remaining steps of the IMPACT system, it is essential that a salesperson have the self-confidence to ask well-focused questions on which to build the remaining steps.

Questioning Strengths

Developing and maintaining the inner confidence to ask probing questions openly and aggressively.

This attribute is closely related to self-confidence, described above. With a solid sense of self-confidence, a salesperson will have no difficulty facing prospects while asking questions during the Probe phase. A good tension-relieving technique in any questioning phase is to know that one is a skillful listener who will put the answers to the questions that are asked to good use. That idea leads naturally to the next topic: *Accurate Listening*.

Accurate Listening

The ability to assess correctly what is being heard.

In the Probe chapter, I provided the best tip on developing one's ability to listen accurately: Get a leather binder and a pen and direct total concentration and attention to what the prospect says while taking accurate notes. This element of IMPACT Selling is crucial as preparation for moving on to the Apply phase.

Understanding Prospects' Needs

Accurately assessing the deepest wants and needs of others.

A salesperson will find plenty of tips on getting to the heart of a prospect's chief dominant need when he or she has a strong sense of *intuitive insight*, discussed earlier in this chapter in the Investigate section.

Patience with People

The ability of an individual to see and accept others as they are and to allow others to proceed at their own pace.

Always remember that some people feel pressured when the salesperson senses it is time for the close and hands them the agreement. No two people will be ready to make a decision at the same time in a presentation. Therefore, salespeople must keep their intuitive insight in high gear for signs that their actions make prospects uncomfortable. If there is any sense of any uneasiness, the salesperson should lay the agreement aside and drop back to some more Probe questions to uncover the true reasons why they are feeling hesitant. A salesperson should never show any signs of frustration with the prospect's inability to make a decision on the *salesperson's* personal timetable.

Goal Focus

The ability of an individual to maintain a sense of targeted direction in the face of obstacles.

This definition was thoroughly discussed in the Investigate section. The same principles reviewed there apply here as well.

INTANGIBLE ATTRIBUTES FOR APPLYING

Assuring prospects that you understand their needs and then showing how a product or service will meet those needs. Unlike traditional demonstration selling, it is the process of meeting the stated or implied needs of the prospect. Showing and telling with power, continually building value, and finding out how prospects feel about what they see, hear, and experience.

Evaluating What to Do

Identification of critical elements in a situation and the development of a plan to resolve issues or needs.

Salespeople who cannot identify the critical elements in specific situations are destined to be stuck performing outdated demonstration selling. Today's crowded niche markets demand salespeople who can develop a flexible plan to resolve issues and fulfill needs in dynamic and varying situations. Since the key to sales success lies in applications selling, salespeople are best able to evaluate what to do when they have good problem-solving skills.

Problem Solving

The identification and evaluation of alternate solutions and the selection of the best options for resolution.

This attribute is at the heart of the new focus for salespeople today: You will no longer be successful selling products; you must sell solutions and fulfill needs (i.e. Application Selling). Salespeople today, more than ever, need well-developed problem-solving skills to build value for their prospects by showing the prospects how to apply their products or services.

Using Common Sense

The ability to see and understand situations in practical terms and to see and understand development of functional solutions.

Common sense is more akin to a reflex than to a value. Reflexes are difficult to learn, whereas values can constantly be upgraded. You most likely have plenty of common sense or you would not be working so intently to improve your career with this book. Nevertheless, it is a valuable quality for sales success and you must view it as if it were a value.

We have observed that common sense is closely akin to a person's practical thinking ability, organizational ability, and capacity to see the varied dimensions of the world clearly. Sales is a real world venture that requires a high degree of common sense applied on a consistent and regular basis. Without common sense, a salesperson is doomed to a common, rather than superlative, career.

Having a positive attitude toward others can help anyone to see these dimensions of the world more clearly. A salesperson could, therefore, develop a positive attitude toward others as a first step toward improving their common sense.

One's practical thinking ability can be augmented by one's intuitive thinking. Since intuitive thinking can be improved by a positive attitude and a basic awareness of body language, a salesperson could improve his or her practical thinking ability by attending training sessions to develop nonverbal communication skills.

Finally, to be sucessful, salespeople must learn to master fundamental organizational skills. It is a simple matter to learn the value of accurate record keeping, scheduling diaries, and other tools that aid salespeople's organizational abilities. We have found that a highly organized person is better able to reach accurate, objective decisions that enhance common sense.

Concrete Organization

The ability to identify and use resources in the accomplishment of short-range goals.

This attribute is equally important for sales success here in the Apply phase as it is for the Investigate phase, where it was thoroughly discussed.

Personal Flexibility

The capacity to adjust to changes in plans caused by unforeseen circumstances.

In traditional demonstration selling, salespeople could succeed without being flexible because they only had to present a standard, rehearsed pitch. Today's value-based selling requires flexibility to be able to adapt to the unique needs of each individual prospect.

However, it *is* possible to be *too* flexible. An IMPACT sales professional must maintain enough flexibility to meet specific needs, yet be able to stay on track well enough to adhere to the IMPACT Selling plan phase-by-phase without skipping steps.

Persuading Others

The ability to convince others to adopt a new point of view.

People who excel in this area can see and speak from another person's point of view. The skill to persuade others depends upon one's intuitive insight and the ability to think clearly on one's feet. Remember that important adage, "Show a person what they want most and they will move heaven and earth to get it." In other words, one of the most important facets of persuading others is giving them the information they need to make a good decision.

An easy way for a salesperson to fail at convincing others would be to assume that the prospect needs to hear only what the salesperson believes to be important. A salesperson who does not clearly see the situation as it exists for the prospect is all too likely to bring up information and make persuasive points that will be irrelevant to the stated or implied needs of that prospect or customer.

In summary, then, having a good attitude toward others will help you to understand their perspective, develop intuitive insight about them, find what they really want to hear, and evaluate their needs and how you can fulfill them. The salesperson can then tell them what they really want to hear, sit back, and watch as they make a buying decision and close the sale themselves.

Balanced Communication

Striking a balance between talking and active listening; not dominating a conversation.

Obviously, any salesperson who talks too much will turn his or her prospects off. Conversely, it is impossible to implement application-based selling without talking enough to explain specific, needs-based applications to each prospect. Members of any sales force must strive to strike a balance between attentive, sensitive listening while still ensuring that every prospect *understands* all the benefits that their products or services offer.

Intuitive insight will serve salespeople well in this area as they watch for nonverbal signs indicating that the prospect needs to talk while they need to listen. Clear goal focus will keep them on track as they make sure they have delivered value to their prospect by fully explaining the key benefits that the prospect will derive from what they sell.

INTANGIBLE ATTRIBUTES FOR CONVINCING

Proving your claims, creating additional value to further justify price, relieving prospect's fears, and making prospects believe enough to act.

Identifying Buying Signals

The ability to rely on intuitive feelings and gut instincts and the awareness of both verbal and nonverbal communication used by prospects.

Intuitive insight is crucial for a value-based sales professional to succeed. An excellent example of identifying buying signals can be seen in the story told earlier in this chapter about David, the salesman who used fax machines to close sales. His strength was in his ability to identify buying signals.

This attribute depends heavily on the next two that I discuss, emotional connection and sense of timing.

Emotional Connection

The capacity to be conscious of the feelings and opinions of others and to value others as people.

To make an emotional connection with others, salespeople must make an extra effort not only to be aware of other people's body language, but to focus intently on exactly what the prospect is verbalizing. They then can respond to the prospect's concerns even if they do not relate to the situation the same way as the prospect does.

During the Convince stage, IMPACT salespeople must be exceptional listeners. One important facet of professional listening is not needing to be heard, or to "get your two cents worth in." This is the time to rely on intuitive insight to maintain an awareness of how a prospect is feeling. The salesperson who is a good listener will never allow his or her feelings to get in the way of objectively convincing prospects to make a buying decision.

Sense of Timing

Knowing when to take appropriate action.

Though already discussed in the Meet phase, sense of timing is also important in the Convince phase; salespeople must watch for nonverbal signals indicating that it is time to move to the phase where they finally get paid: Tie-It-Up.

Correct Use of Resources

The ability to understand the functional use of material resources.

In the Convince phase of IMPACT Selling, it is essential to have a strong aptitude for using the company's products and resources correctly. The correct use of these resources requires a delicate balance between getting a job done and a respect for the resources used.

Ironically, salespeople who are too results-oriented tend to perform poorly in this area. Often they will exhibit tunnel vision, focusing on a short-range goal and ignoring longer-range adverse effects.

Nearly everyone occasionally uses tools or resources designed for one task to perform another. Correct use of resources will balance the job at hand with respect for the tools used. People who do poorly in this area will commonly waste or abuse tools and resources.

To relate this to the Convince phase of IMPACT Selling, one must realize how uninterested a prospect may become if the salesperson tries to build value by illustrating an inappropriate use of the company's products. This type of *reaching* may seem like a desperate measure on the part of someone who does not truly have a solid answer for the prospect's need. Even if the prospect does not see this and makes a buying decision, he or she could easily become dissatisfied when the product fails as a result of improper application.

Building Trust

The ability to coordinate insights and knowledge of others into mutually trusting relationships.

Before moving to the last phase, Tie-It-Up, salespeople must ensure that they have built the trust necessary for the prospect to make a positive buying decision.

As the salesperson and prospect near the end of the Convince phase, both honesty and complete openness are essential. It is important to stop periodically, taking time to ask if a prospect has any unanswered questions. Before one attempts to move to the last phase of IMPACT Selling, all objections must be uncovered and eliminated. A prospect's honest objections should never be brushed off lightly. If trust has not been built, prospects will later seem as though they are wearing earmuffs to block out everything said and tried in closing the sale. Successful sales professionals never hedge on any answer. Doing so can destroy any and all trust build up to that point.

INTANGIBLE ATTRIBUTES FOR TYING-IT-UP

Wrapping up the sale and allowing prospects to take ownership. Negotiating terms and conditions of the sale, clearing away objections to the sale, and asking for the order. Reinforcing the sale after it is complete.

Courage

The confidence to face uncertain circumstances and to ask difficult questions; the ability to face the consequences of one's own actions and decisions.

Lack of courage in salespeople can negate every bit of training and other skills they have if they are unable to face the challenge of asking for the order. However, if one understands that courage means to take action in spite of fears, one can easily see that a key way to appear courageous is to reduce or remove fear.

It is only when a salesperson uses pushy, demonstration-selling techniques that courage becomes an issue when it's time to ask for an order. If the salesperson has no idea whether or not he or she has met any needs of the prospect, asking for an order may be a frightening experience. However, at the end of a properly implemented IMPACT sales presentation, fear vanishes and courage becomes easy. A fully prepared IMPACT sales professional will have enough self-confidence and goal focus that asking for the order becomes organic.

Identifying Objections

Identifying and isolating obstacles that may cause a prospect not to make a buying decision.

Problem Resolution

The ability to keep critical issues in focus and to resolve those issues.

Attaining courage, as cited above, comes most easily once you have thoroughly completed the Convince phase and have cleared away all lingering objections. Clearing away objections is a two-step process involving the identification of the prospect's objections and the subsequent problem resolution. When salespeople recall the old adage that identifying a problem is 90 percent of its solution, it becomes easy to see that neither of these two attributes, implemented without the other, will result in a successful sales career.

Results Oriented

The ability to complete an action in order to bring a situation to a close.

One's ability to be results-oriented is more a measure of focus than of values or capacities. An individual's results-oriented abilities can be enhanced by tackling activities where the outcome occurs within a fairly short time span. Therefore, if a salesperson tends toward a weakness in this area, reference needs to be made to the previous discussions of short-range goals and goal-oriented activities. A results-oriented mentality is difficult to maintain if there are no readily apparent direct rewards.

We frequently find that people who do a lot of long-range planning and analysis often experience difficulty staying oriented toward concrete results. If long-range planning is one's forte, one needs to make an effort to break down long-range plans into manageable short-range plans such as schedules, deadlines, quotas, or performance goals. Creating a mechanism to shift one's mental focus from *planning* to *doing* can certainly improve a salesperson's results-oriented focus.

Self-Control

The capacity to maintain composure in difficult situations; to think and act objectively rather than emotionally.

Emotions are a part of daily life for us all. Every one of us will be exposed to stressful or agitating circumstances at some point in our lives. Our emotions must be dealt with, but they usually add little good to our professional lives. Self-control is the ability to maintain focus and concentration in the face of life's inevitable difficulties; it is one's ability to think and act objectively rather than impulsively and emotionally.

Self-control may therefore be called emotional control. Emotional control is necessary for one to be able to replace emotions that are currently occupying one's thought capacity and burning mental energy with productive thinking. Our logical minds can do very little toward that end. One cannot deal logically with one's emotions. The only use logic has for emotions is to measure one's response to one's feelings. If the response is inappropriate, one should focus on doing something constructive and return to one's feelings later. Emotional control, and therefore self-control, is a simple matter of focusing on the appropriate behavior at the appropriate time. Time spent worrying about anger, sorrow, and frustration is time wasted. A person must allow his or her mind to deal with emotions on its own time and own schedule.

Sense of Timing

Knowing when to take appropriate action.

Though discussed earlier in both the Meet and Convince phases, a good sense of timing is also necessary in this final phase of IMPACT Selling. A salesperson needs to know *when* to say, "Would you like it in red or green?" or "What do we have to do to get started?" A sense of timing for those questions is a critical element in successful selling; all the work done in long-range planning can be wasted if one lacks the skill to know when to close a sale. Without a good sense of timing, a sale can be lost forever with no chance for recovery.

All of the attributes that we have indentified as key elements for sales success in IMPACT Selling are at a much deeper and far more significant level than any treatment of sales *ever* undertaken by traditional sales training technology. It is my hope that you grasp and embrace the power of these attributes as they relate to long-term sales success in niched, competitive markets. These attributes will ultimately separate the winners from the also-rans. These specific qualities are far more critical to success than any memorized words, phrases, scripts, or even in-depth product knowledge.

CLOSING WORDS

The new world of niche selling promises myriad challenges and obstacles yet promises great rewards. Niche selling is not merely a wave of the future; it is the reality of the present. Crowded markets, demanding buyers, price sensitivity, and intense competition will continue. The difference between the long-term winners and the also-rans lies in the sales strategies they employ. Success in the 1990s and beyond will be simple but not easy: It will rely on value-based, needs-directed selling.

It is my wish that the concepts and techniques I've given you in this book will be as powerfully effective for you as they have been for the thousands of others whom we have trained. Here is a final adage that sums up the most important factor in achieving success through what you have learned in this book:

New ideas will never work unless you do.

The challenge is yours. So are the opportunities . . . seize them.

INDEX

ABOUT THE AUTHOR

William T. Brooks is one of the nation's most sought-after authorities on maximizing sales productivity. For over a decade he has been one of America's most in-demand speakers and consultants. Founder of The Brooks Group, he has brought his innovative, creative, and results–producing speaking and consulting services to hundreds of organizations across America and around the world. His custom-designed solutions to unique sales challenges are well-documented and widely respected.

To communicate with William Brooks or to gain additional information about his programs, audio/video systems, or services, contact:

THE BROOKS GROUP
2002 Pisgah Church Road, Suite 25
Greensboro, North Carolina 27408
1-800-633-7762

OTHER
IRWIN *Professional Publishing* TITLES
OF INTEREST TO YOU

MARKETING TO HOME-BASED BUSINESSES
Jeffrey P. Davidson

By 1995, the number of U.S. home-based businesses is expected to reach 54,000,000—more than half of all households in the United States. *Marketing to Home-Based Businesses* shows you how to acquire the knowledge, strategies, and techniques that are needed to effectively market to this affluent, fast-growing market.

ISBN: 1-55623-475-9 $39.95

A Maxwell Sroge Report
THE UNITED STATES MAIL ORDER INDUSTRY

Whether you're a direct-marketing professional, an investor, or an entrepreneur, Sroge helps you find profitable market niches by analyzing both the existing and developing mail order marketplace. Use the information to project probable growth patterns and allocate valuable marketing resources more accurately.

ISBN: 1-55623-486-4 $55.00

THE NEW DIRECT MARKETING
How to Implement a Profit-Driven Database Marketing Strategy
David Shepard Associates

Construct, analyze, use, and evaluate the information in a marketing database to build sales and profits. The authors show you how to cost-effectively acquire the primary and secondary data you need to identify and profile your best customers and prospects.

ISBN: 1-55623-317-5 $52.50

MARKETING TO THE AFFLUENT
Dr. Thomas J. Stanley
A 1989 business book award finalist! Dr. Stanley shows you how to get the true demographics, psychographics, and buying and patronage habits of the wealthy. Includes in-depth interviews with some of the nation's top sales and marketing professionals to help you pinpoint your best prospects.
ISBN: 1-55623-105-9 $55.00

SELLING TO THE AFFLUENT
The Professional's Guide to Closing the Sales that Count
Dr. Thomas J. Stanley
Improve your closing percentage...and income. Dr. Stanley shows you how to approach wealthy prospects at the moment they are most likely to buy. In *Marketing to the Affluent* he tells you how to find them. Here he tells you how to sell them.
ISBN: 1-55623-418-X $55.00

ADVERTISING AGENCY MANAGEMENT
Jay McNamara, former president, McCann-Erickson Worldwide
"Jay McNamara has concisely and comprehensively compiled in one volume what every aspiring agency manager should be learning on the way up and what no advertising manager should ever forget after he or she gets there."
Allen Rosenshine, Chairman and CEO
BBDO Worldwide Inc.
ISBN: 1-55623-230-6 $29.95

Prices quoted are in U.S. currency and are subject to change without notice. Available in fine bookstores and libraries everywhere.